Practical Svelte

Create Performant Applications with the Svelte Component Framework

Alex Libby

Apress®

Practical Svelte: Create Performant Applications with the Svelte Component Framework

Alex Libby
BELPER, UK

ISBN-13 (pbk): 978-1-4842-7373-9 ISBN-13 (electronic): 978-1-4842-7374-6
https://doi.org/10.1007/978-1-4842-7374-6

Managing Director, Apress Media LLC: Welmoed Spahr
Acquisitions Editor: Louise Corrigan
Development Editor: James Markham
Coordinating Editor: Nancy Chen

Cover designed by eStudioCalamar

Cover image by Clark van der Beken on Unsplash (www.unsplash.com)

Distributed to the book trade worldwide by Apress Media, LLC, 1 New York Plaza, New York, NY 10004, U.S.A. Phone 1-800-SPRINGER, fax (201) 348-4505, e-mail orders-ny@springer-sbm.com, or visit www.springeronline.com. Apress Media, LLC is a California LLC and the sole member (owner) is Springer Science + Business Media Finance Inc (SSBM Finance Inc). SSBM Finance Inc is a **Delaware** corporation.

For information on translations, please e-mail booktranslations@springernature.com; for reprint, paperback, or audio rights, please e-mail bookpermissions@springernature.com.

Apress titles may be purchased in bulk for academic, corporate, or promotional use. eBook versions and licenses are also available for most titles. For more information, reference our Print and eBook Bulk Sales web page at http://www.apress.com/bulk-sales.

Any source code or other supplementary material referenced by the author in this book is available to readers on GitHub via the book's product page, located at www.apress.com/9781484273739. For more detailed information, please visit http://www.apress.com/source-code.

Printed on acid-free paper

This is dedicated to my family, with thanks for their love and support while writing this book.

Table of Contents

About the Author

Alex Libby is a front-end engineer and seasoned computer book author who hails from England. His passion for all things open source dates back to the days of his degree studies, where he first came across web development and has been hooked ever since. His daily work involves extensive use of React, Node.js, JavaScript, HTML, and CSS. Alex enjoys tinkering with different open source libraries to see how they work. He has spent a stint maintaining the jQuery Tools library and enjoys writing about open source technologies, principally for front-end UI development.

About the Technical Reviewer

Rami Morrar is a self-taught programmer and has coding experience in languages such as C# and C++ for over three years. He has made different coding projects, such as a gaming tutorial website, several desktop applications, and even games in the Unity game engine. He is currently working on his own independent game project in MonoGame, set to be released next year. He has an abundance of charisma for programming and game development, and talks about both on his blog, and tutorials he has created for the MonoGame framework. He is also cowriting a sequel to the book *MonoGame Mastery*. In his free time, he likes to play games and look at cool new projects by other indie developers.

Acknowledgments

Writing a book can be a long but rewarding process; it is not possible to complete it without the help of other people. I would like to offer a huge vote of thanks to my editors – in particular, Nancy Chen and Louise Corrigan; my thanks also to Rami Morrar as my technical reviewer, James Markham for his help during the process, and others at Apress for getting this book into print. All have made writing this book a painless and enjoyable process, even with the edits!

My thanks also to my family for being understanding and supporting me while writing. I frequently spend lots of late nights writing alone, or pass up times when I should be with them, so their words of encouragement and support have been a real help in getting past those bumps in the road and producing the finished book that you now hold in your hands.

Lastly, it is particularly poignant that the book was written at a time when the world has faced global events of an unprecedented nature; it was too easy to think about those who lost the greatest thing we as humans could ever have. Having a project to work on – no matter how simple or complex it might be – helped me get through those tough times, and with the hope that we face a new, improved, and hopefully better future.

Introduction

Practical Svelte is for people who want to quickly create ecommerce sites that are efficient and fast, using the upcoming Svelte framework and associated tools.

This project-oriented book simplifies the setting up of a Svelte site as a starting point before beginning to explore the benefits of using Svelte in an ecommerce environment and developing it into an ecommerce offer that we can customize according to your needs. It will equip you with a starting toolset that you can use to create future projects, incorporate into your existing workflow, and that will allow you to take your websites to the next level.

Throughout this book, I'll take you on a journey through constructing the front-end UI for our example site. We will touch on subjects such as adding data sources, creating the catalog, and implementing a payment function and more – showing you how easy it is to develop simple ecommerce sites that we can augment later quickly. With the minimum of fuss and plenty of practical exercises, we'll focus on topics such as managing data and state, styling, creating components, and more – right through to producing the final result viewable from any browser!

Svelte uses nothing more than standard JavaScript, CSS, and HTML, three of the most powerful tools available for developers: you can enhance, extend, and configure your site as requirements dictate. With Svelte, the art of possible is only limited by the extent of your imagination and the power of JavaScript, HTML, and Node.js.

Practical Svelte gets you quickly acquainted with creating and manipulating ecommerce sites using tools familiar to all developers. It's perfect for website developers who are already familiar with JavaScript and are keen to learn how to leverage the Svelte framework. You may also be a developer for whom time is of the essence and simplicity is key; you need to produce efficient and properly optimized content in modern browsers using tools already in your possession.

CHAPTER 1

Getting Started

Wait, this new framework has a runtime? Ugh. Thanks, I'll pass.

Let me begin with a single fact: we're shipping too much code to our users.

Yes, it might well be the case that tools, such as React and Angular, are all the rage nowadays. But most of them have one thing in common – they each have a runtime library that must run when rendering websites using these tools. Sure, this might be a necessary evil when creating component-driven websites, but it's okay, as everyone does it, right?

It's not okay. We may think it's acceptable to run a 100Kb+ runtime with the likes of React, but it's not just the code we're using. We have to consider the bandwidth, server resources, external resources (such as third-party libraries or assets), and so on – it starts to add up!

Can we do anything about this? We can, by answering this question: *What if our framework didn't run in the browser?*

Introducing Svelte

Asking this question might seem like a real shocker when we've been used to the likes of React, but it is possible – let me introduce you to Svelte!

Created by Rich Harris in 2016, it was designed to prove that you don't need to create lots of extra component code but could write code that is much closer to vanilla JavaScript. Following this mantra means you can reduce the amount of code you need overall; in a sense, Svelte follows the principle of not reinventing the wheel when you already have perfectly good markup that can do the job. However, what makes it work is that it compiles code into reusable JavaScript modules – **without the need to operate the framework at runtime**.

A. Libby, *Practical Svelte*, https://doi.org/10.1007/978-1-4842-7374-6_1

Not running a framework at runtime is significant: we don't pay the cost of shipping a sizable runtime library (and yes, tools like React get bigger, not smaller), plus our application will be super fast, without the abstraction you otherwise get with other tools.

Throughout this book, I will take you on a journey through creating a simple front-end ecommerce store that we can use on any small to medium online retail site. We'll start with a quick review of how Svelte works in this chapter but then swiftly move through creating the various components required for our store, as well as sourcing data. We'll take a look at a host of different topics on the way, such as managing events, styling, and the like – with the focus on creating our store but learning about the various parts that make up Svelte.

We have a lot to cover – so without further ado, let's dive in. As with all things programming, we will be setting up our development environment, ready for working on our Svelte project.

Setting Up a Development Environment

Okay, with the introductions over, it's time to get to business!

Throughout this book, we will be building up a sample ecommerce storefront, which we can later attach to a back-end payment system such as Shopify. We, of course, need Svelte (after all, that is what this book is about!), but we also need to avail ourselves of a few tools, so without further ado, here is a list of what we need:

- A copy of Svelte – there are two ways to get it; we will explore this shortly.
- A text editor, such as Atom or Visual Studio Code – I would recommend taking a look at `https://svelte.dev/blog/setting-up-your-editor`, which details ways to set up some of the more popular editors for use with Svelte.
- We also need Node.js – not only for Svelte but also for other tools such as webpack. Go ahead and download a version suitable for your platform from `www.nodejs.org` – choosing the default settings will be sufficient for this book.
- A local web server such as Apache (`www.apachefriends.org`) – for Linux users, you may find this already available in your distro. For this, default settings will suffice; it's not necessary to add SSL support.

- A hosting account from a service such as Vercel, Surge, or Now for publishing our site.
- A Git account, with either GitLab or GitHub. I usually use GitHub (as I already have lots of GitHub repositories); please feel free to adapt for GitLab if preferred.
- An optional extra is a custom domain name – this isn't obligatory, but it will give our demo a little extra polish!

If you happen to use the Prettier tool in your browser, then I would strongly recommend checking out `www.rockyourcode.com/prettier-and-es-lint-setup-for-svelte-js/` and in particular for details on setting up Prettier to work with Svelte. The Svelte plugin for Prettier is available at `https://github.com/sveltejs/prettier-plugin-svelte`.

We need a couple of things later in the book, but we will go through details nearer the time. We can download any other Node.js packages as and when needed; I will highlight this at the appropriate point.

Okay, let's move on. I've touched on the fact that we need Svelte, but asked one question: how *do* we get a hold of and install it? There are a couple of options open to us, so let's take a look at them in greater detail.

So How Do We Get Svelte?

One of the great things about Svelte is that as a JavaScript-based framework, it is straightforward to set it up – there are several options open to us:

1. Use the REPL at `https://svelte.dev/repl/hello-world?version=3.31.2` to familiarize ourselves with Svelte – this has several examples at `https://svelte.dev/examples`, which we can tweak to suit our needs.

The example URL will redirect to show the first in the list; you can use that list to select an appropriate option.

---

2. When we outgrow the REPL option, we can download and install a customized version from the Svelte GitHub site, using Node.js/NPM.
3. We can also use degit, a project scaffolding tool available from `https://github.com/Rich-Harris/degit`, to set up a new Svelte project. Using this route would typically require entering these commands:

```
npx degit sveltejs/template my-svelte-project
cd my-svelte-project
npm install
npm run dev
```

4. If you're something of a traditionalist like me, you can also install directly using NPM too – this is perfectly fine.

We will cover Svelte installation in more detail later when we set up our base site for this book.

By default, Svelte comes with the Rollup tool to manage the bundling of ES modules; we can swap it out for different integrations, depending on what tools we already use.

For example, you might choose to work with webpack instead – Svelte has a plugin available at `https://github.com/sveltejs/svelte-loader` to support this system. Alternatively, you can use the `sirv-cli` tool to preview assets directly – this is available from `https://github.com/lukeed/sirv`.

All of the demos in this book were written for Windows, as this is the author's usual development platform. Please adapt if you are using macOS or Linux on your PC.

Now that we have our development environment set up, let's try creating Svelte code using the REPL tool.

Creating Your First Application

We could spend ages talking through how Svelte works, but that's not so interesting – instead, let's dive in and use the REPL tool to start manipulating some simple Svelte code! It's a great way to learn, mainly as Svelte code is structured in a format that closely resembles how you might write a CodePen demo. We will revisit this structure shortly in more detail, but for now, let's dive in and take a quick look at a typical "Hello World" app to get up to speed with using Svelte.

BREAKING INTO USING REPL

To get acquainted with Svelte, using the REPL tool, follow these steps:

1. First, crack open your browser and navigate to `www.svelte.dev`. Click the REPL link at the top right of the page.

The keen-eyed among you will note that you could equally browse directly to the REPL tool once you know the link. Browsing to this URL will work, but be aware though that it includes a version-specific reference to Svelte. You may end up invertedly browsing to and using an older version of Svelte if you're not careful!

---

2. Once at the page, you will see a split code window – on the left is an open file, `App.svelte`, with the Result, JS output, and CSS output tabs on the right. The tool comes with a version of the typical "Hello World" app running, which we can see in Figure 1-1.

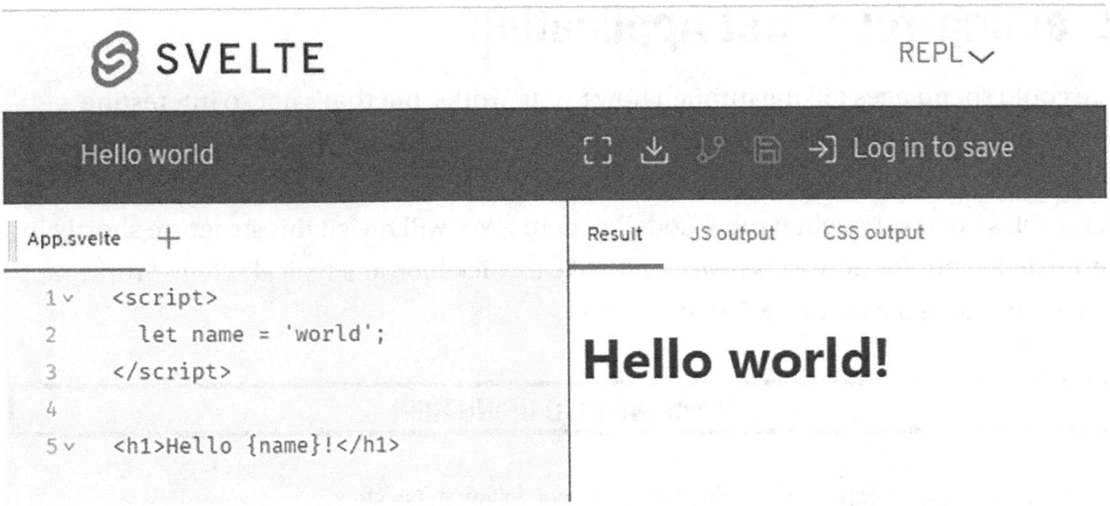

***Figure 1-1.** A screenshot of the REPL tool for Svelte*

3. Try changing the value assigned to the name from `'world'` to your name – see how it changes automatically on the right?
4. Let's add a little color to the result – after the opening `<script>` tag, insert the code as highlighted:

```
<script>
  let name = 'Alex';
</script>
<h1>Hello {name}!</h1>

<style>
  h1 { color: purple; }
</style>
```

5. The results shown on the right will automatically update, so we end up with "Hello…" in a purple font.

6. Okay, let's ramp things up a little. Inside the script block, leave a blank line after the let name= entry, and add this:

```
<script>
  let name = 'world';

  function handleClick() {
    alert('no more alerts');
  }
</script>
```

7. Next, add in this button code immediately after the <h1> tag:

```
<h1>Hello {name}!</h1>
<button on:click|once={handleClick}>
  Click me
</button>
```

8. Try clicking the "Click me" button – what do you get? If all is well, we should see a dialog appear (Figure 1-2, shown overleaf).

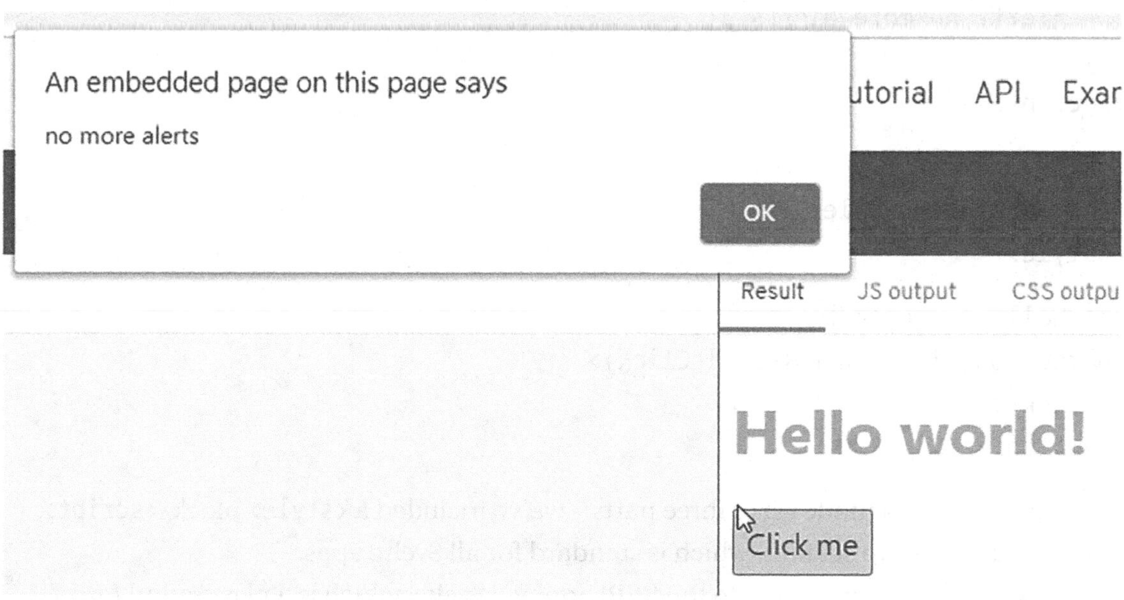

***Figure 1-2.** Clicking the button shows our first dialog box*

You've now completed your first Svelte demo - easy, right? Most of the code we've used is plain vanilla JavaScript, but with some key differences: let's take a moment to review what we've covered in this demo in more detail.

Understanding What Happened

So, what did we achieve in that last demo?

It is fair to say that while it may seem to have been a trivial exercise, this was intentional - it was more about working through the constituent parts of a typical Svelte application than exploring the intricacies of the code itself! We will explore the code in more detail throughout this book, but for now, let's take a quick look at the sections that make up our application.

As a quick recap, here is the code we've just used in full:

```
<script>
  let name = 'Alex';

  function handleClick() {
    alert('no more alerts');
  }
</script>

<style>
  h1 { color: purple; }
</style>

<h1>Hello {name}!</h1>
<button on:click|once={handleClick}>
  Click me
</button>
```

You will see it's made up of three parts - we've included a `<style>` block, `<script>` block, and a markup section, which is standard for all Svelte apps.

We kicked off by browsing to the REPL tool for Svelte, which is a playground for testing code - we understood from earlier that this is perfect for getting started with Svelte, but we will later move to other tools.

The code we entered begins with a style block to add color to an H1 tag we will use in our demo. Next, we then added a script block, where we've defined a variable name to equal the text "`world`" and created a simple event handler. We then created standard markup to render that name and introduce a clickable button. There are two key differences, though – the use of parentheses to act as a placeholder for our `name` variable and the inline event handler to fire a message. If we click that message, we will get a simple alert to say "no more alerts" – it seems a little ironic to display a warning when we no longer want any alerts, but it is only a simple demo, after all!

Don't worry, though, if sections such as the event handler don't entirely make sense at this stage; it's enough to know that the format we've used is a standard way to fire events in Svelte and equates (roughly) to `<button onclick='alert("no more alerts")>Click me</button>`.

We will cover events in more detail later in Chapter 5 of this book.

Okay, let's crack on. Now that we've been introduced to Svelte, it's time for a little theory. Yes, I know: theory isn't everyone's idea of fun, but it's essential to understand how Svelte ticks and what makes it different from its competitors. Don't worry, though, I will keep it short! With that in mind, let's take a stab at answering that very question.

What Makes Svelte Different?

If you've spent any time with frameworks over the last few years, you will no doubt have come across one feature that is common to many of the more popular frameworks in use today – virtual DOM. Say, for example, you create this React component:

```
function HelloMessage(props) {
  return (
    <div className="greeting">
      Hello {props.name}
    </div>
  );
}
```

Looks harmless, right? The object we've just created (using that code) represents how it should display on the page and the virtual DOM. If we update the state in an application with such a component, this will be re-rendered as a new object; the virtual DOM has to reconcile that against the previous version to work out what should now be displayed.

This updating all sounds good, but hold on – if we already have a *physical* DOM, why do we need a virtual one? Doesn't that add overhead to our project?

Tools such as React aim to let you build declarative, state-driven applications without worrying about state and performance – even with a virtual DOM, the speed is usually adequate for our needs. However, there are caveats to this – updating state is still a lot of work, and while features such as React's Fiber will break things into smaller chunks, it won't reduce the overall time it takes to update state.

Let's think about that for a moment – if we updated the name property to use something else, then the diffing algorithm would have to (a) check the elements, (b) enumerate through attributes, and (c) update the DOM – in this case, the text.

That might not seem much, but bear in mind that it's only point (c) that adds any value in this case – points (a) and (b) don't change!

Take, for example, this code example, taken from the Svelte blog:

```
function MoreRealisticComponent(props) {
  const [selected, setSelected] = useState(null);

  return (
    <div>
      <p>Selected {selected ? selected.name : 'nothing'}</p>
      <ul>
        {props.items.map(item =>
          <li>
            <button onClick={() => setSelected(item)}>
              {item.name}
            </button>
          </li>
        )}
      </ul>
    </div>
  );
}
```

Suppose we were to change the `props.item` value, then we would be creating a new array of virtual li elements each time - while it may not be an issue and be sufficiently fast for your needs, it's still unnecessary! We risk ending up landing ourselves with a bottleneck that becomes difficult to optimize at a later date.

What if we could achieve the same result without the use of a virtual DOM? This is where Svelte comes in - instead of compiling code at runtime (and therefore needing that runtime library), we compile at build time into pure, highly efficient imperative code.

Let's say that a typical to-do app in Svelte weighs in at about 4Kb. Compare that to production versions of React and ReactDOM (taken from a CDN), without any application code, weigh in at 128Kb. That equates to 32x the size! Granted, it may not be an entirely fair comparison, but the point is that there is still a hefty increase that we have to consider when using tools such as React. You can see the steps we have to go through when using React, compared to Svelte, in Figure 1-3.

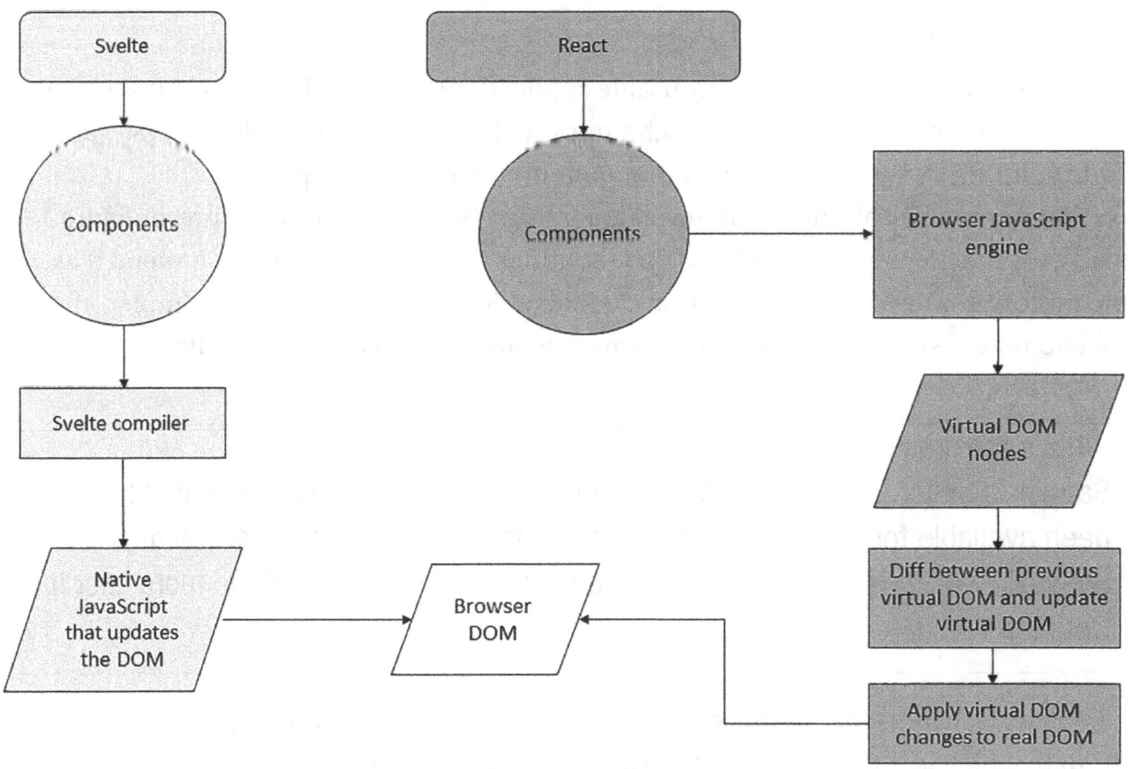

***Figure 1-3.** Comparing the diffing process for Svelte vs. React*

It isn't the only difference, though, when using Svelte – here are two more:

- Interoperability – if you wanted to use an NPM package, you would likely need to find one tailored to your framework, such as React, Ember, or Angular. However, if we had built that package using Svelte, we can use that package with any framework, including Svelte!
- When it comes to code splitting, it doesn't matter how many components you serve – you still have to serve a runtime such as React. It isn't an issue with Svelte; the framework is embedded in each component, which means the code is much smaller, and therefore code splitting is more effective.
- Svelte, from version 3 onward, also took a radical decision not to implement an API. It removes both the need for code that can seem unnatural and reduces the work required for garbage collection; both help keep the size of the framework much smaller than the likes of React and Angular.

Although we can build entirely usable applications using Svelte by itself, this isn't the only option – to take advantage of techniques such as server-side rendering (SSR) and code splitting (essential in today's development), we can use Sapper.

Sapper is an application framework built using Svelte, which comes preconfigured with best practices such as SSR and code splitting. Svelte developers recommend it as the preferred way to build applications. It makes developing applications simpler, and we should consider it when it comes to architecting any project using Svelte.

What's the deal with SvelteKit?

Sapper is undergoing a complete rewrite, as it is based on techniques that have been available for a few years and have become outdated. Its replacement is SvelteKit, which is still in active development – we'll explore this and more later in Chapter 12.

Okay, let's move on. We need to cover one more topic before getting stuck into code, though, which is the issue of browser support. Svelte supports most recent browsers, with at least one exception – to understand what that means for us, let's dive in and take a closer look.

Browser Support

In an age of responsive design, I am sure there will be one question at the top of everyone's mind when using the Svelte framework. Which browsers does it support, and how will this align with my company's requirements?

Fortunately for Svelte, support is excellent - it supports most **recent**, **well-known** browsers, including mobile devices, but with one caveat: it doesn't support IE11, at least not out of the box.

IE11, I hear you say that's an old browser! Many companies still use IE11, primarily because of investment in tools and technologies such as ActiveX.

There is a solution though, of sorts - Svelte will operate in IE11, but only if we include polyfills; the trade-off is that these will bump up the overall size enormously, which means we lose the benefit of tiny, fast files! It is something to think about - can you manage transpiling for IE11, with large polyfills in use, at least until you can move away from supporting IE11?

For more details and some of the support issues raised around IE11, you might like to refer to GitHub issue 2621 on the Svelte repo, at `https://github.com/sveltejs/svelte/issues/2621`. Other developers also provide solutions, such as Ingo Farentholtz's IE11 solution at `https://github.com/ifahrentholz/svelte-3-ie11` or the blog post written by Mark Volkmann at `https://mvolkmann.github.io/blog/topics/#blog/svelte/supporting-ie11/`.

Okay, so we've been introduced to Svelte, explored what makes it different from other frameworks, and dipped our proverbial toes into the water: it's time to get stuck in! Let's dive in and take a look at what's involved in more detail.

Setting Up Our Project

We've already covered the various ways to install Svelte. For this book, I will focus on using option 2, the custom Svelte template, available from the main Svelte site.

It has several useful files and folders already configured for us, such as `package.json` and the `src` folder, making it easier to develop our project. It's a simple process to set up the site, so let's make a start.

DEMO – CREATING OUR INITIAL SITE

To set up our base site, ready for building into a store front end, follow these steps:

1. The first step is to install Node.js and NPM – go ahead and browse to `www.nodejs.org`, and then download and install a version appropriate for your platform. If prompted, please use the default settings.
2. Next, go ahead and extract a copy of the `template-master.zip` file from the code download that accompanies this book – this contains our preconfigured site, ready for installing.

It's also available from `https://github.com/sveltejs/template/archive/master.zip`.

---

3. Go ahead and extract the template-master folder from within the zip file, and save it to your PC. Then rename it to `sveltebook`. Next, fire up a Node.js terminal session, and then change the working folder to the `sveltebook` folder from step 3.

For the exercises in this book, I will assume the location is at the root of your C: drive. Please alter as appropriate if you would like to save it to a different location.

---

4. At the prompt, enter `npm install && npm run dev` to install and run the project. After a few moments, we should see this in the terminal session:

```
Your application is ready~! 🚀

  - Local:      http://localhost:5000
  - Network:    Add `--host` to expose

────────────────── LOGS ──────────────────
```

5. Assuming we do, switch to your browser, and then browse to `http://localhost:5000` to see our base site in all its glory, with the text shown in Figure 1-4.

HELLO WORLD!
Visit the Svelte tutorial to learn how to build Svelte apps.

Figure 1-4. *The base app for our project, running in a browser*

At this point, our site is now ready for us to develop into our store front end throughout this book. It was a simple exercise, but an important one – let's pause for a moment to review the steps we covered in this exercise in more detail.

Reviewing the Changes Made

Setting up any site using Svelte is very easy – to do so, we first installed Node.js (and NPM) before extracting a copy of the custom template site from the code download. We then ran the typical `npm install && npm run dev` commands to install any required dependencies before launching the site in our browser.

With our starting site operational, now is an excellent time to take a quick look at the basic structure of a typical Svelte site and some of the basic principles of using Svelte in more detail.

Exploring the Structure of Our Site

Remember how we worked through setting up a Svelte starter site at the start of this chapter, using the custom template provided by the Svelte developers? If we open the sveltebook folder we created earlier, Figure 1-5 shows us what to expect.

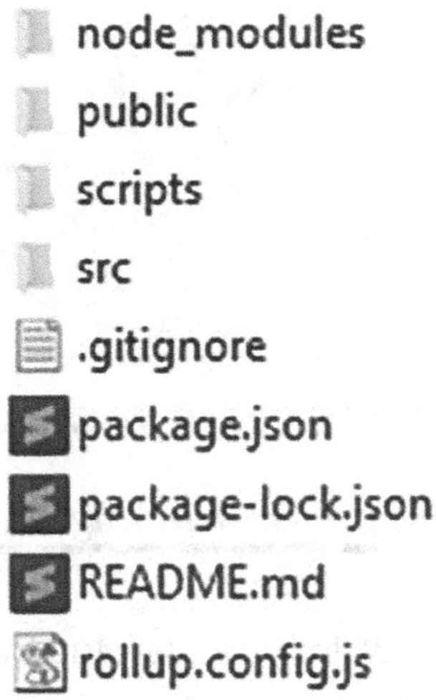

Figure 1-5. *The file and folder structure of a typical Svelte site*

We can see it's created several folders and files; for anyone used to Node.js, some will be familiar. We have the likes of `node_modules`, `public`, and `src` folders, along with `package.json` and `.gitignore`, to name but a few. For now, though, the key files we need to concern ourselves with are in the `\src` folder. Let's take a look at them in more detail, beginning with `main.js`:

```
import App from './App.svelte';

const app = new App({
  target: document.body,
  props: {
    name: 'world'
  }
});

export default app;
```

This `const` initiates every Svelte site. We can pass into it any number of defined property values, or `props` – in our case, `name`, which equates to the value world.

In app.svelte, we set up the placeholder markup for our site - this contains a script block that defines the name variable, plus the markup and styling for our site. Notice the use of curly parentheses in the "Hello {name}" code - this is a placeholder for the value assigned to the name prop value we created earlier and which Svelte will swap out during build:

```
<script>
  export let name;
</script>

<main>
  <h1>Hello {name}!</h1>
  <p>Visit the <a href="https://svelte.dev/tutorial
">Svelte tutorial</a> to learn how to build Svelte apps.</p>
</main>

<style>
  main { text-align: center; padding: 1em; max-width: 240px; margin: 0 auto; }

  h1 { color: #ff3e00; text-transform: uppercase;
font-size: 4em;  font-weight: 100; }

  @media (min-width: 640px) {
    main { max-width: none; }
  }
</style>
```

We've used basic styling here, but Svelte can use external style libraries such as emotion as well – we will cover how in Chapter 7.

Finally, we have package.json, which is standard for all Node.js-based applications – inside it, you can see the packages that have already been installed and configured for use:

```
{
  "name": "svelte-app",
  "version": "1.0.0",
```

```
  "scripts": {
    "build": "rollup -c",
    "dev": "rollup -c -w",
    "start": "sirv public"
  },
  "devDependencies": {
    "@rollup/plugin-commonjs": "^17.0.0",
    "@rollup/plugin-node-resolve": "^11.0.0",
    "rollup": "^2.3.4",
    "rollup-plugin-css-only": "^3.1.0",
    "rollup-plugin-livereload": "^2.0.0",
    "rollup-plugin-svelte": "^7.0.0",
    "rollup-plugin-terser": "^7.0.0",
    "svelte": "^3.0.0"
  },
  "dependencies": {
    "sirv-cli": "^1.0.0"
  }
}
```

The files we've run through are core to making Svelte work – we will, of course, add more when we develop components, but they will hang off these initial files.

Okay, let's crack on. I've hinted that we will be building an online store front end as the theme for this book. The question is, what will our store sell, I wonder?

Setting the Background

Coffee time! Coffee, coffee, coffee, coffee...!

Yes, indeed, our store will be selling coffee! At this point, I'm reminded of that saying from the movie *Dante's Peak*, where Greg, one of the geologists studying a volcano about to cause havoc with the town Dante's Peak, goes a little crazy when given his daily cup by the town's mayor and coffee shop owner. But I digress...

For this book, we will build out an online store that will sell roast coffee beans. Billed as one of the world's most popular drinks, coffee consumption is increasing, with America, Germany, Italy, and Japan being among the biggest importers of the product.

Throughout this book, we will explore the different elements that make Svelte, such as creating components, managing state, and adding data. We'll also cover the logic required to route information, responding to events, and more - all will be based on creating code for our store, but at the same time, I will cover the essential theory for each topic.

We will then finish deploying our project to a host and exploring what we can do to extend it further by adding in payment facilities. So, as you can see, we have plenty to cover!

Summary

We can see creating a website as something of a roller coaster - there will be highs and lows, successes, and challenges to deal with, as we begin to develop what will become our final solution. Over these last few pages, we've started to look at our project's background and get ourselves ready to create the site - let's take a moment to review what we have learned before beginning the real development work.

We started by introducing Svelte before swiftly moving onto set up our development environment and exploring the various options to obtain the framework. We then dipped our toes into our first application, using the REPL playground, before exploring some of the principles behind how Svelte works and what makes it different from other frameworks.

We then rounded out the chapter by setting up the base site for our project. At the same time, we also covered the background details of what we will develop in this book.

Okay, so what's next? Ah, yes, we need to start creating components that will form the basis of our online store! There is a good handful to make, so stay with me, and I will reveal all in the next chapter.

CHAPTER 2

Creating Components

Okay, so we have our tools in place and installed our prerequisites. Let's crack on and build that shop!

First, I want to cover off some of the basics principles around creating components in Svelte.

As I am sure you will already be aware, dozens of frameworks have appeared on the scene like React, Vue, and Angular as examples. With so many appearing, it's almost impossible to have not heard of at least one.

Question though: What do these frameworks have in common? The answer is that they are component driven; Svelte is no different. This component-based architecture allows us to separate features into individual pieces of reusable functionality and make it easier to develop and debug our code.

In this chapter, we will work through the basics of creating components in Svelte. We will use our new-found knowledge to build components for our mini shopping cart that we talked about back in Chapter 1. Let us begin building our first ever component in Svelte.

Understanding the Makeup of Components

If you have ever used CodePen demos, then you already know the basics behind creating Svelte components!

But I digress.

Getting back to reality, though, it doesn't matter which framework those demos used – it might have been Vue, React, or even plain vanilla JavaScript. The same thing applies in each instance: CodePen demos are (broadly) separated into three areas, namely, CSS, HTML, and JS (or JavaScript). We can include links to external libraries, but the same principle still applies: our core code will reside in one of these areas.

A. Libby, *Practical Svelte*, https://doi.org/10.1007/978-1-4842-7374-6_2

Svelte works on precisely the same principle - we split code into three areas, each contained within their relevant markup tags. To see what I mean, let's go ahead and create some examples, so you can see how this works in practice.

Creating an Example Component

The best way to get started with creating a Svelte component is to use the REPL tool. Although this might sound a little odd as a name, it is just a playground for writing code; it works in the same way as CodePen demos, so you should have no difficulty using it!

We can use the browser version, which is available at `https://svelte.dev/repl`, which is perfectly fine for our needs.

The URL for the Svelte REPL playground will redirect to a version-specific URL – this is normal and expected.

I you run the URL in Chrome, you can install the playground as an app in your browser - click the link highlighted in Figure 2-1 to install the app when prompted.

***Figure 2-1.** The REPL playground in a browser*

Wait for it to show this window (Figure 2-2).

Figure 2-2. *The same REPL playground as an installed app*

We can then use the download symbol (second from left in the blue-gray bar) to download the finished code or create an account to save our work online if desired.

Okay, assuming you've added the app (or are on the REPL playground in the browser), let's start creating our demo component as part of the next exercise.

Building the Example Component

To start our foray into creating components in Svelte, we will warm up with a quick demo by creating a Button component – this may be very simple, but it shows off some key features of creating and importing components in Svelte. Let's take a look at how it works in more detail.

CREATING A CUSTOM BUTTON

To set up the Button component, go ahead and follow these steps:

1. First, fire up your browser, and head over to `https://svelte.dev/repl`; the URL will redirect to show a version-specific address – this is normal.

2. Next, in the tab marked App.svelte on the left, add this code:

```
<script>
  import DefaultButton from './DefaultButton.svelte';
</script>

<DefaultButton />
```

3. Next, click the plus symbol to the right of the word App.svelte to add a new component.

4. When prompted (it will show Component2.svelte), change the name to DefaultButton.svelte.

5. Go ahead and add in this script code to that tab:

```
<script>
  export let buttonAction = () => alert('Welcome to the world of
  Svelte!');
</script>
```

6. In the same tab, miss a line and then add in this style block:

```
<style>
  button {
    color: #ffcc00;
    background-color: #333;
    border-radius: 5px;
    padding: 8px;
    border: none;
    font-size: 20px;
  }
</style>
```

7. Finally, leave a line blank, and then add in this markup:

```
<button on:click={buttonAction}>
  <slot>Hello World</slot>
</button>
```

8. The editor will automatically save the code – after a few moments, you will see the button shown in Figure 2-3.

***Figure 2-3.** The finished button displayed in the REPL playground*

9. Go ahead and click it – you will see the message appear as indicated in Figure 2-4.

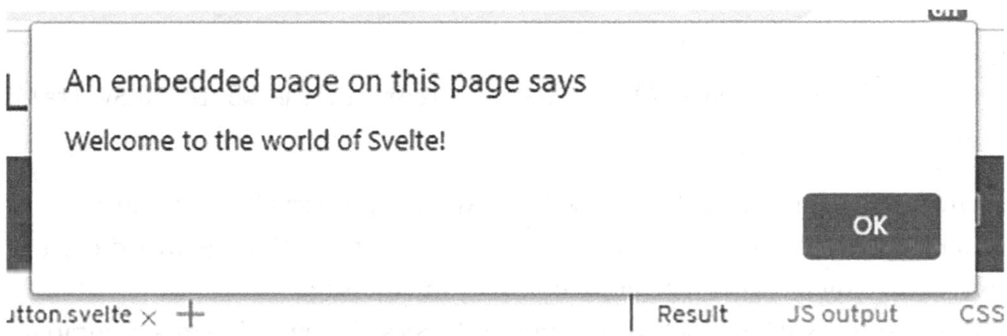

***Figure 2-4.** The message displayed from our button*

10. The demo is now complete – you can either download the code for future use or save it if you have logged in with an account.

Congratulations, you've now created your first component in Svelte! I know that some of you might wonder what all the fuss is about, as that was a straightforward exercise. But his simplicity is what makes Svelte so fantastic; it was designed to require minimal code and operate very much like writing CodePen-style demos.

However, it hides a lot of the code required to create and run the demo; if you look at the JS output window in the REPL playground, you will see what I mean! Our less than 24 lines are multiplied by a factor of almost 5 when it comes to building the final code!

But I digress. Although the code looks very straightforward, it does include a couple of essential points that are worth noting – let's take a look at the code in more detail.

Reviewing the Code

So, what did we achieve in the last demo?

If we take a closer look at the code again, we can see that much of what we wrote was plain HTML markup and CSS styling - this in the main is just standard code, so easy to understand.

However, what makes it different is the simple, easy-to-read style of coding - Svelte uses the same principles used by CodePen, where we focus on the key elements and let Svelte build the code into valid JavaScript. In this last demo, we created a simple Button component - we started in `App.svelte` by adding an import to our base component before calling an instance of it on the page.

We then switched to creating that component; at the top of `DefaultButton.svelte`, we first inserted a script block that contains an export statement:

```
<script>
  export let buttonAction = () => alert('Welcome to the world of Svelte!');
</script>
```

In a nutshell, export in Svelte allows us to expose a property from within a component, which we can call from a parent component. In this case, we exposed `buttonAction`, which triggers the alert to display the message.

Next up came a styling block, using standard CSS styles available to any component that supports them. We then moved onto the last block, which is the markup:

```
<button on:click={buttonAction}>
  <slot>Hello World</slot>
</button>
```

At face value, this looks like any other standard markup for a `<button>` element, but notice the presence of `<slot></slot>`? It is a placeholder for any child elements that should reside inside the parent button element, **which will override any text or elements present in the original component**.

That last statement is crucial - if we were using React, for example, then we would have done something like this:

```
<Button label={"This is a label"} />
```

"There is nothing wrong with using prop values, right?" I hear you say we override what's already in the component, right? I would 100% agree with you: but what if we didn't have to specify that prop value? Svelte is clever enough to work out if there are any child elements and drop them into the `<slot>` placeholder – no need to specify a prop value!

To prove it, change the `<DefaultButton />` tag to this in your demo:

```
<DefaultButton>
    This is an overridden button
</DefaultButton>
```

Watch how it changes automatically in the Result window on the right (Figure 2-5). See how easy that was to change the text?

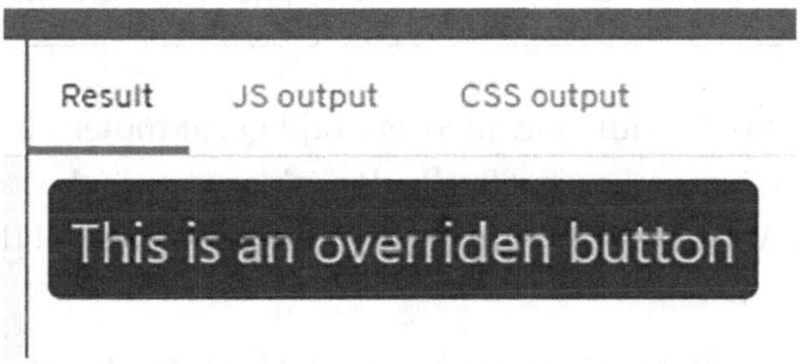

***Figure 2-5.** The updated button in the REPL demo*

Okay, now that we've become acquainted with the basics of using components, let's put some of that knowledge to good use and begin to create the first components for our shopping cart demo. Over the following few pages, we'll reuse some of these principles to build out components to make a simple cart icon at the end of the chapter, which we will then style later in the book.

Setting Expectations

At this point, it's an excellent time to set some expectations – after all, we simply don't have the space to build something that replicates the likes of Amazon!

It's important nonetheless to set a few boundaries, so with that in mind, here they are:

- The site we will create won't be production-ready by any stretch of the imagination: we would need to add security, a lot more error checking, and scale it up to handle a lot more products!
- We will focus on using Svelte to provide a front end to our site. Svelte can work with tools such as GraphQL for managing data, but support is not enabled by default; we would have to use a third-party plugin for this purpose. To keep things simple, we will define a small JSON-based data block; in an ideal world, we would scale up to the likes of GraphQL to better manage expected volumes.

We will explore what would be required to hook into GraphQL later in Chapter 3.

- We can use Svelte with tools such as GraphQL or routers, but it's important to remember that Svelte doesn't operate in the same way as React or Angular, which comes with many of these tools built-in as standard.
- The demo we will build will act as a sound basis for developing your projects – there will be features that we won't include in this demo, but we would need to later. I will go through some suggestions later in the book.

Okay, let's continue. Before we start coding, let's quickly cover an essential part, which is understanding the architecture we will use in our demo.

Working Out the Architecture

Architecture is an essential part of any site – this is what makes it easier to manage features such as data or state and help keep our code DRY, so we're not repeating ourselves too often. For this book, we will keep the structure very simple, with all of the various elements we create in the `\src` folder.

If we take a look at the folder structure, we can see that the `\src` folder contains the files and folders listed in Figure 2-6 – note that `App.svelte` and `main.js` come as standard; we will create the others.

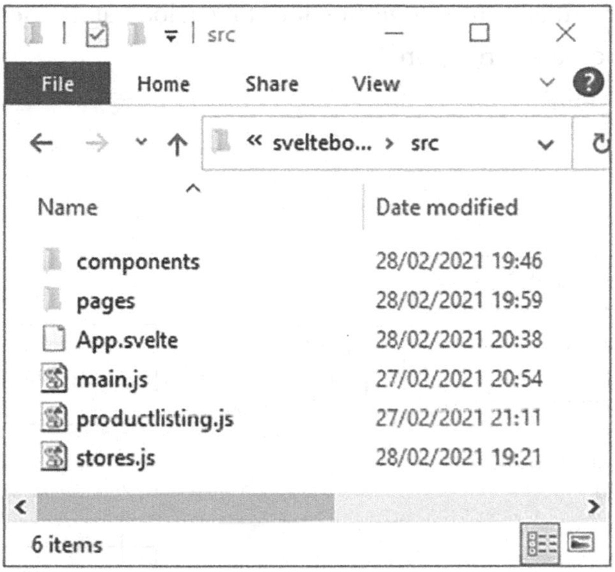

Figure 2-6. *The list of components for our project*

Inside the `\components` folder, we will create the following:

- `Button.svelte` – We'll use this for the add-to-cart feature in the product gallery and on individual product pages.
- `Cart.svelte` – This is the main shopping cart component for the site.
- `Header.svelte` and `Footer.svelte` – These we will use to create the header and footer for the page layout.
- `Products.svelte` – This forms the main product gallery for the site.
- `Product.svelte` – This is the product card with individual details of a chosen product.

Switching to the `\pages` folder, we will add three pages: About, Coffee, and Home. These are not compulsory, but give a little context to the site and make it look a little more realistic. The About and Home pages will be self-explanatory; the Coffee page is a little history about the coffee we would be selling from our site.

There are two ancillary files we will also create and store at the root of the `\src` folder in the next chapter – these are `productlisting.js` and `stores.js`.

To understand how it all hangs together, let's take a look at a schematic of the site architecture that I've created in Figure 2-7.

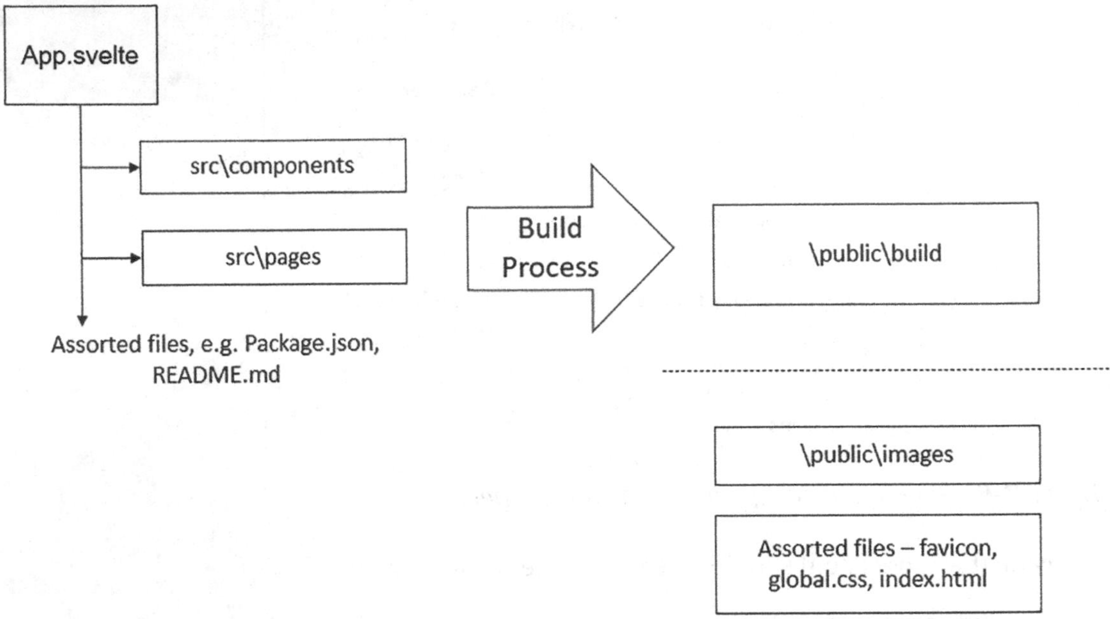

***Figure 2-7.** Architectural schematic of the site*

Here, we can see the parent `App.svelte`, which calls components and pages from the `src` folder. During the build process, Svelte pulls the script code into a compiled `bundle.js` file, with styles in `bundle.css`. We can directly call images from within the `\public\images` folder, at the same time.

As you've been working through the demo, notice anything particular about filenames, say in comparison to React? It doesn't matter if we're developing a page or component; they are effectively the same thing when it comes to file naming in Svelte. It comes with a big proviso, though: they all follow the same structure, but when it comes to adding code, there are some differences.

We will cover it later in more detail.

Moving on, the first task is to update the main application component, `App.svelte`.

Making a Start with App.svelte

For our first exercise, we need to update the `App.svelte` file – this is effectively the master file, of which all of the other files will hang. We'll use this to generate the structure for our page – let's take a look at what is involved in more detail.

CREATING APP.SVELTE

To update the `App.svelte` file, follow these steps:

1. We'll start by opening a copy of `App.svelte` – delete the line of code between the `<script>` tags, and replace it with this:

```
<script>
  import { Products, Footer, Header, Product, CartLength, Cart } from
  "./components";

  import About from "./pages/About.svelte";
  import Home from "./pages/Home.svelte";
  import Coffee from "./pages/Coffee.svelte";

  import { Router, Link, Route } from "svelte-routing";
  import {products, cart, counter } from "./stores.js";
  export let url = "";
</script>
```

2. Next, leave a line blank, and then add in this block – this will take care of managing the navigation for the site:

```
<Header />
<Router url="{url}">
  <nav>
    <Link to="/">Home</Link>
    <Link to="/products">Shop</Link>
    <Link to="/about">Our Story</Link>
    <Link to="/coffee">Our Coffee</Link>
  </nav>
```

3. Although we've added in navigation, it won't work immediately – it's reliant on setting up a plugin, which we will cover momentarily. For now, go ahead and remove the markup between the existing <main> tags, and then replace it with this:

```
<main>
  <Route path="/" component="{Home}" />
  <Route path="products" component="{Products}" />
  <Route path="about" component="{About}" />
  <Route path="coffee" component="{Coffee}" />
  <Route path="/product/:id" component="{Product}" />
</main>
```

4. We're almost there – to close off the markup, we need to add in the closing tag for <Router>, followed by the call to what will be our footer:

```
</Router>
<Footer />
```

5. Next, leave a line blank, and then add in this block – this is a placeholder for styles that we will add in a later chapter:

```
<style>
...TO BE ADDED LATER...
</style>
```

6. Go ahead and save the file and close it – we have finished with the file for now.

7. Now fire up a Node.js terminal session and change the working folder to our project area.

8. At the prompt, run this command to install our missing plugin:

```
npm install svelte-routing -s
```

9. We've completed the changes – if we were to run npm run dev to fire up the Svelte dev server and preview the changes, we wouldn't get anything! It will result in our code generating several errors; this is to be expected. Don't worry, though – we will fix most (if not all) of them in this chapter!

We now have the basics for our site, but I'll bet you're wondering: what exactly have we added? It is what makes Svelte so easy to use; we focus on producing clean, easy-to-read code!

Most of what we add will be standard JavaScript, CSS, and HTML markup, with only a few Svelte keywords in the mix. That said, we should cover a couple of essential points from this demo, so let's take a moment to review the code in more detail.

Reviewing the Code Changes

So, what did we create? Well, we can consider `App.svelte` as the root component for our site; all other components hang off this one. To set ours up, we kicked off by including a handful of imports. Most of these are for pages, such as About, Coffee, and Home, but we also import the svelte-routing plugin and `stores.js` file simultaneously.

We will cover the significance of `stores.js` later in the book, but for now, let's explore what this svelte-routing plugin does in more detail.

To understand how it works, move down to the `<Router...>` line of code at the start of our markup. This line is where our navigation starts; Svelte takes each page we want to display and displays it as a module within the parent page, `App.svelte`. So, if we were to navigate to Shop

```
<Link to="/products">Shop</Link>
```

Svelte-routing uses the Route line a little lower to display the `Products.svelte` component on the page:

```
<Route path="products" component="{Products}" />
```

Sounds straightforward enough, right? Well, svelte-routing can achieve a lot more; imagine if we needed to navigate to a dynamic link such as in a blog:

```
<Link to="/blog">Blog</Link>
```

In this case, svelte-routing would take the ID of the post link and use it to route to the blog page, using a link such as this:

```
<Route path="blog/:id" component="{BlogPost}" />
```

I would strongly recommend looking at the GitHub site documentation for this plugin at `https://github.com/EmilTholin/svelte-routing`. We've only touched the surface of what is possible with this plugin!

Moving on, with the main `App.svelte` file in place, we can start to build out the components needed for our mini site. We could link to them individually, but a better method is to build a component index - to see why, let's take a peek at the code in more detail.

Setting Up the Component Index

Now we need to set up a component index!

I suspect those of you who have used tools, such as React or Vue, will be familiar with this principle. For the uninitiated, we create a file that contains references to each of the components we use.

How is this of use to us? Well, take another look at the top of the `app.svelte` file we've just created - notice this statement?

```
<script>
  import { Products, Footer, Header, Product, CartLength, Cart } from
  "./components";
```

Typically, when importing files into a project that uses a framework such as React, we might do something like this:

```
  import About from "./pages/About.svelte";
  import Home from "./pages/Home.svelte";
  ...
```

It works perfectly fine but is wordy - instead, we group the import statements into one file (usually called index) and replace it with a single call that references all of the components in one shot.

The index file then knows where to get that component from; this process makes it easier as we don't have to alter `app.svelte` each time; we simply add a reference to the index file. Let us now quickly create this index file.

CREATING THE COMPONENT INDEX

To set up the component index, work through these steps:

1. First, open a new file, and save it as index.js at the root of the `\src` folder.
2. Next, go ahead and add this block of import statements:

```
import Products from "./Products.svelte";
import Footer from "./Footer.svelte";
import Header from "./Header.svelte";
import Product from "./Product.svelte";
import CartLength from "./CartLength.svelte";
import Cart from "./Cart.svelte";
```

3. We need to finish it with an export statement – this tells Svelte to make the components available for importing into our project. Leave a line blank, and then add this line:

```
export { Products, Footer, Header, Product, CartLength, Cart }
```

4. Go ahead and save the file, and then close it – we've completed the changes for now.

Great, we now have our component index in place! If we run the code, it will still cause an error, but we are one step closer to fixing it. We still have a few more components to write, so let's move on and look at the next one: the header.

Creating the Header

Now that we have our main `app.svelte` file in place, along with a component index, it's time to create some of the missing components.

There are seven in total that we need to create; all follow similar principles. We also have three pages to assemble too; for convenience, we will lift copies of the relevant files from the code download that accompanies this book. At the same time, we will also copy across various images required for the site. I've sourced these from multiple locations, such as FreeSVG.org (`https://freesvg.org`), but feel free to use your own versions if you prefer.

Let's make a start with setting up the header component.

BUILDING THE HEADER

This first component is very easy – it's a basic header for our site, which will appear across all pages. To get this component set up, follow these steps:

1. Crack open a new file in your editor, and then add in this `<script>` block:

```
<script>
  import { writable } from "svelte/store";
  import { cart } from "../stores.js";
</script>
```

2. Next, leave a line blank, and add in this placeholder – this is something we will update later in Chapter 7:

```
<style>
...TO BE ADDED LATER...
</style>
```

3. Finally, we also need to add in our markup – for this, go ahead and leave an empty line, and then add in this code:

```
<header>
  <div>
    <span>Small Coffee Company</span>
  </div>
  <div>
    <span>{$counter}</span>
  </div>
</header>
```

4. Extract a copy of the images folder from the code download that accompanies this book, and save it to the `\src\public\` folder – this will provide images for the various components and pages for our mini site, including the header.

5. Save the file as `header.svelte` in a new folder called `components`, under the `\src` folder – we can close it.

Short, sweet, and straightforward - that's how I like my exercises. Okay, yes, I know that might open me up to various - shall we say - comments, but there is some truth in the matter: anything for a simple life!

There is, however, one crucial point that we should explore more from this demo - the use of the writable import. Ordinarily, I would go into detail here, but we will cover it and more when we explore data and state management in the next chapter. For now, all we need to know is that it deals with passing values between components and that this (in a way) is similar to the principles used by React's props facility.

Let's move on. The next component we will set up is the footer - this one is purely markup, although we use a plugin. To see what I mean, let's dive in and take a look.

Setting Up the Footer

We have the main app file in place, along with our component index and the header - we can't have the latter without top and tailing it with a footer! Fortunately, this is just as easy to set up - let's take a look at what's involved in more detail.

BUILDING THE FOOTER

To get the footer set up and ready for use, work through these steps:

1. First, fire up a new file in your editor – go ahead and save it as `Header.svelte` in the `\src\components` folder.

2. Next, go ahead and create a new folder inside our project area – call it `public`.

3. Extract a copy of the `images` folder from the code download that accompanies this book, and drop the entire folder into the `\public` folder.

4. Next, go ahead and add in this script block at the top of the file – this will take care of handling some SVGs that we use in the footer:

```
<script>
  import InlineSVG from 'svelte-inline-svg';
```

```
  $: attributes = {
    width: 30,
    height: 30,
    fill: "#fff",
  }
</script>
```

5. As before, we need to add in a placeholder for some styling that will come later – for this, leave a blank line, and then add in this block:

```
<style>
...TO BE ADDED LATER...
</style>
```

6. The remaining code is markup that forms our footer – go ahead and add the following below the style block, leaving a blank line before it:

```
<footer>
  <div>
    <span>&copy; Small Coffee Shop 2021</span>
  </div>
  <div>
    <span>
      <a href="https://facebook.com/smallcoffeeshop"><InlineSVG
      src="/images/facebook.svg" {...attributes} /></a>
      <a href="https://instagram.com/smallcoffeeshop"><InlineSVG
      src="/images/instagram.svg" {...attributes} /></a>
      <a href="https://Twitter.com/smallcoffeeshop"><InlineSVG
      src="/images/twitter.svg" {...attributes} /></a>
    </span>
  </div>
</footer>
```

7. Save the file – you can now close it.

That's another step closer to getting the basic site set up - we still have a few more components to add, though! Most of what we added in this demo is just plain HTML markup; the CSS styling we will add later when we cover styling in Chapter 7. There is one point of interest, and that's the plugin we've used: `svelte-inline-svg`.

The plugin is available from `https://github.com/robinscholz/svelte-inline-svg`; it does as it says on the tin by inlining SVG images into our markup. We inserted three SVGs using code similar to this:

```
<a href="https://facebook.com/smallcoffeeshop">
  <InlineSVG src="/images/facebook.svg" {...attributes} />
</a>
```

The plugin turns that code into this (Figure 2-8).

```
▼<div class="svelte-1r7nbp7">
  ▼<span>
    ▼<a href="https://facebook.com/smallcoffeeshop" class="svelte
    -1r7nbp7">
      ▶<svg xmlns="http://www.w3.org/2000/svg" width="30"
      height="30" fill="#fff" contenteditable="true" viewBox="0 0
      24 24" enable-background="new 0 0 24 24" id="regular" xmlns=
      "http://www.w3.org/2000/svg">…</svg>
      </a>
```

Figure 2-8. *Example of inline SVG code using the InlineSVG plugin*

It is preferable to in-line SVGs where possible, as we can style individual elements within the SVG. SVGs in image files will be treated as images and can only be styled via externally facing properties such as `width` and `height`.

Okay, let's keep going and turn our attention to setting up the product gallery, which will be the shop window to our store.

Creating the Product Gallery

Assembling the product gallery is the most critical part of our project – after all, we clearly wouldn't be able to sell without products and therefore make money!

For this book, we'll keep to just a handful of products that we will source from a data block – we will explore sourcing data using other methods later in the book. To get things started, let's take a look at the code required in more detail.

CONSTRUCTING THE PRODUCT GALLERY

To get the product gallery wired up, follow these steps:

1. We'll start by cracking open a new file, saving it as `products.svelte`, at the root of the `\src\components` folder.
2. Next, go ahead and add this script block – this will take care of adding products to our basket directly from the product gallery:

```
<script>
  import {products, cart} from "../stores.js";
  import Cart from "./Cart.svelte";

  export let location;

  const addToCart = (product) => {
    for (let item of $cart) {
      if(item.id === product.id) {
        product.quantity += 1
        $cart = $cart;
        return;
      }
    }
    $cart = [...$cart, product]
  }
</script>
```

3. Go ahead and miss a line, and then add in this placeholder – we will come back to adding styles later in this book:

```
<style>
...TO BE ADDED LATER...
</style>
```

4. Finally, we need to add in the markup that will render the products on the page – for this, go ahead and add in this code, leaving a line blank first after the style placeholder:

```
<div class="product-list">
  {#each $products as product}
    <div>
      <div class="image" style="background-image:
      url({product.image})"></div>
    <h4><a href="product/{product.id}">{product.name}</a></h4>
    <p>${product.price}</p>
    <button on:click={() => addToCart(product)}>Add to cart</button>
    </div>
  {/each}
</div>
<Cart />
```

5. Go ahead and save the file, and then close it.

Although we are getting close to a starting site that runs, if we were to run our code now, it would error - we still need to add several components! One of these components is the product detail (or description) page - let's run through what's required in more detail.

Building the Product Card

With the product gallery now set up, our shop is beginning to take shape. We could stop there, but who has ever used a site without some form of product detail page (or PDP)?

It is an essential part of the site for the customer - it is where they can learn more about the product, the options available, pricing, and more. We will keep things simple for now and show just some basic details, but there is no excuse not to develop the content further should we go into production use.

CREATING THE PRODUCT CARD

This exercise is a little more involved – you will see it uses similar principles to the product gallery but begins to extend it by including a Svelte-driven conditional check. Let's take a look at the steps required to create our product page:

1. To get started, create a new document, saving it as `Product.svelte` at the root of the `\src\components` folder.

2. Next, go ahead and add in this block of code – this contains some variable declarations, an import statement and (another) add-to-cart function:

```
<script>
  let individualID = document.location.pathname.split("/")[2];
  let individualName;

  import {products, cart} from "../stores.js";

  const addToCart = (product) => {
    for(let item of $cart) {
        if(item.id === product.id) {
          product.quantity += 1
          $cart = $cart;
          return;
        }
    }
    $cart = [...$cart, product]
  }
</script>
```

3. You will recognize this next step – we need to add in the now-familiar placeholder folder for our styling:

```
<style>
...TO BE ADDED LATER...
</style>
```

4. The last block to add in is the HTML markup – leave a line blank, and then drop in this code:

```
<a href="/products">{"<< Back to Shop"}</a>

<div id="productdetails">
  {#each $products as product }
    {#if product.id == individualID}
      <div>
        <p><img src="{product.large_image}" alt="{product.name}" /></p>
      </div>
      <div>
        <p>{product.name}</p>
        <p>SKU: {individualID}</p>
        <p>{product.description}</p>
        <h2>${product.price}</h2>
        <button on:click={() => addToCart(product)}>Add to cart</button>
      </div>
    {/if}
  {/each}
</div>
```

5. Go ahead and save the file, and then close it.

We are now close to completing the construction of the components! We now have a working (if albeit somewhat simplistic) product page in place – this shows off a few valuable techniques specific to Svelte, so let's take a moment to review these in more detail.

Reviewing the Code

By now, I am sure you will start to see a theme for creating Svelte components – notice how we have three blocks, starting with `<script>`, followed by the CSS, and rounded off with our markup?

Creating the `Product.svelte` is no different; we follow the same format for structuring our code. However, we've started to use more Svelte keywords in this component; the first is the `import` statement near the top of the file.

We're importing two values from `stores.js` to source the data required for the page; we're not using a source such as GraphQL to manage data. Instead, we're using what is effectively a flat-file structure (of sorts) to hold our data. I'll come back to this later in the book.

For now, let's move down to our markup and come back to the `addToCart` button. We imported our data at the top of the component (using the `import` statement - that's a good hint as to what it does!). We then iterate through all of the products using an `#each` block. If `product.id` matches the chosen ID, we display the details using HTML markup formatted with string literal placeholders.

What makes it all hang together is the statement at the top of the script block:

```
let individualID = document.location.pathname.split("/")[2];
```

We get the ID of the product we want to display from the URL and then use it to iterate through all of the product data imported into the component. Once that data is rendered on-screen, we have an `on:click` handler assigned to the button, to add products to our cart; the addToCart function takes care of this process.

There is one catch here - owing to how Svelte updates values, we need to use the `$cart = $cart` statement to force it to update values displayed in the cart. These are then re-rendered by the spread operator at the end of that function.

Phew, it sounds a bit complex! Don't worry, we will go through managing data more in the next chapter; this refreshing process will make more sense once we've covered how Svelte handles data changes.

Right, let's crack on with the next part: adding products to our shopping cart. Before we do so, there is one component we need to add - has anyone noticed anything about the references to `<Button...>` in the last couple of exercises?

Creating a Button Component

Yes, the sharp-eyed among you should spot that we've not created the component, even though we've added references to one! Let's quickly correct that omission, by adding one in now.

ADDING A BUTTON COMPONENT

To add in the button, follow these steps:

1. First, crack open a new file in your editor, and save it as `Button.svelte` in the `\src\` components folder.
2. Go ahead and add in the following code:

```
<style>
...TO BE ADDED LATER...
</style>

<button on:click>
  <slot />
</button>
```

3. Save the file and close it – no further changes are required.

Excellent, now that we've gotten that out of the way, let's carry on with adding the cart to our demo.

Adding the Cart

It is the last part of our site and the most important - without it, customers can't pay for the goods they order! Everything else is in place, so all that is left for us to do is add in the cart and checkout button, ready to connect to a payment provider at a later date.

> We will cover the checkout part later in Chapter 10 when we look at using third-party libraries with Svelte.

This code is a little more complex than that we've seen so far - let's take a look at what is involved to add a cart to our site in more detail.

PUTTING TOGETHER THE CART

To get the cart feature set up, follow these steps:

1. First, create a new file called `Cart.svelte` – save it in the `\src\components` folder.
2. We have a good chunk of code to add, so go ahead and add in this block, beginning with an `import` and the `removeItem` event handler:

```
<script>
  import { cart } from "../stores.js";

  const removeItem = (product) => {
    for(let item of $cart) {
      if(item.id === product.id) {
       if(product.quantity > 1 ) {
         product.quantity -= 1
         $cart = $cart
       } else {
         $cart = $cart.filter((cartItem) => cartItem != product)
       }
       return;
      }
    }
  }
```

3. Next, leave a blank line, and then add in the `addItem` event handler, thus:

```
const addItem = (product) => {
  for(let item of $cart) {
    if(item.id === product.id) {
      product.quantity += 1
      $cart = $cart;
      return;
    }
  }
}
```

4. We have a couple of lines left to cover, so skip a line and drop in the following code:

```
  $: total = $cart.reduce((sum, item) => sum + item.price * item.
  quantity, 0)
</script>
```

5. You'll recognize this next bit – yes, we need to add in the now-familiar style placeholder! Leave a line, and then add in this code:

```
<style>
...TO BE ADDED LATER...
</style>
```

6. Last but by no means least, let's add in the HTML markup for our cart:

```
<div class="cart-list">
  {#each $cart as item }
    {#if item.quantity > 0}
    <div class="cart-item">
      <img width="50" src={item.image} alt={item.name}/>
      <div>{item.quantity}
        <button on:click={() => addItem(item)}>+</button>
        <button on:click={() => removeItem(item)}>-</button>
      </div>
      <p>${item.price * item.quantity}</p>
    </div>
    {/if}
  {/each}
  <div class="total">
    <h4>Total: $ {total}</h4>
  </div>
</div>
```

7. At this point, we have finished with the file; go ahead and save your work, and then close the file.

So far, the exercises we've completed have been relatively straightforward; all use code that is mainly self-explanatory, with little functionality required for each component.

The cart is the odd one out, in as much as this contains a lot more functionality in comparison! This component uses some features of Svelte that are of particular interest; let's take a moment to review the code in more detail before finishing up with creating the remaining pages for our site.

Breaking Apart the Code Used

We've added a good chunk of code for this last demo - the question is, though, what does it all mean? Well, most of it is just standard HTML markup and CSS, but there are nonetheless some important features we should explore.

Let's start with the first - we began by creating a `removeItem` event handler; this iterated through each item of `$cart` (our cart). If we found a product ID match, we then subtracted one from `product.quantity`, before refreshing the cart value. If we found that the `product.quantity` was equal to 1, we would remove it from the cart altogether. We used the same principles in the `addItem` event handler, but this time added 1 to the count and didn't remove anything!

Next up came this line:

```
$: total = $cart.reduce((sum, item) => sum + item.price * item.quantity, 0)
```

This line is of particular interest - it might seem odd to use a $ symbol to start it, but there is a reason. It tells Svelte to update the value of `total` each time a change is made. This function uses a reducer to add up our basket's total cost by multiplying the `item.price` with `item.quantity`, to arrive at a single value calculated from multiple inputs (hence the name reducer!).

For the last part, we skip to the HTML markup, which contains three items of particular note: the use of `#each...as`, `#if.../if`, and the `on:click` handlers. In a nutshell, the first two iterate through a handful of items and determine whether to action something, in much the same way as we might use a `for...each` block or `if...else...then` check. The latter is the Svelte syntax for defining `on:click()` style handlers for elements when using Svelte.

> We will explore the first two in more detail in Chapter 4, while we will cover events in Chapter 5. We also included an import into our component for stores.js – I will go into the significance of this file in more detail in Chapter 3. Suffice to say it relates to handling data; I will reveal all in that chapter!

Okay, we should do one more task: we've added in some references to three pages for our site. As these are standard markup and CSS, we will get these from the code download that accompanies this book - let's cover this off before moving onto testing our site for the first time.

Creating the Remaining Pages

At this point, we've now added the bulk of the code required for our store - there remain only three files to source, `About.svelte`, `Coffee.svelte`, and `Home.svelte`.

These are some additional pages to help make our mini site look a little more realistic. They are not obligatory, but if you don't include them, you will need to remove references to allow the site to work!

All three files can be sourced from the `\src\pages` folder in the code download that accompanies this book; copy and paste the folder as-is into the \src folder of our project area.

File Formats and Svelte – A Note

By now, I'm sure you will have noticed that we've used two file formats - `.svelte` and `.js` - when constructing our components.

It's important to note that you will simply need to use `.svelte` for constructing pages and components in most cases. The only time we need to use `.js` as a file format is when importing content that is **not** a component. By this, I'm thinking of files such as `stores.js`; all other files should use the `.svelte` extension during development.

Okay, that aside, everything is now in place: it's time to start.

Testing the Initial Site

We now have the basics of our mini store - granted, it won't be perfect, but it will at least show the core elements of how we might begin to create such a store using Svelte.

It's at this point we can now run the site; to do this, switch to a Node.js terminal session, and then run `npm run dev` at the prompt (making sure you change the working folder first). If all is well, we should see something akin to Figure 2-9.

Small Coffee Company
0
Home Shop Our Story Our Coffee
Welcome to Small Coffee Company - high quality great coffee, roasted with love in the heart of Yorkshire
Lorem ipsum dolor sit amet, consectetur adipiscing elit. Maecenas sed odio id nulla gravida rhoncus. Suspendisse potenti. In volutpat nibh

Figure 2-9. *The site running without styling*

Okay, it won't win any styling awards anytime soon, but, hey, it is at least running, albeit a little functional! It gives us an excellent base to start fleshing out how it looks and works – this is something we will do through five chapters before deploying it into production in Chapter 9.

Summary

Building a site should be considered something of a journey – it's not about the end product, but the journey, which is more important! It is no different with Svelte; we still use the same principles, irrespective of the framework. We've started on that journey to construct our microsite; let's take a moment to review what we learned thus far in this chapter.

We began working through the principles of creating a simple component, using the playground that comes with Svelte. We then moved onto setting expectations for our project before exploring the proposed architecture for the site.

Next up came the start of the construction process – here, we began with the core app file before working our way through each of the various components. We then finished pulling the product pages from the code download (as they are simple markup pages) before testing the site for the first time. Granted, it won't win any style awards any time soon, but we will quickly fix that later in this book!

Right, we still have a lot more to cover, so let's move swiftly on: it's time to get down with data! All right, that was a terrible play on words, but data plays a fundamental role in any site. We've added in simple data to start things off, but what if we wanted to use a third-party source, for example? No problem – stay with me, and I will show you that and more when we explore how to link in data to our Svelte site.

CHAPTER 3

Managing State and Data

So far, we've worked our way through constructing components for our site, but they are no good without one thing – data!

I'm sure someone once said "Content is king" – it doesn't matter if this is product content, or the results of asking our customers for information such as product quantity, decent data is essential for any website.

Not only is producing accurate and valid data vital, we also need to manage it properly. It's no good if we ask customers how many items they want to purchase, yet present completely inaccurate values or keep asking for the same data! For this chapter, we will explore the world of passing information around components used in our site, while taking a look at how to maintain state between said components and what happens when components react to changes made on our site.

We have to start somewhere, so let's first take a look at answering a single question.

Why Is Data So Important in Svelte?

There is a simple answer to that question, although the question we should really be asking is what makes state and data so important in Svelte? This has a lot to do with what makes Svelte tick: reactivity. You see, Svelte is all about keeping the DOM in sync with changes we make in application state. This could be anything from changing a value to performing multiple actions in response to a triggered event.

This principle is something that features heavily in frameworks such as React, and Svelte is no different. For example, I'm sure you will have seen code similar to this:

```
<script>
  let count = 0;

  function handleClick() {
    count += 1;
  }
</script>
```


A. Libby, *Practical Svelte*, https://doi.org/10.1007/978-1-4842-7374-6_3

```
<button on:click={handleClick}>
  Clicked {count} {count === 1 ? 'time' : 'times'}
</button>
```

While it is true that it is written in Svelte, the same principle applies to frameworks such as React and Vue, where we trigger the execution of a function on clicking a button. When this happens, Svelte will tell the assignment with code that tells the DOM to update the state.

This seems straightforward, right? Well, what if you came across this piece of code?

```
let numcount = 0;
$: doubled = numcount * 2;
```

This is specific to Svelte and is called a **reactive declaration** – it is used to compute a value from more than one base value. It will recompute automatically when any of the base values change: in this example, this would be `numcount`.

There is one thing we should note when it comes to using Svelte though. Svelte's reactivity is triggered by assignments, so using array methods like push and splice won't automatically cause updates. For example, try running this code in an instance of the Svelte playground:

```
<script>
  let numbers = [5, 6, 7, 8];
  function addNumber() {
    numbers.push(numbers.length + 1);
  }

  $: sum = numbers.reduce((t, n) => t + n, 0);
</script>

<p>{numbers.join(' + ')} = {sum}</p>

<button on:click={addNumber}>
  Add a number
</button>
```

The output should be 26, but it's not rendering at all in our output. What gives? The answer lies in a lack of assignment in the `addNumber()` function – we need to do something that assigns a value, before Svelte will update. To fix the code, try changing the line in the `addNumber()` function to this:

```
function addNumber() {
  numbers = [...numbers, numbers.length + 1];
}
```

We can also add `numbers=numbers` to the original code which will work just as well; a spread operator makes it clearer as to what we're doing.

It works now! It does mean that we can't use keywords such as pop, `shift`, `unshift`, or `splice`; instead, we have to use assignments to trigger an update in state within Svelte.

Moving on, although we talk about maintaining (or updating state), in reality we're updating values or data in code. There are several different ways to do this – let's take a look at the options.

For exercises in this chapter, we will use the REPL playground for convenience; these exercises will work just as well if you want to run them locally.

Passing and Setting Values in Code

If we need to update data or values (and therefore change state), we can use any one of several different techniques to affect the update.

These split roughly into two groups – reacting to events or changes and passing data. If we need to react to an event or change, then we can

- React to an event using a handler, such as `on:click`, where we perform one or more tasks in the event handler
- Use the `$:` operator to update a value, particularly if that value has to be computed from several different values

If, however, we need to pass values around the site, we can use one of these three methods:

- Using prop values (similar to React or Vue), to pass data around components from parent to child
- Creating a store to make data available and accessible from any component
- Using context to pass values around a site

It's important to note that each has its own quirks; we will explore the difference between each later in this chapter and understand when we should use each method.

Okay, let's move on. Throughout this book, we're focusing on building a mini ecommerce site to sell coffee. We will use some of the techniques we've covered so far, but before we do, let's build some quick demos to see how some of what we've explored so far works in action. We'll begin with passing prop values between components.

Exploring the World of Props

Cast your mind back to the start of this chapter – we talked about how to manage state inside of a component, but doing so between components requires a whole different approach. We've briefly covered the three ways to do this; our starting point (and which is similar to the likes of React) is to set and pass properties between components.

This is arguably the simplest method, but also the most clunky – we have to pass a property down through each layer, which can get cumbersome if doing this for a component more than two to three layers deep. There are ways to get around that which we will cover in more detail shortly, but for now, let's take a look at how to pass props within Svelte in more detail.

PASSING PROPS

To set up this demo, run through these steps:

1. First, go ahead and browse to `https://svelte.dev/repl` – as before, just be aware that it will redirect to a version-specific URL, to indicate which version of Svelte is being used.
2. Next, in the first tab which should be labeled `App.svelte`, add this code:

```
<script>
  import Button from "./Button.svelte";

  function Twitter() {
    console.log("Twitter button clicked");
  }
  function Instagram() {
    console.log("Instagram button clicked");
  }

  function Facebook() {
    console.log("Facebook button clicked");
  }
</script>

<div>
  <h1>Get me on social media!</h1>
  <Button name="twitter" handleClick={Twitter} />
  <Button name="instagram" handleClick={Instagram} />
  <Button name="facebook" handleClick={Facebook} />
</div>
```

3. Next, click the + symbol to the right of the tab name, and replace the (highlighted) word `Component2` with `Button`:

```
<script>
  export let name;
  export let handleClick;
</script>

<button on:click={handleClick}>{name}</button>
```

4. If all is well, we should see something akin to the screenshot shown in Figure 3-1.

***Figure 3-1.** The results of passing props to our Button component*

Cool – it's a simple demo, but illustrates perfectly how we can pass properties to a single component!

Although we've passed distinct values in each instance, there is more we can do: we can even set default values or use a spread operator if we want to pass multiple values to that component. In the meantime, let's take a quick look at the code we've created, ready to see how we might use it in our shop demo later in this chapter.

Reviewing the Code

If you've spent any time developing with frameworks such as React or Vue, then you will likely be familiar with the concept of passing props – we pass values as part of calling a component and that these can be single properties, variables, or even functions.

It's no different with Svelte, as the last demo illustrates – we began with importing our `<Button>` component, before creating three simple functions to render a statement to the console. In the markup section, we then call that Button component three times, in each instance passing the name of the function we want it to run from within the Button component, and the name tag that should be applied to each instance of `Button`.

The real magic to making this work lies in the `Button.svelte` tab – here, we have defined two export statements. The first is the `name` tag for each button, and the second is the function it should execute when clicked. We insert the values into the placeholders (marked with parentheses), before executing the `on:click` handler when the appropriate button is clicked.

It's worth noting that we are not limited to passing static values in props – we can equally pass variables as well or functions as we have done in this last exercise.

There is one thing we need to be aware of though, and that relates to the architecture of using props. Props only work when we are walking up and down the same tree, not across different trees.

What do I mean by this? Well, imagine your components are on the same branch of a tree, with the top most at the root of the branch and the child some way down the branch. We can navigate up and down fine, but what if the target child component was on a different branch of that tree? That wouldn't be accessible using props - instead, we have to use a different method to pass values down to that component.

Making Use of Context in Svelte

If we need to pass values between components (be they static, dynamic, or even a function), then this is straightforward when the components are very close together and in the same hierarchy. By default, we must maintain state at the parent level and pass down - if we pass upward, Svelte will complain that we are creating a circular effect.

If the components are some ways apart, or not even in the same tree, then using props becomes less practical; instead, we have to use the Context API. This is perfect for communicating with multiple components and descendants, but avoids the need to pass props - instead, we communicate with a central store (not to be confused with Svelte stores - more later!).

The API is part of Svelte and provides two functions we can use - `getContext` and `setContext`. It works on a key-value pair arrangement, where we set an object in our context and associate it with a key or identifier. Take a look at this example:

```
<script>
  import { setContext } from 'svelte';
  const myObject = {};
  setContext('myKey', myObject)
<script>
```

Granted, this is just an example, so I certainly wouldn't advocate using my naming convention, but it's the principle of how it works that counts!

Once defined and set, we can then use getContext to pull the object assigned to our key:

```
<script>
  import { getContext } from 'svelte'
  const myObject = getContext('myKey')
</script>
```

We can only use `getContext` to retrieve a key either within the component which used `setContext` or in one of its descendants – this descendant can be several layers deep, but the important point here is we do not have to pass values via intermediate descendants.

If we need to communicate with a component in a different tree, then we need to use Svelte store tool – more on this later in this chapter.

Okay, enough talking: it's time to get dirty with context, so to speak! To really understand how it works, let's take a look at a quick demo using the Svelte playground.

MAKING USE OF CONTEXT

In this demo, we're going to switch from one color to another, after a two-second delay:

1. First, browse to the Svelte REPL site at `https://svelte.dev/repl` – don't forget that the URL will redirect, as from previous exercises.
2. In the `App.svelte` tab, add this code, which will perform the change using `setContext`:

```
<script>
  import {setContext, getContext} from 'svelte';
  import {writable} from 'svelte/store';
  import Child from './Child.svelte';

  let state = writable({color: 'hotpink'});
  setContext('state', state);

  setTimeout(() => {$state = {color: 'red'}},2000);
</script>

<Child />
```

3. Switch to a new tab, and then rename it to be `Child.svelte` – in the main part of this tab, add this code:

```
<script>
  import {getContext} from 'svelte';
  const state = getContext('state')
</script>

<h1>
  This is the {$state.color} value
</h1>
```

4. If all is well, we should see the color change from hot pink to red, as indicated in Figure 3-2.

Figure 3-2. *Changing the color value to red using setContext*

You might want to increase the `setTimeOut` value to something larger to see the effect happening – the change is very quick!

Another simple exercise – this is what I love about Svelte! Svelte makes writing code simpler, as it uses standard markup and JavaScript where possible, with very little extra required that is specific to Svelte. It makes it a cinch to use tools such as `setContext` and `getContext` – let's take a look at the code we've used in the last demo to understand how it works.

Breaking Apart the Code

In creating our demo, we began by setting three imports in `App.svelte`; these reference the `setContext` and `getContext` methods from Svelte, as well as use the `writable` tool from Svelte (more on this later). We also import a child component into our demo.

Next up, we set a variable `state` and assign to it the key-pair value `of color: 'hotpink'`; this we add the `state` variable to context using the `setContext` command. We then run the `setTimeout` command to change the value from `hotpink` to `red` with a two-second delay; this automatically updates context.

It's at this point we then reference the Child component - inside of this, we import the `getContext` tool, before obtaining the value of state using `getContext` and rendering it on-screen.

If you want to get into the guts of how context works, take a look at `https://imfeld.dev/writing/svelte_context`. It is based on the author's own research, but nevertheless provides a useful insight into how context works and provides some alternatives to using it.

In that breakdown, I made a reference to the writable tool from within Svelte - it is used for this line:

```
let state = writable({color: 'hotpink'});
```

Given I've already mentioned that it is not part of the Svelte Context API, you might be forgiven for wondering why we're using it! Now would be a good opportunity to delve into this a little more.

In this instance, we're using the `writable` keyword simply to assign a key/value pair to a variable and **not** to a Svelte store file (as you will see in the next section). We could simply assign the value of "hotpink," but we wouldn't have a meaningful way to reference it in code. Making use of writable in this instance allows us to use `$state.color` to both reference the value and give a clear indication of what it means in our code.

Okay, let's crack on. There is one more way to pass values between components, which will make it even more useful. We've just touched on it in the last exercise, so let's continue with that theme and explore the world of stores in more detail.

Creating and Maintaining Svelte Stores

Over the last few pages, we've explored how using props can help with passing information between components. While it works well in principle as a technique, it isn't without its flaws; it can only handle components in the same tree, and we have to pass the values down through each layer which can become cumbersome. Context goes some way to resolving this, but still only within the same tree.

The real question is, how can we manage passing components across *different* trees? There is a way to do this, and we touched on using it in the last demo: Svelte `stores`.

The basic principle is that instead of passing values down, we store them in a central location, so we can access any value needed from any component. It requires a little more code to operate, but removes the need to pass down values through multiple layers - definitely a win for us! To see what I mean, let's take a look at a quick example in more detail, as part of our next exercise.

OPERATING STORES

To set up and operate a Svelte store, follow these steps:

1. First, browse to `https://svelte.dev/repl` – this URL will redirect to show which version of Svelte we are using (currently 3.35.0 at the time of writing).
2. Next, in the `App.svelte` pane on the left, add this code:

```
<script>
  import { username } from './stores.js'

  username.set('new username');
  const newUsername = 'Alex';

  username.update(existing => {
    console.log(`Updating username from ${existing} to
    ${newUsername}`);
    return newUsername
  })
</script>
<h1>
  Hello, {newUsername}! </h1>
```

3. Now go ahead and hit the + symbol next to `App.svelte` – rename the tab that appears to `stores.js`.

4. In the window below it, add in this code:

```
import { writable } from 'svelte/store'
export const username = writable('Guest');
```

5. Take a look at the right – if all is well, we should see the text shown in Figure 3-3.

***Figure 3-3.** Creating and using a value from store*

6. Next, press Ctrl+Shift+I (Win, Linux) or Cmd+Shift+I (mac) to bring up the browser console – we should see the update logged, similar to Figure 3-4.

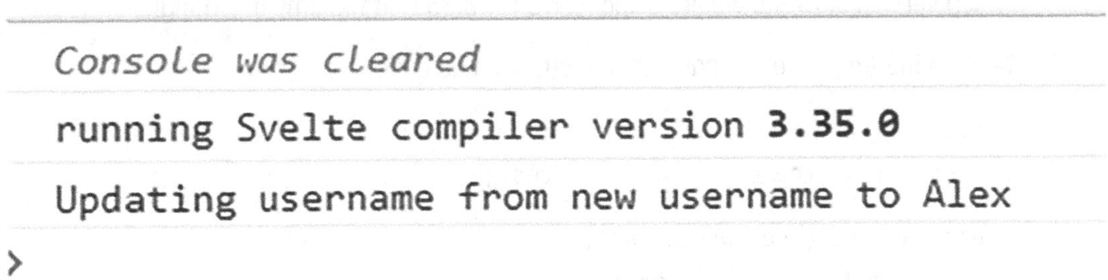

Console was cleared
running Svelte compiler version 3.35.0
Updating username from new username to Alex
>

***Figure 3-4.** Confirmation that the store value has changed*

And with that our Svelte store has been easily set up. The great thing about stores is that we can access values from any component and do not have to pass values down the chain from parent to child (as is the case for props). It is true that this last exercise was a little simplistic, but the real value will come when calling values from any component – these we treat as if they were standard variables in our code.

Leaving that aside, creating a writable store is only part of the picture; there are a few more tips and tricks we can use to really take advantage of stores. Let's take a moment to explore the code we've used in more detail, to see how it fits into the wider picture.

Understanding the Code in Detail

Implementing `stores` is a process that requires a little extra code, but is one that gives us the greatest flexibility when it comes to passing values across different components. In the same way as we did for context, we use a central location; this time though it uses a text file as our starting point, not an in-browser-based location.

In the demo we've just created, we made use of the `writable` tool part of the `store` function. To really understand how it works, we should first skip to the `stores.js` file – here, we import the `writable` tool from Svelte, before creating our `writable` store and assigning it to the `username` variable:

```
import { writable } from 'svelte/store'
export const username = writable('Guest');
```

With our store created, we then import it into `App.svelte`, before setting a value of `newUsername` to our exported variable:

```
import { username } from './stores.js'

username.set('newUsername');
```

With the `username` variable set, we now assign a new value of `Alex` to the `newUsername` property, before updating the `username` store, displaying it on-screen, and piping out a report to the browser console:

```
  const newUsername = 'Alex';

  username.update(existing => {
    console.log(`Updating username from ${existing} to ${newUsername}`);
    return newUsername
  })
</script>
<h1>
  Hello, {newUsername}!
</h1>
```

Notice how even though `newUsername` comes from a store, we can return and use it as a normal variable in our code.

In this example, we've focused on using the `writable` function; this is only part of the story though. We could equally just use the `readable()` option if we just need to source a read-only value. We could also use the `derived()` option if we want to source a value based on one or more store values.

A great example of this would be calculating the total cost of items in a shopping basket – this is something we will use in our site later in this chapter.

The important point to note is that if we need to pass values between components in different trees, then we should use stores. Now that we've covered props, context, and stores, it's vital we understand when best to use each method – let's take a moment to go through this in more detail.

Understanding the Differences

Svelte props, Context API, or stores, which one do I use? It's a very good question. We've covered three useful tools, but you thinking it might seem confusing as to which we should use and when!

Don't worry – deciding which to use boils down to two things:

- Do we need to cross between different trees?
- Do we need our "props" to be reactive, that is, respond to changes in values?

I've produced a flowchart that summarizes which option to use, which is shown in Figure 3-5.

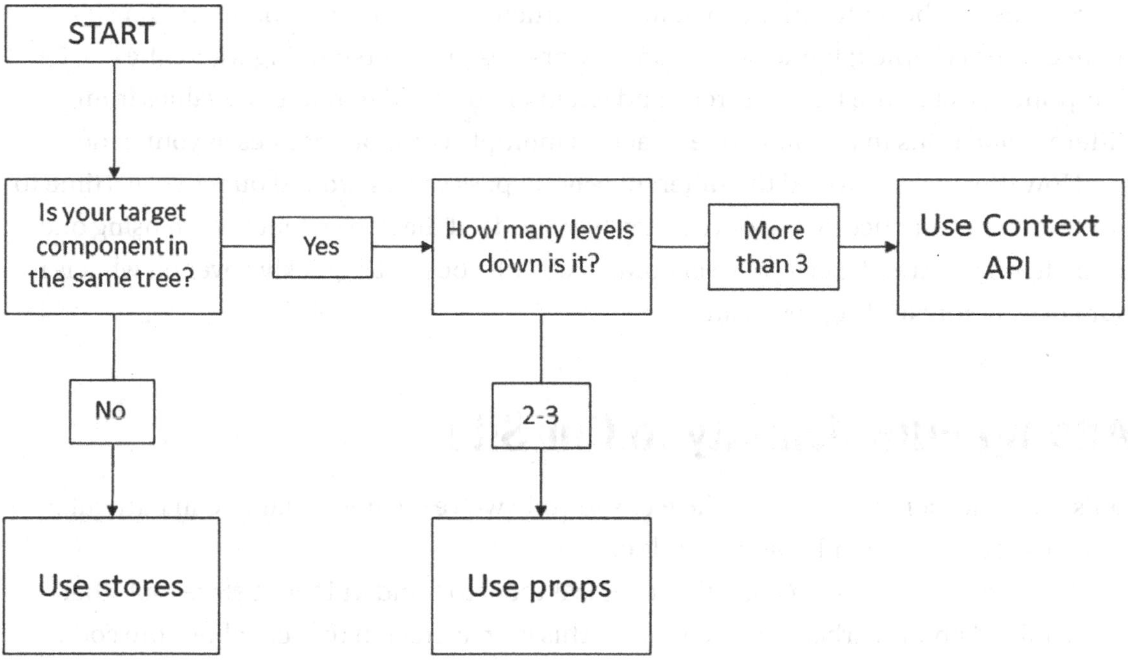

Figure 3-5. *Selecting which method to use for passing values*

The first question to ask is if we need to cross over between different component trees – to use the real branch analogy, is that component further down the same branch, or on one round the other side of the tree, or maybe even higher? If it is lower down on the same branch, then we can use props or the Context API. Either will work, but bear this in mind: if we need to pass values down more than say two to three levels, using the Context API will be the better option.

If, however, our target component is elsewhere on that proverbial tree (say round the other side, for example), then the best option to use is `stores`. This allows us to use a central location which is accessible from anywhere in our code, irrespective of where the component is in the tree (virtual or real!)

As we will see soon, the latter is particularly advantageous for our website demo, for two reasons:

- Using stores allows us to have a central repository for our product listing – it avoids the need for duplicating data.
- Stores are reactive – we can create new store values from existing stores, which is something we will use to display the basket total in the header of our site.

Stores can be a little tricky to manage, particularly if a project you're working on becomes complex; the key to making it work lies in understanding where the components sit in the tree hierarchy and whether you need to reference values from different locations in the same tree or across multiple component trees in your code.

Now that we've covered the different ways to pass values around our code, it's time to put them into practice. Some of you may have noticed that we've touched on using one of the features already; before we get practical with code, let's quickly cover off what is in our code, before adding new features.

Adding Functionality to Our Site

Let's take another closer look at the website code we've created so far and in particular two files: `stores.js` and `Header.svelte`.

These two files contain code that uses the `readable` and `writable` store tools that we've talked about earlier in this chapter – this is an extract of the readable store code from `stores.js`:

```
let products = readable([{
  id: 1,
  name: "Italian House Blend",
  ...
}
```

We use the readable store in two places within the site – the first is `Products.svelte`:

```
<script>
  import {products, cart} from "../stores.js";
  import Cart from "./Cart.svelte";
  import Button from "./Button.svelte";
...
<div class="product-list">
  {#each $products as product}
    <div>
      <div class="image" style="background-image: url({product.image})">
      </div>
```

And the second is Product.svelte:

```
<script>
  import {products, cart} from "../stores.js";
  import Button from "./Button.svelte";
  ...

  <a href="/products">{"<< Back to Shop"}</a>
  <div id="productdetails">
    {#each $products as product }
      {#if product.id == individualID}
        <div>
```

We could use standard props, but this would be cumbersome. Not only would we have to pass multiple values down from parent to child, we would likely have had to implement data twice as the product data would have been inaccessible from within the Header component. Using a `store` makes it simpler to access from anywhere in the site and allows us to maintain a single source of truth for data.

Moving on, over the next few pages, we will focus on adding in two techniques. We will add in a derived store to help calculate the total cost of our basket shortly, but first, let's work on adding support for props.

Adding Props Support

For this exercise, we will simulate the appearance of a logged in user - the next demo will add in a name to the left of the shopping basket icon. If we don't provide a name, it will fall back to a default of "Guest." Let's take a look at the code required to put this change in place, in more detail.

For now, we will focus on markup – we will deal with styling later in the book.

FAKING A CUSTOMER NAME

To add a fake customer name on login, follow these steps:

1. First, crack open the `main.js` file, and add in the props value as highlighted:

```
const app = new App({
  target: document.body,
  props: {
    name: "Alex"
  }
});
```

2. Next, save the file, and then switch to `App.svelte` – we need to pass the prop value down the chain, so go ahead and add this statement in before the closing `</script>` tag:

```
export let url = "";
export let name = "Guest";
```

3. Scroll down until you see the `<Header />` tag at the top of the markup, and then alter it to this: `<Header` **name={name}** `/>`.

4. We have a couple more changes to make – save the changes in `App.svelte`, and then crack open `Header.svelte`. We need to alter the markup as indicated:

```
<div>
  <div class="basket">
    <div>Hi, {name}</div>
    <div><InlineSVG src="/images/shoppingcart.svg"
    {...attributesCart} /></div>
  </div>
```

5. Go ahead and save and close the files – the changes are complete.

That may have been a quick exercise, but it's not without one downside - notice how we had to add entries to first the `main.js`, then `App.svelte`, before adding to the Header?

This is one of the disadvantages of using props: we have to chain them through from top to bottom; otherwise, we will end up with `undefined` values appearing in our code. With that in mind, let's take a look at the code we've added in more detail, to see how it works on our site.

Exploring the Changes

If you spent any time working with frameworks such as React, then the concept of passing props will be familiar; Svelte uses the same principle to communicate between different components.

For the exercise we've just completed, we first initialized the name prop in `main.js`; this holds the author's name, but it could equally be any name! We then set a variable called name in App.svelte and marked it as exportable, so it is available to other components throughout the site.

The key to making props work effectively is to limit the number of layers we pass information down; anything more than two to three is likely to get very cumbersome! In our case, we limited it to two layers which keeps this feeling of being clunky to a minimum. We then updated the call to the Header component to include the name prop, before editing the markup in Header to display the value of name on the page.

Okay, let's move on. We've seen how props can be implemented and understand that we have to pass them through each intermediate layer, to allow them to render correctly on the target page. Let's turn our attention to using stores, to see how we can implement that tool within our site.

Adding New Functionality Using Stores

Okay, so we can share data between different components, but this is only a small part of what is possible. What if we could calculate values *based on store values*? You're probably thinking that we could simply assign store values to variables and then calculate using these values, right?

Nothing technically wrong with that per se, but there is one small point - our calculations would be based on values in two different locations. This makes it riskier that calculated values returned to us will still be accurate, as other elements might cause a state change that affects our calculation.

Instead, we can use a **derived store** to work out that value in the `stores.js` file and return this - we can be sure that the result is accurate! To see what I mean, let's make a few changes to our site, to return a total value for our cart that will be visible across all pages.

ADDING DERIVED STORES

To add a derived store to display the cart total value, follow these steps:

1. First, crack open the `stores.js` file, and then change the first line to this:

```
import { readable, writable, derived } from "svelte/store";
```

2. Scroll down until you see the start of this line:

```
let cart = writable([])
```

3. Add in this block of code to calculate the total value of our cart:

```
let totalprice = derived(
  cart,
  ($cart) => {
    let price = 0
    $cart.forEach(e => price = price + e.price)
    return price
  }
);
```

4. To make this value available to other components in the site, we need to add it as an export – change the export statement at the end of the file to this:

```
export { cart, products, totalprice }
```

5. Go ahead and save and then close the file. Next, open `Header.svelte`, and change the initial import statement as highlighted:

```
import { cart, totalprice} from "../stores.js";
```

6. Scroll down to the end of the file, and then change the markup to include a new reference to the `totalprice` value, plus a count of products in the cart:

```
  <div>
    <span>
      <InlineSVG src="/images/shoppingcart.svg" {...attributesCart} />
    </span>
    <span>{$cart.length} items: ${$totalprice}</span>
  </div>
</header>
```

The count reflects the number of *different types* of products, not how many units of each are in the basket.

This exercise is one of those changes where we might not alter much of the code, but it provides a nice touch to the customer. Granted, there are things we can do to develop this feature further, but we must start somewhere!

That aside, this exercise exposes a couple of important points, so let's take a moment to review the changes to see how they fit into the wider picture, in more detail.

Breaking Apart the Code

For the penultimate exercise in this chapter, we worked on creating a derived store – this is a tool that can be very powerful, but equally should not be abused: in some instances, it can be overkill for our needs! That aside, the principles of setting up a derived store are straightforward; let's take a closer look at the code used from that exercise.

We began by updating the `stores.js` file to include the derived tool – this is the function that allows us to perform operations on existing stores, to arrive at a new value. We then added a new function, which is where things get a little more complex: `derived()` takes two arguments. The first is the existing store value, but the second is a function that itself receives the initial store value as its first argument.

```
let totalprice = derived(
  cart,
  ($cart) => {
    let price = 0
```

```
    $cart.forEach(e => price = price + e.price)
    return price
  }
);
```

So, to match that with the function we created, we have a cart on the second line which is the existing cart value (and itself a store). We then have `$cart` which is a reference to the existing store, but which we can then perform any function we like - here, we iterate through each $cart value, to create a cumulative price total. Finally, we return that total price, ready for importing into the Header component and displaying on-screen.

Making use of stores opens up some interesting possibilities – while researching this book, I came across an article on the Chasing Code website, at `https://chasingcode.dev/blog/svelte-persist-state-to-localstorage/`.

One of the downsides of using stores is persistence: how do we stop stores resetting back to their default or initial value? This is particularly true if we're not using a data source such as GraphQL; one way to achieve it is using the browser's local storage feature, although this comes at the risk of privacy and security!

Exploring Alternative Data Sources

So far, we've concentrated on constructing front-end features using Svelte - after all, this is what Svelte is all about, right? We used a Svelte store to create our data "back end," which works great for a small site.

This point did get me thinking though: What if we needed to scale out? How would this look? We of course would need something such as GraphQL; in this current environment, it would be a popular choice. The key though would be to connect the two: there are several ways to achieve this connection.

One of the more well-known ones we could use is a package called svelte-apollo, available from `https://github.com/timhall/svelte-apollo`. Created by Tim Hall, the package is designed to integrate support for GraphQL when using Svelte. It's written to return data in a Svelte store format which we can read and update as needed. There is an excellent demo and two articles on how to add GraphQL support, on the Techformist website - note you will need to read and complete both; otherwise, the first won't operate correctly!

The articles are available at `https://techformist.com/posts/2019/2019-08-15-todo-app-using-svelte-graphql/` and `https://techformist.com/spin-up-your-own-local-graphql-server-within-15-min/`.

To give you a flavor of how it might work, here is an extract from one of the Techformist articles:

```
let todoEdit = "";
function addTodo() {
  const todoAdd = mutate(client, {
    mutation: ADDTODO,
    variables: {
      todoEdit,
    },
  })
    .then((data) => {
      todoEdit = "";
      todoOp.refetch();
    })
    .catch((e) => {
      console.error("error: ", e);
    });
}
```

Once we have retrieved the data, we can iterate through it using standard Svelte code – note though that it's wise to use an `#await` clause to ensure the data is successfully retrieved first:

```
<div style="text-align:center">
  <h2>Svedos</h2>

  {#await $todoOp}

  <p>.. loading</p>
```

```
  {:then data}
    {#each data.data['allTodos']['nodes'] as todo, i}
    <p class:done="{todo.done}">{todo.title}</p>
    {/each}
  {:catch e}
    {e}
  {/await}
</div>
```

Hopefully this gives you a flavor of what is possible – while Svelte focuses more on the front-end UI, it doesn't mean to say we can't hook it into a back-end system such as GraphQL. Doing so will open up a world of possibilities – we could connect it to any manner of databases that support GraphQL or even into a third-party cloud-based system such as DatoCMS (`https://datocms.com`) or Hasura (`https://hasura.io`)!

Summary

Over the course of this chapter, we've covered a variety of different concepts around passing data between Svelte components, as well as updated our site demo; let's take a moment to review what we have learned in this chapter.

We kicked off by answering that all-important question of why data is so important in Svelte; we learned that this all stems from the concept of reactivity and how Svelte manages state within the application. We then moved onto understanding the different methods for passing information, before exploring each one in turn to understand how each operates and the constraints we may face when using the method.

We then turned our attention to adding new features to our website demo – at this stage, we covered just the markup, as styling will feature in a separate chapter later in the book. We worked through examples to add in prop support and new functionality using derived stores, before rounding out with a quick discussion about using alternative data sources such as GraphQL to scale up data for a Svelte application. We still have a lot more to cover however. The next chapter is where things will start to really get interesting, as we add logic to HTML markup within our Svelte application. Yes, my friends, it's time to make some decisions and write logic.

CHAPTER 4

Controlling Logic

We're making good progress with our demo site – we have the core components in place and can now manage data and the overall state of interacting with our customers.

So, what's next? It's time for decisions. Decisions such as "should element X be displayed, or should we show element Y?" "What happens if we log in or out – should the content on the page change?" These are just two questions I am sure developers will ask when determining what should happen if condition X becomes valid.

Controlling what happens is a fundamental part of any website; the principle of "if X happens, then do Y, else do Z" has been around for years. We can apply the same principles when using Svelte; in this chapter, we'll explore how to render elements or content based on satisfying one or more conditions in our code; we'll also apply some of these techniques to update our site. Let's first begin with exploring how to implement basic `if-else` logic in Svelte.

Creating If-Else Conditions

Take a look at this code for a moment:

```
{#if user.loggedIn}
  <button on:click={toggle}>
    Log out
  </button>
{/if}
```

Look familiar? Sure, it's written in Svelte, but that is purely syntax – it should be easy to work out to only display a logout button if the user has already logged in.

A. Libby, *Practical Svelte*, https://doi.org/10.1007/978-1-4842-7374-6_4

This simplicity is the beauty of Svelte - when it comes to exploring functions such as this one, Svelte doesn't overcomplicate things; it strives to keep code as clean as possible. The only difference is the hash or slash symbols; many other frameworks already used brackets or parentheses.

Keep that thought in mind. To see what I mean, let's take a look at implementing a simple `if-else` block in Svelte to display a QR code provided that the input string is not empty.

CREATING A QR CODE

To show a QR code on the screen, follow these steps:

1. First, go ahead and browse to `www.svelte.dev/repl` – don't forget about the by-now-familiar redirection that will happen!

2. Next, in the `App.svelte` tab, enter this code:

```
<script>
  let inputText = "I love Svelte!";
  let textPresent = false;
  let API_URL = "https://api.qrserver.com/v1/create-qr-code/
  ?size=150x150&data=";

  if (inputText !== "") {
    textPresent = true;
    API_URL += inputText;
  }
</script>
```

3. Leave a line blank, and then add in this markup:

```
<h1>
  A Random QR Code...
</h1>
{#if textPresent}
  <img src={API_URL} alt="qr-code"/><br>
```

```
{:else}
  <h2>
    Are you sure you can see me?
  </h2>
{/if}
```

4. If all is well, we should see a QR code appear on the right (Figure 4-1).

***Figure 4-1.** Creating a QR code using an if-else block*

This exercise was a simple one, highlighting how we can use the classic `if-else` statement in our Svelte code. Indeed, the syntax might look a little different, but the underlying principle is identical to most other languages that support this function! That said, it's essential to understand how this code works, so let's pause for a moment to review it in more detail.

Breaking Apart the Code

Although we created a demo about 20 lines long, there are, in reality, only three lines of interest to us from that demo – they are

```
{#if textPresent}
...
{:else}
...
{/if}
```

Seems a little crazy, huh? Granted, it's a fair comment – I'm sure there would have been a way to create a shorter, more straightforward demo. But I digress.

That aside, most of our demo contains standard JavaScript and HTML code in the now-familiar script/markup blocks. We started by defining three variables – one to store the text used for our QR code, one as a control variable, and the other as the base URL for sourcing the QR code.

We then created a simple check to see if `inputText` was not empty. If this was true, we set a boolean variable `textPresent` to `true` and concatenate `inputText` to the `API_URL` variable.

The remaining code is the markup to render the QR code on-screen – we use Svelte's `#if` statement to check `textPresent` (defined in the script block and accessible within the markup). If this is `true`, we render the QR code on-screen, else render a message to ask if it is still visible.

It's worth noting we could have included an `{:else}`, statement in this demo. To learn more, I would recommend consulting the documentation on the Svelte site at `https://svelte.dev/tutorial/else-blocks`.

I am sure many of you will have recognized similarities in that demo between Svelte and other frameworks such as React or Vue when using `if-else` blocks in code.

This similarity applies to if-else blocks and another condition check that we can use: the #each statement. Each block iterates through a list of items, with no condition checks applied – instead, the logic is in the looping around each item before parsing the next step in our code. To see what I mean, let's take a closer look at using #each in Svelte.

Implementing Each Conditions

Cast your mind back a few years – anyone remembers doing a `for...while` or `for...until` type loop in their code? Yes, that blast from the past is something you would likely have had to do when iterating through a bunch of items – it was admittedly clunky, but it worked!

Fast forward a few years, and we now have the `each` block – it's become a standard way to iterate through any number of different objects, irrespective of how many we might have.

As a function, `each` exists in all manner of different frameworks, such as React or Vue – Svelte is no different. It works in much the same way as other frameworks, with only minor differences in syntax; let's take a closer look at an example as part of our next exercise.

DEMO – ITERATING THROUGH AN EACH BLOCK

Iterating through an #each block is very straightforward in Svelte. To see how, follow these steps:

1. First, browse to `www.svelte.dev/repl` – don't forget the URL redirection that will kick in!

2. Next, we need to add in the script and markup – in the `App.svelte` tab section, start by adding this script block:

```
<script>
  let coffees = [
    { id: 'coffee1', name: 'Peruvian Blend' },
    { id: 'coffee2', name: 'African Inca' },
    { id: 'coffee3', name: 'Ristretto' }
  ];
</script>
```

3. Next, leave a line blank, and then add some rudimentary styling:

```
<style>
  ul {
    list-style-type: none;
    display: grid;
    grid-template-columns: 1fr 1fr 1fr 1fr;
    grid-template-rows: 1fr 1fr 1fr;
    gap: 10px 10px;
  }

  li {
    padding: 10px 5px;
    border: 1px solid black;
    text-align: center;
  }
</style>
```

4. We have one more section to add – this is the markup for our page. Go ahead and leave a line blank, and then add in this code:

```
<h1>Coffees for Sale</h1>
<ul>
  {#each coffees as { id, name }, i}
    <!-- open each block -->
    <li>
      <a target="_blank" href="{id}">
        <img src="https://via.placeholder.com/150"
        alt="placeholder">
        <span>{name}</span>
      </a>
    </li>
    <!-- close each block -->
  {/each}
</ul>
```

5. If all is well, we should see our three fake products appear on the right after a few moments, as shown in Figure 4-2.

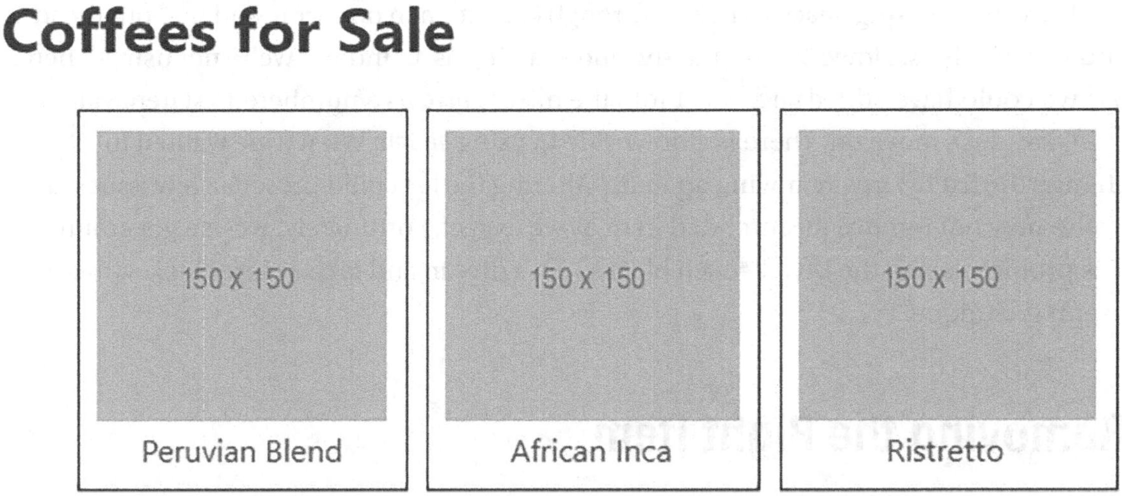

***Figure 4-2.** Displaying the three products using an #each block*

Mmm... the thought of coffee is making me thirsty... but I digress! We will come back to coffee later, but for now, it's worth taking a closer look at the code we've just created in the last exercise. Most of it is standard HTML markup and CSS styling, but we should cover a couple of essential points in more detail.

Exploring the Code

Anyone familiar with using `#each` blocks in JavaScript will no doubt begin to recognize some of what is happening in the last exercise – the syntax may look a little different, but the principles are the same.

We started by defining an array of coffees, in which we specified both `id` and `name` values. We then moved onto adding some basic styling so that our demo made sense on-screen – after all, this is not an exercise about aesthetics!

In the last stage, we added our all-important markup. Here, we added the title and opening unordered list tag before using `#each` to iterate through each item in the `coffees` array and render both the `name` and `id` in a list item, along with a placeholder dummy image. This we closed out with the appropriate `</li>` tag and `{/each}` closing tags.

There is one particular point of note, though, which is this line:

```
{#each coffees as { id, name }, i}
```

Here, we're using #each to iterate through each item in our array and pull out the id and name values. However, the `i` at the end is acting as an index – we're not using it here, but we could have added an `i += 1` into the mix, to give us a numbered list item value.

Okay, let's move on. There is a downside to using #each. What if we wanted to change the list by, say, removing an item? Altering the list could present a few issues, as Svelte may not remove the intended item as we expect. Fortunately, we can get around this problem using the keyed #each blocks – let's dive in and take a closer look at this useful technique.

Removing the Right Item

If you need to modify or remove items in an #each block, by default, Svelte will remove the items from the end, which is not always where you want them to be removed! Removing an item will drop it out of the list, but it will update other items when we want to leave them alone.

Fortunately, there is a way to get around this, which is to use keyed #each blocks – we assign an identifier to each item and reference it by ID rather than position. That way, we can be sure to remove the correct item **and leave the rest alone**.

The best way to understand how this works is to see it in action. For our next exercise, we will adapt the previous demo. It only requires some minor changes, but it's worth it if we want to retain some sense of sanity!

REMOVING A SELECTED ITEM

Removing a specific item is easy with Svelte – to do so, follow these steps:

1. First, browse to `www.svelte.dev/repl` – note that the now-familiar warning about redirection still applies!
2. Next, go ahead and add this script block at the top of the `App.svelte` tab:

```
<script>
let coffees = [
  { id: 'coffee1', name: 'Peruvian Blend' },
  { id: 'coffee2', name: 'African Inca' },
  { id: 'coffee3', name: 'Ristretto' },
```

```
  { id: 'coffee4', name: 'Peruvian Blend Decaff' },
  { id: 'coffee5', name: 'African Inca Decaff' },
  { id: 'coffee6', name: 'Ristretto Decaff' }
];

function handleClick() {
  coffees = coffees.slice(5,6)
}
</script>
```

3. Next, leave a line blank, and then add in these styles – they are not obligatory, but will help make the demo look a little more presentable:

```
<style>
  ul { list-style-type: none; display: grid; grid-template-
  columns: 1fr 1fr 1fr; grid-template-rows: 1fr 1fr 1fr;
  gap: 10px 10px; width: 200px;
  }

  li { padding: 10px 5px; border: 1px solid black;    text-align:
  center; }
</style>
```

4. Finally, it's the turn of the markup – for this, miss a line, and then add in the following:

```
<h1>Coffees for Sale</h1>
<button on:click={() => handleClick()}>
    Remove selected item(s)
</button>
<ul>
  {#each coffees as coffee (coffee.id)}
    <!-- open each block -->
    <li>
      <a target="_blank" href="{coffee.id}">
        <img src="https://via.placeholder.com/150"
        alt="placeholder">
```

```
            <span>{coffee.name}</span>
          </a>
          </li>
        <!-- close each block -->
      {/each}
    </ul>
```

5. If all is well, we should see something similar to the previous demo, but this time with the addition of a button, as shown in Figure 4-3.

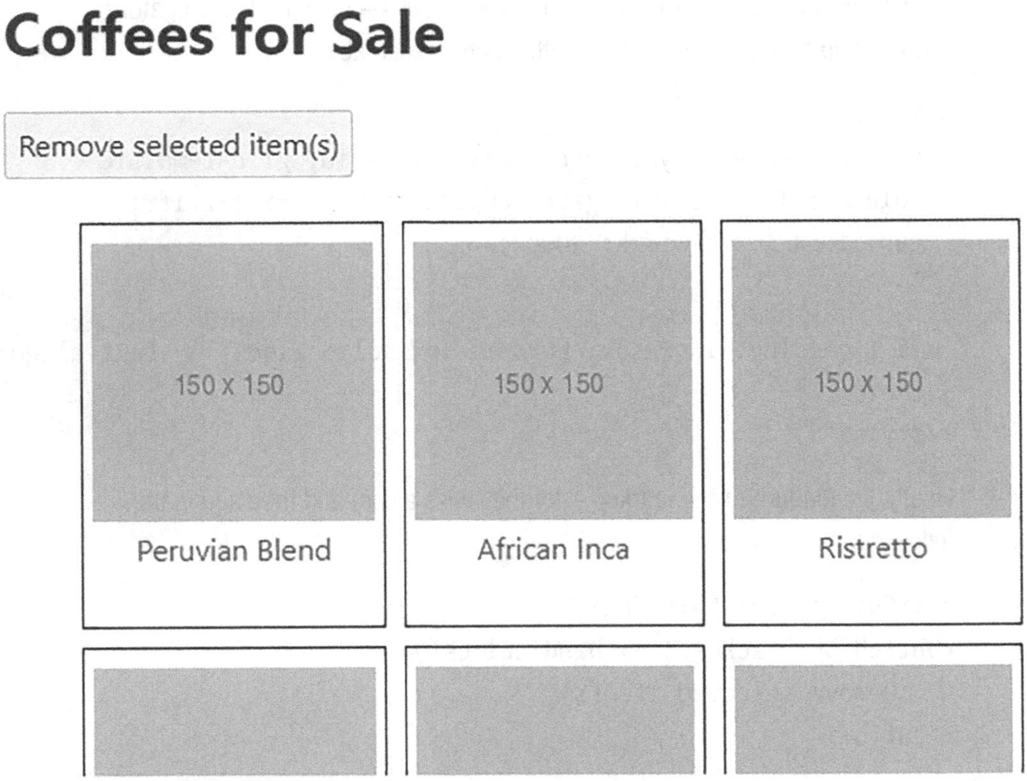

Figure 4-3. *The updated each demo, now with a button to remove elements*

6. You will notice that I've extended the number of items this time around to make it a little more interesting – if we click the button, we should see that Svelte has removed all except `Ristretto Decaff`. We can verify this too in the browser console, as it returns the results of what is left in `coffees`, as shown in Figure 4-4.

```
                                        about:srcdoc:157
▼[{…}] ℹ
  ▶0: {id: "coffee6", name: "Ristretto Decaff"}
   length: 1
  ▶__proto__: Array(0)
```

***Figure 4-4.** The results of removing our selected element*

At first glance, it might not look like we're changed that much - granted, we've doubled the number of products. Apart from adding an event handler (a subject we will revisit in the next chapter), there is only one other minor change. Take a look at the #each block carefully - notice what it is?

Breaking Apart the Code in Detail

The slight change I'm referring to is using `each coffees` **as coffee**, rather than destructuring the individual properties as we did in the previous demo.

There is a reason for this - it may look like an insignificant change, but that change allows us to apply a unique identifier to each item in the block. We effectively use the ID for each item from within the `coffees` block to identify which item (or items) to remove correctly.

Let's keep that thought in mind as we take a closer look at the code - we started by defining an object array with the `ID`s and `name`s of six coffee products (the names are not critical - it's the structure that is important here). I will come back to the event handler at the bottom of the script block in a moment.

Next up came some rudimentary styling - these are not essential to the demo, but help make it a little more presentable! The key to making this demo work is in the markup, in the third and final block.

Here, we start by setting a title and button - the latter using Svelte format to reference the `handleClick()` event we created near the top of the code. Note that using standard JavaScript markup will not work; this has the effect of automatically triggering the event on page load, not on demand. This event handler triggers the `handleClick` function we skipped past just now; this uses standard JavaScript `to .slice` the array and return the required products.

If you're not familiar with how `slice()` works, then have a look at the W3Schools link online at `www.w3schools.com/jsref/jsref_slice_array.asp`, which details how it works.

In the markup, we use the same #each block as in the previous demo. This time though, we use `coffees as coffee (coffee.id)` instead of destructuring the various properties referenced in the markup. Adding the unique identifier (similar to React's key function) allows us to reference items correctly.

There is a more detailed explanation of how Svelte's keyed each block works, available on the StackOverflow website at `https://stackoverflow.com/a/62503366/15301592`.

Okay, let's move on. There is one more topic that we should explore to control what happens and when in a Svelte site. That topic is data – yes, I'm aware we've already talked about it back in Chapter 3! But there is one more part to it that is crucial to managing data: fetching it at the right point in the execution process. To understand what I mean, let's take a closer look at how this can impact a Svelte site.

Fetching Content

When it comes to sourcing data for a project, there will undoubtedly be instances where it might take a few seconds to retrieve, right? Without some form of control, our code will simply keep iterating through each step – with the likely result that it falls into a complete heap of errors due to no data!

What can we do? Well, we can use await. Anyone who's worked with JS promises will know this is a great technique to pause execution until a promise to complete another task is completed successfully or rejected. As long as that task finishes without issue, then the original job can resume execution.

Svelte includes such functionality by default, in the form of `await` – this works in the same way as standard JavaScript, although the syntax may look a little different. In reality, the only differences are the use of special characters to signify Svelte keywords; the rest of an await block works in the same way as standard JavaScript.

There is a perfect example of how we can illustrate the use of await - fetching data for a shop catalog. As it so happens, this will be the theme for our next demo, but before we get there, there are a couple of things we should do:

- We need some dummy data - for this, I would suggest using an online generator such as `www.fakestoreapi.com/products/`. Browse to that URL, grab the contents, and save it to a plain text file (the location is not critical, as it's a temporary measure).
- Copy the contents of that file into a JSON viewer, such as the one at `https://codebeautify.org/jsonviewer`.
- Go ahead and grab the first product, which should look similar to this example:

```
[
  {
    "id": 1,
    "title": "Fjallraven - Foldsack No. 1 Backpack, Fits 15
    Laptops",
    "price": 109.95,
    "description": "Your perfect pack for everyday use and walks
    in the forest. Stash your laptop (up to 15 inches) in the
    padded sleeve, your every day",
    "category": "men clothing",
    "image": "https://fakestoreapi.com/img/81fPKd-2AYL._AC_
    SL1500_.jpg"
  },
```

Excellent, we're now good to go with the demo, so let's crack on and see how `await` works in Svelte.

DEMO – SOURCING FAKE PRODUCTS

We can easily retrieve data using Svelte's fetch command – to do so, use these steps:

1. We'll start by browsing to `www.svelte.dev/repl` – don't forget the redirection!

2. In the `App.svelte` tab on the left, go ahead and add this script block:

```
<script>
  const fetchImage = (async () => {
    const response = await fetch('https://
fakestoreapi.com/products/1');
    return await response.json();
  })()
</script>
```

3. Next, leave a line – we need to add some rudimentary styling, so drop in this code:

```
<style>
  div {
    width: 200px;
    border: 1px solid black;
    display: flex;
    flex-direction: column;
    align-items: center;
    padding: 10px;
    animation: fadeIn ease 1s;
  }

  @keyframes fadeIn {
    0% {opacity:0;}
    100% {opacity:1;}
  }

  img {
    display: block;
    width: 150px;
    height: auto;
  }

  span {
    text-align: center;
  }
</style>
```

4. We have one more section to add, which is the markup for our demo – for this, miss a line in the `App.svelte` tab, and then add in this code:

```
<h1>My Fake Store</h1>

{#await fetchImage}
  <p>...loading products</p>
{:then data}
  <div>
    <img src={data.image} alt="product" />
    <span>{data.title}</span>
  </div>
{/await}
```

5. If all is well, we should see this fade in on the right after a few seconds (Figure 4-5).

***Figure 4-5.** Returning a product using Svelte's fetch command*

There is one thing missing from the image at the end of the last step of that exercise – the image fading into view! Unfortunately, the marvels of modern printing mean it's not something I can demonstrate on paper, so hopefully, you will have seen it when running the demo.

That aside, this demo highlights a few critical points around using await and fetch, so let's take a moment to review the code in greater detail.

Understanding the Changes Made

If I were to say this last demo has some similarities between it and the `#each` demo from earlier, you might at first think I've completely lost the plot! There is a reason for this, though, so let me explain.

Take a closer look at some of the keywords used in the demos in this chapter. You will see that most (if not all) start with a hashbang (`#`), with intermediate steps (such as `then`) preceded with a `:` and the closing tags beginning with a `/`. It's a helpful way to identify which keywords are Svelte and which are pure JavaScript – you will see some similarities between them, but not always!

That aside, we've created a simple demo that perfectly illustrates how we can control the code execution without the need for using `if-else` blocks. Granted, each step might execute linearly, but the critical thing to note is *how* we control when we complete each step.

In this demo, we created an async function `fetchImage` to fetch data from an external source – this we assigned to a variable response and returned it only when both this step and `response.json()` were no longer undefined.

The next critical step (after the styling) was to call the `fetchImage` function and `await` for it to complete; while this is happening, we display some placeholder text on-screen. Once the browser returns the JSON, we execute the `:then` statement – the data returned is stored in the data object. The placeholder text is swapped out and replaced with an `<div>` element that contains an image (using `data.image` as the source) and text.

An important point to note is that Svelte only considers the most recent promise when using await and promises. This point means you should not have to worry about race conditions.

It's time to apply some of what we've learned in this chapter to update our store demo! Yes, we've covered a lot of theory over the last few pages, so let's turn our attention to the store demo and start to apply some of that theory in the form of extra features.

Exploring Existing Code in the Demo

Right, take a good look through the code. Notice anything?

The keen-eyed among you spot something - we've already used some of the code we've covered in this chapter in our shop demo. Yes, I confess: it was unavoidable. Otherwise, we might have had to wait even longer to get something working!

That said, the code already included isn't that extensive - it centers around three files, namely, `Cart.svelte`, `Product.svelte`, and `Products.svelte`. In reality, the latter two are very similar; I suspect that we could create a component that served both purposes with a bit of work.

So, given we've just worked on `Products.svelte`, let's focus on `Cart.svelte` - here is the code we have used in the shop that uses the keywords covered in this chapter:

```
  <h4>Total: $ {total}</h4>
</div>
  {#each $cart as item }
    {#if item.quantity > 0}
      <div class="cart-item">
       ..
      </div>
    {/if}
  {/each}
</div>
```

In this instance, we're using it to iterate through the cart - if it sees a quantity greater than zero, we add an image of the product, the product name, quantity, and add or remove buttons into the cart.

It is that simple - there is nothing more to it! To see what I mean, let's dive in and look at adding a couple of features to our shop, starting with adding a login button.

Updating the Shop

A login button, I hear you say? What does that have to do with controlling logic, I wonder?

Well, the answer is simple - it's not the button, but the condition check behind it that is of interest to us! It's effortless to implement something to fake the appearance of a logged in user, so let's dive into our first update and take a closer look at the code.

Adding Login Functionality to Our Site

We will add a simulated logged in user to our shop for the first of two demos that relate to our shop. We won't cover the back end but instead focus on the UI - it will use the if-else function we've covered, plus the `getContext` and `setContext` feature from earlier in the book.

ADDING LOGIN/OUT LINKS

To set up the appearance of a fake logged in user, follow these steps:

1. First, go ahead and crack open `App.svelte` from within the `\src` folder – scroll down until you see this line:

```
export let name;
```

2. Leave a line blank, and then add in these two statements:

```
  import { setContext } from "svelte";

let loggedIn;
```

3. Immediately below that line, add in this condition check:

```
if (name == "") {
  loggedIn = false;
} else {
  loggedIn = true;
}
```

```
setContext('key', {
  loggedIn
});
```

4. Go ahead and save the file – we can close it at this point.
5. Next, switch to the `Header.svelte` component from the `\src\components` folder, and look for this line:

```
let loggedInText = "Hi, {name}";
```

6. Immediately below it, leave a line blank, and then add in this code:

```
import { getContext } from "svelte";
const { loggedIn } = getContext('key');
```

7. Scroll down to the markup, and then replace the code in the `<div class="basket">` block with this code, as highlighted:

```
<div class="basket">
  {#if loggedIn}
    <div>Hi, {name} | Logout</div>
  {:else}
    <div>Hi, Guest | Login</div>
  {/if}
  <div><InlineSVG src="/images/shoppingcart.svg"
  {...attributesCart} /></div>
</div>
```

8. Save the file and close it – the changes are complete.
9. Switch to your browser – if you don't already have it running, browse to `http://localhost:5000`. If all is well, we should see something akin to the screenshot in Figure 4-6.

***Figure 4-6.** Our updated header, showing a fake logged in user*

Perfect use for a conditional check feature - something HTML should have had a long time ago! Admittedly, our demo only touches on the UI and assumes our customer has logged in, but that doesn't matter - it's the principle of using an if-else statement block in HTML markup which counts for this demo.

This demo shows off some valuable points around using the if-else block in Svelte, so let's pause for a moment to review the code added from the last demo.

Understanding the Changes

This change was an interesting exercise - although the main focus was to add in the condition check, we also used Svelte's context feature. We could have achieved this using props, but that can get messy - instead, using context makes for cleaner code. Let's take a moment to review what we've added to see how it operates in more detail.

We kicked off by adding a reference to the `setContext` function from Svelte in `App.svelte` - this is key to making this demo work: it acts as a store for holding information for child components (not to be confused with Svelte's `store` function, of course!)

We then set two variables - one called `loggedIn` to track if a customer has logged in and one as `loggedInText` to store a placeholder for the welcome greeting. Next up, we added in an `if-else` condition to determine if the name property was empty; based on this, we could determine if the user had logged in. The last change we made added a command to use `setContext` to set a property of key, with the value from `loggedIn`.

We then switched to editing `Header.svelte`; in this component, we imported the `getContext` command and retrieved the value of key using this command. We then updated the markup displayed on-screen to determine `#if loggedIn` was true; if so, we showed the Logout message, otherwise displayed the Login equivalent label.

Okay, let's move on. For the second demo, we will revisit a subject from earlier in the book: loading data. Yes, I can hear the questions - what does this have to do with using a condition check, I wonder? There is a good reason for it; I will go through it and more in the explanation that will follow, but let's first look at the demo itself.

Loading Products

For the second of two demos, we're going to take a different tack - instead of adding a complete function, we're going to create a partial effect only!

Yes, it won't be an entirely complete one: don't worry, though, as it will still work. We're going to revisit using the await and fetch functions from earlier to help refactor importing data and better control the loading process. There is a twist, though, as this demo will open up options for us. To learn more, let's first look at the code as part of our next exercise.

LOADING PRODUCTS

To add in better loading facilities, follow these steps:

1. First, we need to install a plugin – for this, crack open a Node.js terminal session, and then change the working folder to our project area.

2. At the prompt, enter this command and press Enter:

   ```
   npm install "@rollup/plugin-json" --save
   ```

3. Once done, minimize the session, and then switch to stores.js from within the `\src` folder.

4. Go ahead and comment out the entire `let products=...` block – all 70-odd lines!

5. Immediately below `import { readable, writable, derived } from "svelte/store";`, add in this code:

   ```
   import * as myjson from '../public/stock.json';
   ```

6. Miss a line, and then add in this declaration:

   ```
   let products = readable(myjson.default);
   ```

7. Go ahead and save the file – we can close it at this point.

8. Next, switch to `Products.svelte`, and add in the highlighted code as indicated:

   ```
   {#await $products}
     <p>...loading products</p>
   {:then}
     {#each $products as product}
       <div>
         <div class="image" style="background-image: url({product.
         image})"></div>
         <h4><a href="product/{product.id}">{product.name}</a></h4>
   ...
       </div>
     {/each}
   {/await}
   ```

9. Save the file and close it – the changes are complete.

10. Fire up your browser, and browse to `http://localhost:5000`, and then click Products in the menu – if all is well, we should see our products appear as before, but this time sourcing it from the JSON file, not inline. We can see the effect in Figure 4-7, where I've already gone ahead and added in some basic styling (and which we will cover later in this book).

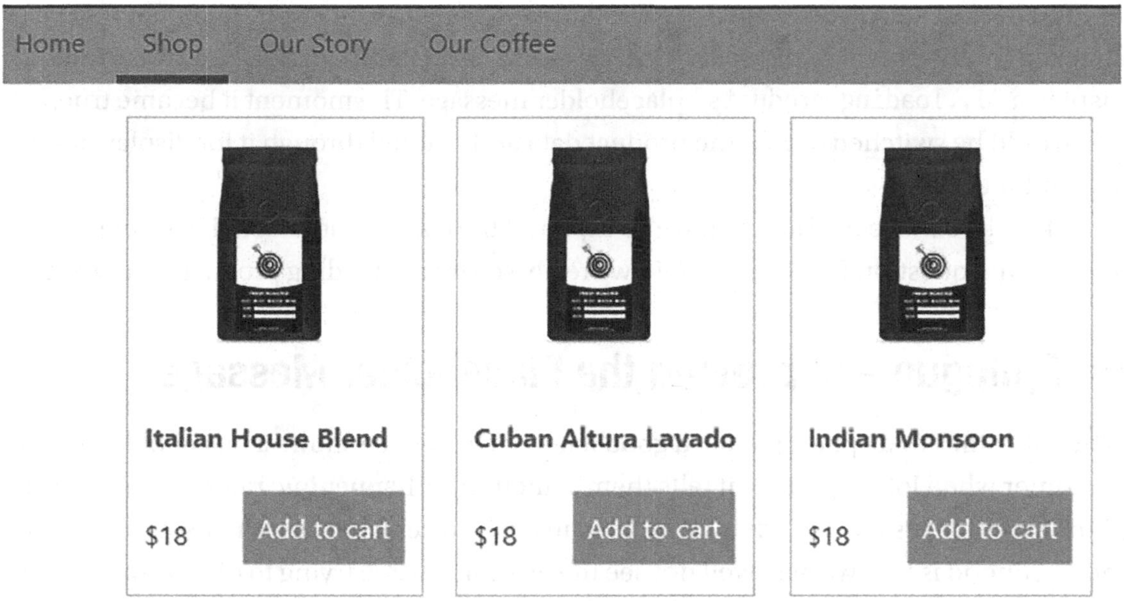

Figure 4-7. *The products list, sourced from a JSON file*

All looks good, right? When you ran the demo, did you see anything happen, or not, as the case may be?

Exploring the Code in Detail

Okay, that last question might have been a little leading, but with good reason – I'm not sure that the "..loading products" text appeared! Before I explain what I mean by that statement, let's first cover the changes made in the last demo.

Cast your mind back to Chapter 3, where we explored iterating through data in Svelte using stores – it's a helpful technique but does have one inherent flaw.

We're only running a small site, so hard-coding data is something we can live with – what if we wanted to run something more significant or source our data from a third-party offering, such as a database? This change would be infinitely more preferable – for one, it means not having to edit code all of the time!

To illustrate this principle in our site, we first installed the `@rollup/plugin-json` plugin to consume the JSON file – we could have done this manually, but there is little reward for what would effectively be reinventing the wheel. We then moved onto editing the `stores.js` file – inside this, we added an import reference to the `stock.json` file before calling Svelte's `readable` function to consume the contents and assign it to a variable `products`.

For the last step, we wrapped the existing #each block in an await statement that checked for the presence of `products`. If this were false (i.e., it did not exist), we would display a `"...loading products"` placeholder message. The moment it became true, this would be switched out for the product data and iterated through it for display on-screen for the user.

Okay, let's move on. Now that we've explored the code in more detail, it's time to answer that question from earlier: Did we really see that "...loading products" message?

An Epilogue – Improving the Placeholder Message

When it comes to displaying data, a good tenet of UI practice shows a placeholder for the customer when loading data – it tells them something is happening, rather than seeing a blank screen. This effect is what we've tried to achieve here, but as we're using localhost, the likelihood is that we may well not see the one thing we're trying to display on-screen!

As part of researching this book, I tried an alternative way to source the data, which made the "loading product..." message a little more visible. Below `let products = readable(myjson.default)...` I added this:

```
console.log("test1", myjson.default)

const fetchData = (async () => {
  await fetch('../stock.json')
    .then(function(response) {
      return response.json();
    })
    .then(function(data) {
      const items = data;
      console.log("test2", data);
    })
});

let a = fetchData();

let products2 = readable([]);
products2 = readable(a);
console.log(products2.data);
```

When running the code in my browser, I got the response shown in Figure 4-8, which shows we can get identical information using either format. However, trying to get it into a Svelte readable store was something else – I got very close, but as we say in England, "close but no cigar!"

```
test1
▼(6) [{…}, {…}, {…}, {…}, {…}, {…}]
  ▶0: {id: 1, name: "Italian House Blend", description: "Lorem ipsum dolor sit amet, consectetur adipisci
  ▶1: {id: 2, name: "Cuban Altura Lavado", description: "Lorem ipsum dolor sit amet, consectetur adipisci
  ▶2: {id: 3, name: "Indian Monsoon", description: "Lorem ipsum dolor sit amet, consectetur adipiscing…n
  ▶3: {id: 4, name: "Robusta Uganda", description: "Lorem ipsum dolor sit amet, consectetur adipiscing…n
  ▶4: {id: 5, name: "Yemen Matari", description: "Lorem ipsum dolor sit amet, consectetur adipiscing…n ar
  ▶5: {id: 6, name: "Salvador Pacamara", description: "Lorem ipsum dolor sit amet, consectetur adipiscing
   length: 6
  ▶ __proto__: Array(0)
test2
▼(6) [{…}, {…}, {…}, {…}, {…}, {…}]
  ▶0: {id: 1, name: "Italian House Blend", description: "Lorem ipsum dolor sit amet, consectetur adipisci
  ▶1: {id: 2, name: "Cuban Altura Lavado", description: "Lorem ipsum dolor sit amet, consectetur adipisci
  ▶2: {id: 3, name: "Indian Monsoon", description: "Lorem ipsum dolor sit amet, consectetur adipiscing…n
  ▶3: {id: 4, name: "Robusta Uganda", description: "Lorem ipsum dolor sit amet, consectetur adipiscing…n
  ▶4: {id: 5, name: "Yemen Matari", description: "Lorem ipsum dolor sit amet, consectetur adipiscing…n ar
  ▶5: {id: 6, name: "Salvador Pacamara", description: "Lorem ipsum dolor sit amet, consectetur adipiscing
   length: 6
  ▶ __proto__: Array(0)
>
```

Figure 4-8. *Comparing data from both methods*

The issue here was extracting data in a format **that the Svelte store could understand**. This last bit is critical, as Svelte stores only accept values that we can iterate through as an array. Getting the data out from a promise wasn't too tricky, but altering it into something that didn't show the message in Figure 4-9 proved to be an entirely different matter!

```
Test ▶(6) [{…}, {…}, {…}, {…}, {…}, {…}]
⊗ ▶Uncaught (in promise) Error: {#each} only iterates over array-like objects.
    at validate_each_argument (index.mjs:1642)
    at create_then_block (Products.svelte:52)
    at update (index.mjs:1055)
    at index.mjs:1090
>
```

Figure 4-9. *The error generated using the alternative method*

Still, it was a useful exercise – it's something we should bear in mind when using promises and no less so than with Svelte.

Summary

The ability to control what happens on a website has been around for years in some form or another – indeed, it even dates back to the days of the old BBC Micro or ZX Spectrum computers, if not even farther! Does anyone remember those? Now, there's a blast from the past.

But I digress – back to more practical matters. This chapter has all been about implementing logic to control what happens in Svelte – we started looking at creating the Svelte equivalent of the classic if-else condition, known throughout most programming or scripting languages today. We learned that the syntax is very similar to vanilla JavaScript, but with the bonus of being part of HTML markup and not just within a script block.

We then worked our way through several different types of controlling logic: #each, keyed each statements, and how to use Svelte's fetch/await keywords to control the flow of data into a project.

Next up came the exciting part – this focused on updating the shop, with two demos. The first explored how we could fake a logged in user with the appropriate message, using the equivalent of an if-then-else statement. The second was more of a proof of concept on improving the control overloading data into our site. We then rounded out the chapter with a brief look at why the last demo might not all seem as it should and explored the importance of getting the correct data into a readable store which can sometimes be tricky in Svelte.

Phew, we've worked our way through quite a bit there! This is what makes Svelte so easy to learn: it makes coding features a cinch – the markup is significantly lighter and easier to understand and allows us to create content without half of the associated baggage seen in other, larger frameworks!

We've made significant progress, but there are still two areas we should explore – what happens if we click on elements or interact with forms in Svelte? Both need handling – stay with me as we take a look at the first, events, in the next chapter.

CHAPTER 5

Managing Events

So far, we've constructed the bare bones of our site, added data, and started to implement state and some form of controlling logic – it's time to step it up and allow people to interact with our website.

Interacting with a website will, of course, create different events – we need to respond to them accordingly so that the website can continue to function correctly. It might even be as simple as clicking a button to something more complex such as logging into a website. For this chapter, we will start to add some simple events to the demo website – before we do so, let's have a quick look at how events work in Svelte.

The Theory of Reactivity

Think back to Chapter 1, where we talked about what makes Svelte different – I want to try a little test.

INSTRUMENTING THE DOM

You can run this little test in a single browser window, but I would recommend running in two separate windows so that you can get a before and after effect:

1. Head over to `https://svelte.dev/repl` – go ahead and paste this code into the `App.svelte` tab on the left:

```
<script>
  let count = 0;

  function handleClick() {
  // event handler code goes here
  }
</script>
```


A. Libby, *Practical Svelte*, https://doi.org/10.1007/978-1-4842-7374-6_5

```
<button>
  Clicked {count} {count === 1 ? 'time' : 'times'}
</button>
```

2. Now, on the right, click the JS Output tab – take a good look at the code. I'm not expecting you to understand it at this stage – it's more about the *quantity* of code, rather than understanding what it does!

3. When you're ready, replace the `function handleClick()` code and `button` markup in the `App.svelte` tab with this:

```
  function handleClick() {
    count += 1;
  }
</script>

<button on:click={handleClick}>
  Clicked {count} {count === 1 ? 'time' : 'times'}
</button>
```

4. Go ahead and click the JS Output tab, as you did in step 2 – notice how much extra code has been included this time?

You might be asking why we've done this little test - let me explain.

In a nutshell, it boils down to something I like to call the theory of reactivity. We talked about how Svelte likes to be the odd one out, or the kid that likes to be different - doing away with a virtual DOM, unlike its bigger and perhaps more experienced cousins!

Instead, Svelte wraps our scripts with extra code to tell it when the DOM needs to be updated. This reactivity means that the DOM updates only when is necessary, but at the same time, we don't need to run a virtual DOM to perform this operation. Thankfully, we don't need to see all of that code - Svelte allows us to focus on what is necessary and abstracts away the remaining code as part of the build process.

Okay, we should crack on. Now that we've had a quick refresher on reactivity in Svelte, let's take a look at the different types of events that we can create in Svelte in more detail.

Choosing from Different Event Types

Okay, so when it comes to working events, what can we achieve in Svelte?

I'm sure you are familiar with standard events such as `onClick()`, albeit under a different syntax; if you look closely at some of the code we've already written for the demo website, you will see at least one example in use. We've created a separate function as the event handler, but we could equally have written it inline.

This event isn't the only one we can use - Svelte supports all of the (hopefully) familiar event types, such as `mouseover()`. Also, there are a few other event types we can use, which are:

- Event modifiers - These are perfect for overriding certain behaviors such as `preventDefault`, where we need the effect of an event such as `onClick`, but not the default action associated with it.
- Component-driven events - Components in Svelte can also trigger events, albeit they must use a different mechanism; you will frequently see `eventCreateDispatcher` function used in this instance.
- Event forwarding - In some instances, we might want to respond to an event triggered by a component several layers deep. The trouble is it's not possible as component events do not bubble in Svelte; to get around this, we can forward events to the component and respond accordingly.
- DOM event forwarding - We might want to create an event handler that we want to decouple from a component; we can build a reusable component (such as a `button`) but pass in different event handlers as needed.
- Life cycle events - This is slightly different: each event has a life cycle, where we can intercept specific actions and trigger a function at that point. We might typically use `onMount()` most, but other methods also exist, such as `beforeUpdate`.

Right, with this in mind, let's turn our attention to putting some of this theory into practice; it's time to get coding!

Creating Events

Now that we've seen some of the different types of events available in Svelte, it's time to see some in action.

For those of you used to frameworks such as React or Vue, you will see some similarities - indeed, if you use vanilla JavaScript, you will equally recognize the same principles in use! To see what I mean, let's dive into the first exercise for this chapter, with a quick look at how to create standard events in Svelte.

EXPLORING EVENT HANDLERS

To see how event handlers operate in Svelte, follow these steps:

1. First, fire up your browser and head over to `www.svelte.dev/repl` – don't forget the by-now-familiar redirection!
2. Next, go ahead and add this code into the top of the `App.svelte` tab on the left:

```
<script>
  function handleClick(event) {
    window.alert('Message from the click handler');
  }
</script>
<button on:click="{handleClick}">Click me</button>
```

3. After a few moments, you should see a button appear – if you click it, you will see the message displayed in Figure 5-1.

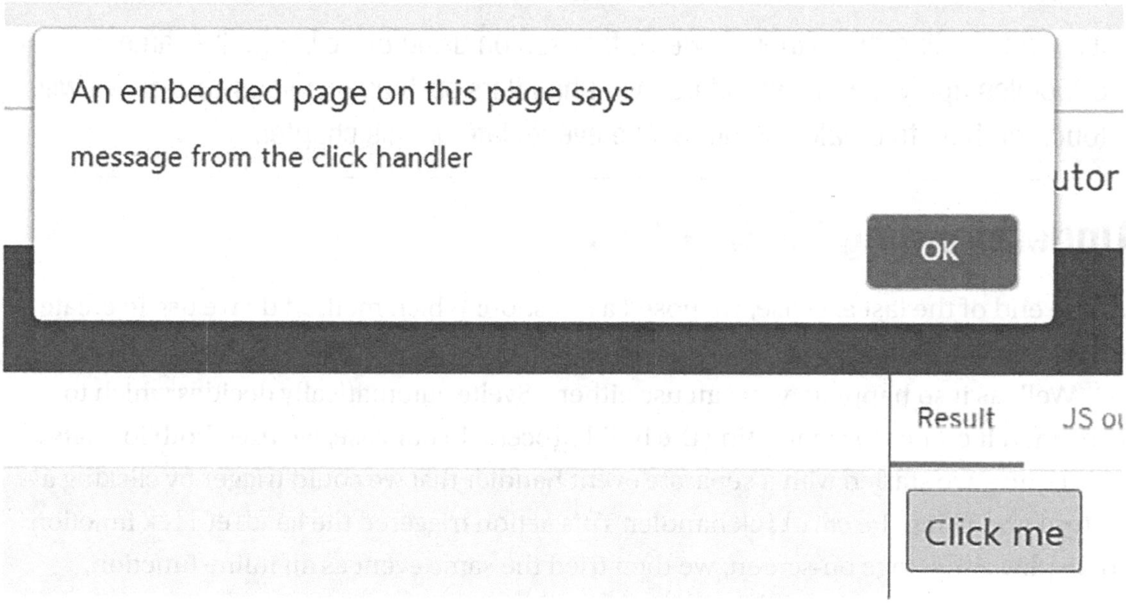

Figure 5-1. *The results of clicking the event handler*

4. Try changing the code to this in `App.svelte`:

```
<button on:click="{e => window.alert('message from the click
handler')}">Click me</button>
```

This in-lines the event handler, but clicking it will produce the same result.

That was a simple exercise that highlighted an important point: Which one do we use? Is one better than the other? I know some of you will have likely seen recommendations to steer away from using inline event handlers, owing to performance concerns, particularly when it comes to iterating through loops.

This recommendation might be valid for other frameworks, but not for Svelte – it doesn't matter which format you use! I can already hear the comments to the effect that this surely can't be true – it is indeed true: you can use either format as you wish. To understand why, let's first take a quick look at the code before understanding more about what happens under the covers with Svelte.

It's worth noting that although we've focused on using `on:click`, the same principles apply to other standard event handlers such as `on:mouseover`. We will touch on how to create custom Svelte events later in this chapter.

Understanding the Changes

At the end of the last exercise, we posed a question: Which method do we use to create events? Inline or not?

Well, as it so happens, you can use either - Svelte automatically decides which to use when it comes to completing the build process. In our case, we tried both formats in the demo - we started with a separate event handler that we could trigger by clicking a button and firing the `on:click` handler. This action triggered the `handleClick` function to display a message on-screen; we then tried the same event as an inline function, which gave us the same result once compiled by Svelte.

To see what I mean, revert to a copy of the code where we used a separate event handler. Switch to the JS Output tab, and you will at first see a swathe of code - the key parts I reproduce here:

```
function handleClick(event) {
  window.alert("message from the click handler");
}
...
class App extends SvelteComponent {
  constructor(options) {
    super();
    init(this, options, null, create_fragment, safe_not_equal, {});
  }
}
```

Now try the code again that had the inline form of the event handler – in the JS Output tab, we should see the same two functions:

```
function instance($$self) {
  const click_handler = e => window.alert("message from the click handler");
  return [click_handler];
}
...
class App extends SvelteComponent {
  constructor(options) {
    super();
    init(this, options, instance, create_fragment, safe_not_equal, {});
  }
}
```

As you can see, even though we've used two different forms of event handler, the resulting code is very similar, with only minor differences in the event handler itself!

Modifying Event Handlers

In the previous exercise, we explored how to add event handlers using Svelte – it was easy to see from the demo that the syntax bears a remarkable similarity to standard JS.

There will be occasions where we might want to override the default behavior; fortunately, we can do this with only a slight change required. Event modifiers in Svelte take this format:

```
<div on:click|<name of event modifier>={() => ...}>
```

where the event modifier might be any one of several event modifiers listed in Table 5-1.

Table 5-1. *List of event modifiers available in Svelte*

Event handler	Purpose
`preventDefault`	Calls `event.preventDefault()` before running the handler. Useful for client-side form handling, for example.
`stopPropagation`	Calls `event.stopPropagation()` to prevent the event reaching the next element
`passive`	Improves scrolling performance on touch/wheel events (Svelte will add it automatically where it's safe to do so)
`Nonpassive`	Explicitly set `passive: false`
`capture`	Fires the handler during the capture phase instead of the bubbling phase
`Once`	Remove the handler after the first time it runs
`Self`	Only trigger handler if `event.target` is the element itself

Source: Adapted from Svelte.dev website

A bonus is that these modifiers can be chained together – for example, we can do this: `on:click|once|capture={...}`.

It's all well and good talking about it, but the best way to understand how these modifiers work is to see them in action! We will do this in the next exercise, using two chosen at random from Table 5-1.

ADDING EVENT MODIFIERS

Assigning an event modifier requires only a small change. To see how, work these steps:

1. First, browse to `www.svelte.dev/repl` – don't forget the redirection that takes place!

2. For our first example, we will use `preventDefault` – go ahead and add this code into the `App.svelte` panel on the left:

```
<script>
  function handleSubmit() {
    console.log("success");
  }
</script>

<form on:submit|preventDefault={handleSubmit}>
  <input type="text" placeholder="Name" />
  <button>submit</button>
</form>
```

3. After a few moments, you will see a form appear on the right – click the submit button to see the response shown in Figure 5-2.

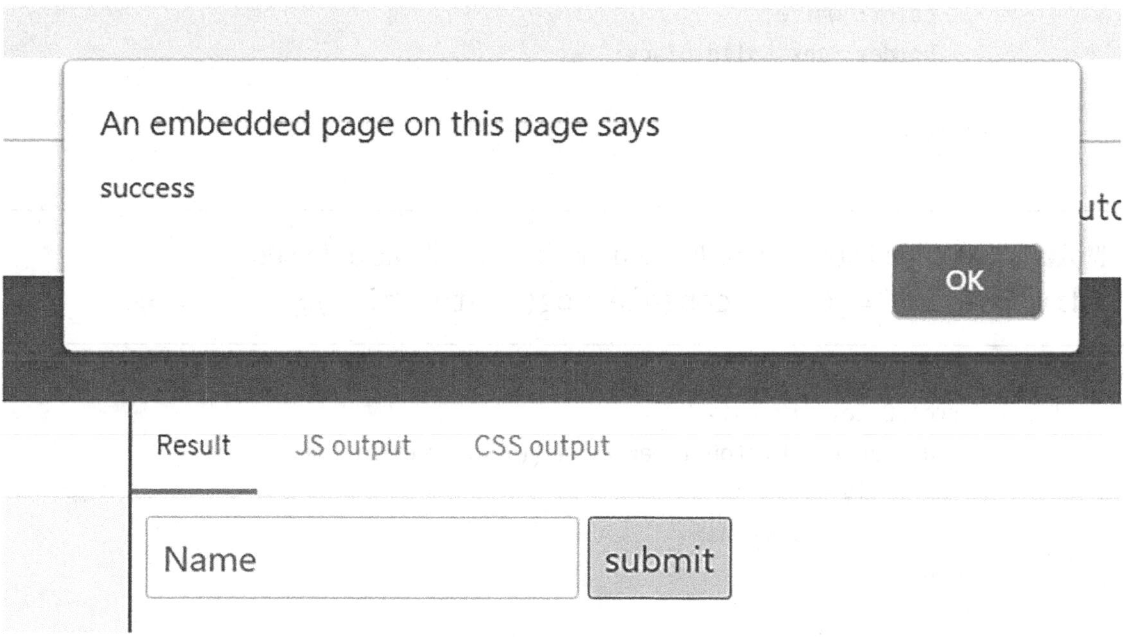

***Figure 5-2.** Using preventDefault in a Svelte event*

4. Go ahead and remove the `|preventDefault` text from the code, and then hit the Submit button once the screen has refreshed. You will see the same message appear, but if you click the OK button, the pane behind it will blank out.

The second example we will look at is `stopPropagation` – as with standard JavaScript, this will have more of a pronounced effect.

5. Go ahead and save a copy of the code if you have set up an account with the REPL tool, or bring up a new REPL window.

6. As before, add this code into the `App.svelte` tab on the left:

```
<style>
  div {
    padding: 1rem;
    border: 1px solid;
  }

  div:nth-child(1) { background-color: gainsboro; }

  div:nth-child(2) {
    background-color: grey;
    color: white;
    border: 1px solid black;
  }
</style>
```

Note I've added some color to each div, to make it easier to see `<div on:click={() => console.log('Outer div')}>`.

```
    <h1>Outer div</h1>
    <div on:click|stopPropagation={() => console.log
('inner div')}>
      <h1>Inner div</h1>
    </div>
</div>
```

7. Go ahead and click the Outer and then Inner div tags – in the console log, you should see the name of the clicked div appear, as indicated in Figure 5-3.

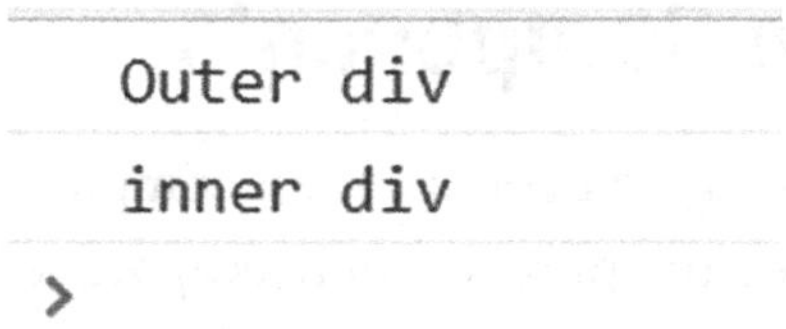

***Figure 5-3.** The results of clicking each div when stopPropagation is used*

8. Try removing |stopPropagation from within the code and clicking the div tags as before – you will get a completely different result!

Adding an event modifier is an effortless change which can have a dramatic effect on the overall behavior of our code. Let's take a moment to quickly explore the code we've created in more detail before moving on to looking at the next type of events in Svelte.

Exploring the Changes in Detail

Event modifiers in Svelte are so easy to set up. The syntax for each modifier is the same; we add the |<name of modifier> immediately after the on: directive name.

Although event modifiers in Svelte are a cinch to add, they each apply the same effect as their JavaScript equivalents; in our case, we used preventDefault and stopPropagation.

We started by creating a function handleSubmit(), which logs a message to the browser console - this we trigger using the on:submit event handler bound to the button element in our markup. We then switched to creating a more complex demo with two div elements; this time, we used two event handlers. Notice, though, we only applied the event modifier to the child div element to stop the outer event handler bubbling down to the parent and trigger clicks on both elements.

Okay, let's move on. We've focused on creating standard events and how to pass in modifiers to override the default action if needed. While this works very well, we should bear in mind that we may need to take a slightly different approach when writing components. The question is - how would that code differ compared to writing standard event handlers?

Creating Events in Components

It's a good question: we could create events within components - if we triggered them, they would work fine. However, the parent (such as `App.svelte`) won't listen to them and consequently won't react. A good example could be to click an add-to-basket button; with an ordinary event, features such as mini basket counts may not respond (and therefore could become out of sync with the main basket).

To get around this, Svelte has the `createEventDispatcher` feature - this allows the parent to listen for any instance where a child component triggers an event and responds accordingly. Hold that thought, though - there is a twist on this tale: What if we had to trigger an event held several levels deep rather than just one?

Forwarding Events

Well, we could use `createEventDispatcher`, but this is likely to generate a lot of extra code. Instead, Svelte provides a shortcut called `on:message`. This shortcut allows us to forward events down from the parent through intermediaries to the target component, but the net effect means less code to write!

It does raise an interesting question, though, as to whether this is better than simply passing events as part of a call to a native function, but for now, let's take a look at an example of how we can use both `on:message` and `createEventDispatcher` to trigger events from nested components.

FORWARDING EVENTS

To see how we can mix both `createEventDispatcher` and `on:message`, follow these steps:

1. First, browse to `www.svelte.dev/repl` – as before, don't forget the URL redirection that will kick in!
2. Next, in the `App.svelte` tab on the left, add this code:

```
<script>
  import Outer from './Outer.svelte';
```

```
  function handleMessage(event) {
    alert(event.detail.text);
  }
</script>

<Outer on:message={handleMessage}/>
```

3. We need to add another component, so click the plus sign to the right of the App.svelte tab, and rename it to Outer.svelte.

4. Go ahead and add in this code:

```
<script>
  import Inner from './Inner.svelte';
</script>

<Inner on:message/>
```

5. There is one more component to add – Inner.svelte. Click the plus sign as before, but this time, rename the component to Inner.svelte.

6. Go ahead and add in this code:

```
<script>
  import { createEventDispatcher } from 'svelte';

  const dispatch = createEventDispatcher();

  function sayHello() {
    dispatch('message', {
      text: 'Hi, Alex!',
    });
  }
</script>

<button on:click={sayHello}>
  Click to say hello
</button>
```

You will note I've used my name in the greeting, but feel free to substitute yours if you like!

---

7. After a few moments, we should see this button appear – if we click it, we get a suitable response from the inner component created in the demo (Figure 5-4).

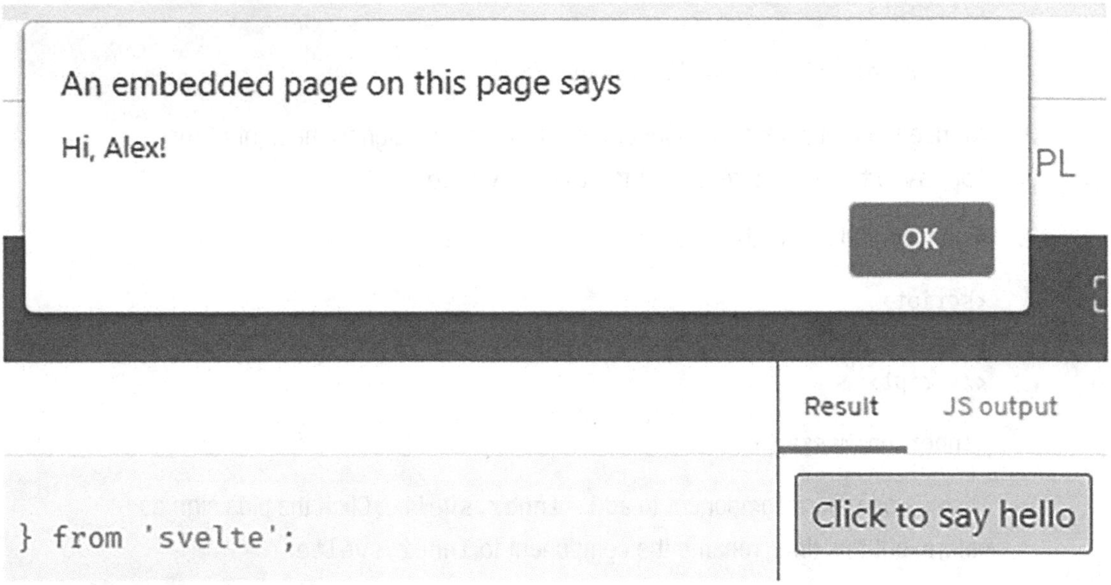

***Figure 5-4.** Response from the "forwarded" event*

This exercise shows how we can track and trigger events in a nested component from pretty much anywhere in our application. The only proviso is that we must maintain the forwarding chain (i.e., pass the event from component to component). Otherwise, a break means the event will not be triggered correctly.

To understand how it works, let's pause for a moment to review the code we've created in this demo in more detail.

Breaking Apart the Changes

Forwarding events in Svelte can be seen as something of a double-edged sword – while it allows us to provide two-way interaction (a parent can pass to child and respond to events from children), we should take care over how we forward events.

This means that we have to pass values down from the parent through each layer to the target child component when forwarding events. Granted, this is technically feasible for, say, six to seven layers, but it doesn't mean we should do it. As a general rule of thumb, I would follow the same principle as for CSS styling - anything more than two to three layers, and we should reconsider the architecture of our site.

Architecture aside for a moment, it's worth exploring how our code works - we started by creating the `App.svelte` parent, where we imported an Outer component (more anon) before constructing the `handleMessage` function. The format of this function is essential as the real action is in the `Inner.svelte` component. The `handleMessage` function is effectively a placeholder for the `sayHello()` function within `Inner.svelte`.

The trick to making this work is the `on:message` directive - this passes the `handleMessage` function down through to `Outer.svelte`, which then hands it off to `Inner.svelte` as a parameter. Once in `Inner.svelte`, we have a button tag, bound to which is an `on:click` handler that triggers the `sayHello` function.

This next point is where it gets interesting. As we are in a component, we use the `createEventDispatcher()` function to listen out for the message response and dispatch an appropriate message on-screen using the alert handler in the parent `App.svelte` component. If we were to remove any part of the alert in `App.svelte`, or even the `on:message` tag in the Outer component, then we won't see anything happen - even though we might call an instance of `Inner.svelte`, it won't respond to clicks as the alert function is in the parent component, not the child!

In our demo, we used `on:message` with the function's name to be passed down as a parameter. It's worth noting that if we didn't pass a parameter, Svelte will forward every message automatically.

A Point of Note

In our demo, we used `createEventDispatcher` and passed functions inline as parameters - is there any difference between the two?

If all you're worried about is the result, then the simple answer is no: we can use both to produce the same effect. However, you might end up with a mix of code, such as this:

```
<Child clickHandler="{childClick}" />
<button on:click="{buttonClick}">click</button>
```

While there is little difference between the two in terms of characters, you would need to remember which to use when working with Svelte. Having both styles could get messy – instead, it's better to be more consistent and stay with one. The second method might require a little more code, but this is the trade-off we have to face when working with event forwarding.

The equally important point is that passing down events as props more than six to seven layers deep is considered prop drilling and frowned upon by some as bad practice!

You can see some interesting comments on this subject on a StackOverflow posting starting at `https://stackoverflow.com/q/61569655/15301592`. Doniel Smith has also produced a more detailed article at `www.donielsmith.com/blog/2020-04-21-props-vs-event-dispatcher-svelte-3/`.

Okay, let's move on. We've covered standard events in some detail, but two topics remain, which play an equally important role in creating and managing events. I'm talking about managing life cycle events and creating actions – let's first look at life cycle events and how they fit into the broader picture of event management.

Life Cycling Events in Svelte

Over time, there will be critical moments where we might need to perform an action, during the life of a component. This life cycle starts when we create or mount the component and finishes once we have no further need for that component and it is destroyed.

A perfect example of performing this action might be to fetch data when a component is mounted; we might also want to load a library used to perform a function essential to the component's operation.

As with many component-based frameworks, we can use several methods, depending on what point we need to intercept the component. These are listed in Table 5-2.

Table 5-2. *List of Svelte component life cycle methods*

Svelte life cycle method	Function/use case – called when
`OnMount()`	The component is mounted on the DOM
`OnDestroy()`	Just before the component unmounts and is destroyed
`beforeUpdate()`	Before state updates the DOM
`afterUpdate()`	After state has updated the DOM
`tick()`	We can use this life cycle method at any time to help batch together changes to the DOM more effectively and reduce the number of instances we have to update the DOM

The theory of each type of life cycle event is all good, but nothing beats a little hands-on practice, right? With that in mind, let's play with a couple of these event handlers to see how they work in Svelte.

Working with onMount

If you've spent any time developing with the likes of React and Vue, then you may well be familiar with the first of our examples – `onMount`. This event works in much the same way as React; we can use it to intercept when a component is mounted and ask Svelte to execute an action during this process.

The Svelte tutorial has a great example of how this works – we can use it to fetch data from a mock placeholder service, ready to render slots on-screen, for, say, a gallery. I've used it as the basis for our next exercise, with some minor tweaks – let's look at how it works in action.

LIFE CYCLE METHODS PART 1: ONMOUNT

To understand how `onMount` works in Svelte, follow these steps:

1. As from previous exercises, we will start by browsing to `https://svelte.dev/repl` to use the Svelte REPL tool – don't forget the redirect that will kick in!

2. In the `App.svelte` tab, go ahead and add this script block:

```
<script>
    import { onMount } from 'svelte';

    let photos = [];

    onMount(async () => {
        const res = await fetch(`https://jsonplaceholder.typicode.com/
        photos?_limit=4`);
        photos = await res.json();
    });
</script>
```

3. Next, we need to add some rudimentary styling, so the demo at least looks presentable – for this, skip a line, and then add in this code:

```
<style>
    .photos { width: 100%; display: grid; grid-template-columns:
    repeat(2, 1fr); grid-gap: 8px; }

    figure, img { width: 100%; margin: 0; }
</style>
```

4. Our demo will be meaningless without some form of markup to display – for that, we need to add in this code, first leaving a line blank after the styling block:

```
<h1>Photo album</h1>

<div class="photos">
  {#each photos as photo}
    <figure>
      <img src={photo.thumbnailUrl} alt={photo.title}>
      <figcaption>{photo.title}</figcaption>
    </figure>
  {:else}
    <!-- renders when photos.length === 0 -->
    <p>loading the album...</p>
  {/each}
</div>
```

5. Excellent, our code is now in place: after a few moments, we should see something akin to the screenshot shown in Figure 5-5.

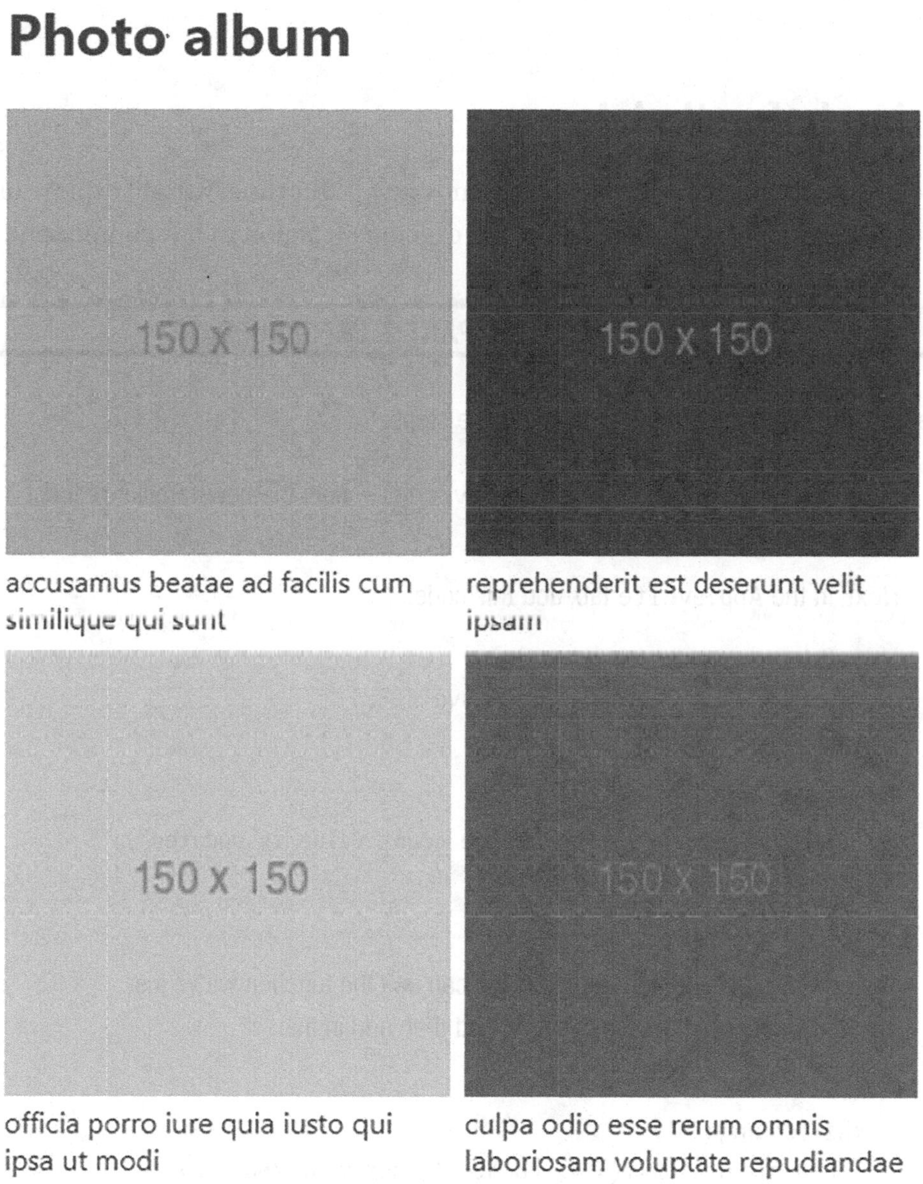

Figure 5-5. *The results of using on Mount to fetch data*

This example is a great way to show how we can use `onMount` to fetch data for a component – it does require us to use the await block to get the desired effect. Still, we can at least delay the loading of data or media until we are ready to render the component.

Exploring beforeUpdate

Let's take a look at the second of our two demos now – this time, we will explore using `beforeUpdate` to throw a message before we execute an action in our component.

LIFE CYCLE METHODS PART 2: BEFOREUPDATE

To see how we can refine the code, follow these steps:

1. First, browse to `https://svelte.dev/repl` – note the now-familiar redirect that will kick in!
2. Next, in the `App.svelte` tab, add this code:

```
<script>
  import { beforeUpdate} from "svelte";
  let count = 1;

  beforeUpdate(function() {
    alert("You can see me before count value is updated");
  });
</script>
```

3. We now need to add in markup, so we can use the function we've just created – go ahead and miss a line, and then add in this:

```
<div>
  <h1>{count}</h1>
  <button on:click={() => count++}>Increment</button>
</div>
```

4. After a few seconds, you will see a button appear – try clicking it: each time, a message will appear before the count is updated, similar to that shown in Figure 5-6.

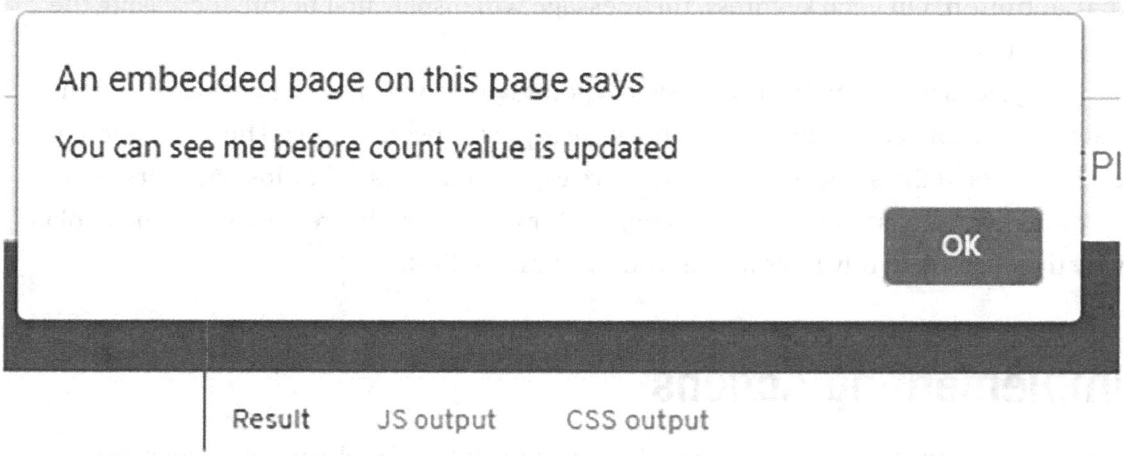

An embedded page on this page says
You can see me before count value is updated
OK
Result
JS output
CSS output

Figure 5-6. *The result of beforeUpdate*

Most of the code in the last two demos should be reasonably self-explanatory, but there are a couple of important points we should explore further, so let's pause for a moment to consider the code in greater detail.

Understanding How It Works

When it comes to working with life cycling events, you might see a few similarities with other frameworks, such as React - one such example that comes to mind is `componentDidMount()`. You might be tempted to follow suit and use them in the same way as React, but React now considers many of these to be legacy, so the direct comparison is less valid now!

That aside, in the first example, we kicked off by importing the `onMount` function from Svelte before creating an anonymous function to fetch placeholder photos from the JSONPlaceholder service asynchronously. Once retrieved, we assigned the results to an object named `photo`. Next up, we then iterated through each item in the `photo` object and rendered the various properties from each member of that object on-screen.

In the second exercise, we used a similar principle of importing the life cycle event – this time, we used `beforeUpdate`. We then set a variable `count` to 1 before implementing that handler to kick in and display a message before each increase of `count`. In the markup, we then rendered a button on-screen and bound this function to that button. On each keypress, the message will display first before increasing the value of `count`.

Okay, let's move on. We're almost at a point where we can start to use some of this newfound knowledge, but there is one more topic to cover: actions. These are not life cycle events in the same manner that we've explored thus far; they instead work at an element level. Let's take a peek at some, see how they work in greater detail, and explain why they can be handy tools to use when working in Svelte.

Implementing Actions

Imagine for a moment that we needed to call `onMount` in a Svelte project – let's say for arguments' sake this was all within the `App.svelte` file. Chances are we would need to import the `onMount` function, write our custom function, and then call that custom function from within `onMount`.

Sounds sensible, right? It serves our needs fine – we have the custom function in place, it's called when we need it, and we can destroy it at the appropriate time. What if I said that that was potentially a terrible way to write code and that we can do so much better?

I hear you say, "What do you mean we can do better?"

There are two issues here: when using `onMount` on an element, we could end up with an instance of `onMount` returning an undefined element, as Svelte hasn't yet initialized it. The second is that `onMount` code isn't reusable; we could shift it to `App.svelte` from a component, but we still need extra code to call it in each component where it is required. So, what is the solution? Let me introduce Actions – put simply, we can abstract code into reusable actions (think of them as components in a sense) and call the action on an element when needed in code. Perfect!

To see what I mean, let's dive into a before and after demo to see how it helps keep code clean and concise.

CREATING CUSTOM ACTIONS: PART 1

Let's take a look at how we can improve the code from the previous demo:

1. In a new window, browse to `https://svelte.dev` – the URL will redirect to indicate the version of Svelte in use.

2. In the `App.svelte` window, add this code:

```
<script>
  import { onMount } from "svelte";
  let node;

  function tellMeAboutTheNode(node) {
    console.log("Information: ", node.tagName);
  }

  onMount(() => {
    tellMeAboutTheNode(node);
  });
</script>

<h1 bind:this={node}>Hello onMount!</h1>
```

3. Go ahead and fire up your browser's console log, and then refresh the screen – if all is good, then you should see this message appear, as indicated in Figure 5-7.

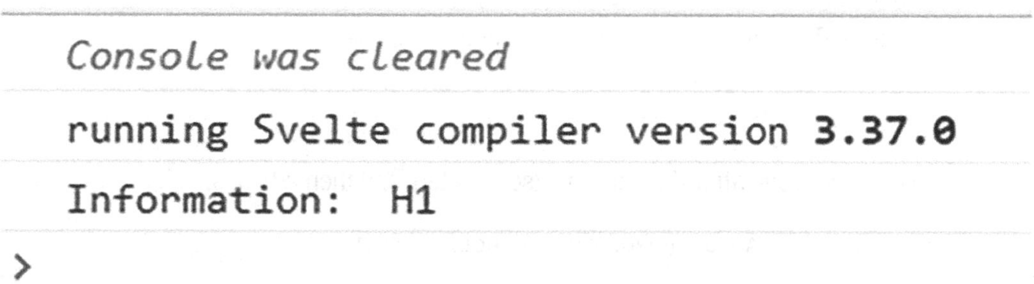

***Figure 5-7.** Piping out the name of a DOM node*

That was probably one of the shortest exercises I've ever written, and I've created more than a few in my books over the years! The key here is the number of lines of code we've used - ten in total, excluding the script tags but including blank lines. We can certainly improve on it. To see how, let's move onto the next exercise.

Reworking the Code

We've mentioned that Svelte Actions are the perfect tool to help refine this function - not only do they work in the same way as (in this case) onMount(), we can turn them into reusable modules that we can import as if they were just another component!

I'm sure you will agree this makes this type of function infinitely more appealing - to see just how one might look, let's dive into our next exercise where we will refine the code from part 1 to produce something reusable in our projects.

CREATING CUSTOM ACTIONS: PART 2

To see how we can improve the original code, follow these steps:

1. First, fire up a new session of the REPL playground, at www.svelte.dev/repl – this will give you a before and after effect.

2. In the App.svelte tab of this new instance, go ahead and paste in this script block:

```
<script>
  function tellMeAboutTheNode(node) {
    console.log("Information: ", node.tagName);
  }
</script>
```

3. Leave a line blank after the closing </script> tag, and then add this:

```
<h1 use:tellMeAboutTheNode>Hello Action!</h1>
```

4. After a moment or two, we should see the results shown in Figure 5-8 – you will need to resize the Console section at the bottom of the Result window to see the full effect.

***Figure 5-8.** Implementing a Svelte Action*

I am sure you will agree that the changes we've made already make the code more concise and easier to read!

That keyword `use` may look innocuous, but it hides a lot of potential: there are all manners of different applications we could use this feature for, which will help when writing our code. Let's take a moment to pause and explore the code in more detail.

Understanding What Happened

At this point, I would typically write some spiel about how each part of the code works, but I'm going to flip things on their head for once! Instead, let's talk a little about how the two demos differ.

In the first one, we've created a simple function to log the name of our chosen node to the browser console and then used the (imported) `onMount()` function to call it when Svelte mounts the component in the browser. Seems sensible, right?

Mmm... as I alluded to earlier, we can do better! Let's assume for argument's sake that the tellMeAboutTheNode function is a more complex example; to make it "reusable," we would have to move it to a higher level, such as `App.svelte`. It makes the code a little more flexible, but we still have to add code that imports `onMount`, the function, etc.... not great.

Instead, as we did in part 2, we did away with the onMount function. We created a similar function as before, but this time used a Svelte Action to call it on our chosen element directly. Using an action cuts down the amount of code we have to write and, above all, makes it far more reusable!

Gone is the import for onMount(), plus initiating an instance of it - instead, we call the function with the use: command. It means we can now move that function into a separate library or component and just import it if we needed. Yes, if we follow this route, we would still have an import. But we could put all of the functions called by use into that one file, then import it into App.svelte, and call each as needed with the use: function. A much better arrangement, I'm sure you will agree!

Continuing on, we've covered a lot of valuable tips throughout this chapter: let's put them to use! For the remaining demo in this book, we will add a modal feature to the home page to advertise a fake 10% discount offer. Before we do so, let's quickly cover off in more detail some of the features we've explored and already exist on our site.

Adding Functionality to Our Site

Throughout this book, we've focused on creating a simple ecommerce site using Svelte. It's a great way to show off some of this fantastic framework's valuable techniques and features. At this point, I would typically say, "let's add a new feature," but - as it so happens - we've already done it in more than one place!

That is indeed true: we've used the on:click event handler in several places in our code. Take a look at Cart.svelte, Button.svelte, or Products.svelte; inside each, you will find at least one example of the on:click handler in use. Here, as an example, is a code extract from Products.svelte, showing the on:click handler in use:

```
<div class="cta">
  <p>${product.price}</p>
  <Button on:click={() => addToCart(product)}>
     Add to cart
  </Button>
```

The reality is that the syntax is very similar to React or vanilla JavaScript, which makes it easy to understand how they operate in Svelte.

Let's continue with this theme, though, and add in a few more examples - we will add to the tally for `on:click`, but at the same time, including examples for `createEventDispatcher`, the `onDestroy()` life cycle event, and `on:keydown` handler. Let's crack on with the final exercise for this chapter and set up a modal display for our site.

Adding a Modal

A modal for our site, I hear you say? I wonder why...?

Ah, yes, you might well ask why, but it's with good reason: how many times have you visited a site, only to be bombarded with offers of discounts, or cookie consent forms, for example? I've personally lost count - sometimes you might come across a site which uses them sensibly and others... not so much. That criticism aside, models are an essential part of a developer's toolkit - we could spend time creating one from scratch, but why reinvent the wheel? There are several components out there for Svelte that will do just fine, including one created using code from the main Svelte website! We use this latter component for our next exercise, so let's dive in and make a start.

The plugin in question is available from the central NPM registry at `www.npmjs.com/package/modal-overlay`.

DEMO – ADDING A MODAL OVERLAY

Adding a modal is easy to add in for a Svelte site and uses several features we've touched on in this chapter – to see how to, follow these steps:

1. First, fire up a Node.js terminal session, and then change the working folder to our project area.

2. At the prompt, enter this command and press Enter:

   ```
   install npm i modal-overlay
   ```

3. Next, go ahead and open Home.svelte in your text editor, and then find this line:

```
{#if display}
```

4. Immediately below it, add this block of code:

```
  <Modal on:close={close}>
    <h1>Get 10% off your first order!</h1>
    <p>
      <span>Use code 10PERCENT at checkout</span>
      <img src="images/3.png" alt="image3" />
    </p>
    <button on:click={close}>X</button>
  </Modal>
{/if}
```

5. Save the file and close it.

6. Next, go ahead and open global.css – scroll to the bottom, and then add in this styling:

```
.modal-background { background-color: rgba(0, 0, 0, .7) !important; }
```

7. Save and close the file – the changes (for now) are complete.

8. Revert to the Node.js terminal window, and then make sure you have set the working folder as the project folder. At the prompt, enter npm run dev and press Enter.

9. Give it a few moments, and then when prompted, browse to http://localhost:5000 in your browser – if all is well, we should see something akin to Figure 5-9.

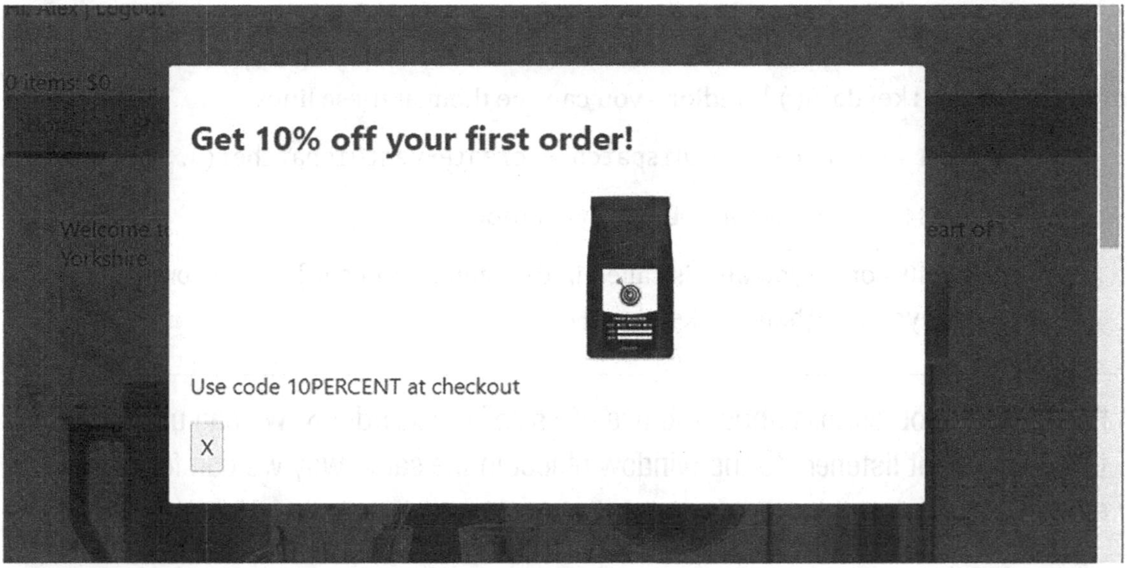

Figure 5-9. Displaying a modal on the home page of our site

Setting up a modal is a cinch technically, but using them does raise a few UX (user experience) questions, potentially becoming issues if we are not careful in how we use them. We should consider these questions further – before we do so, let's quickly run through the steps we took to create our demo in more detail.

Exploring Changes Made to Code

So, what did we change? This last exercise was very straightforward technically, but one that raises several questions, which we will come to in a moment.

For now, though, we kicked off by first installing the modal-overlay plugin, using a standard `npm install` command – once installed, we then added some example markup into `Home.svelte`, which we will render on-screen as our modal content. Simultaneously, we added an override for the modal opacity – the original comes in much lighter and makes it harder to view the modal content. Sounds simple, right? Or is it?

Exploring the Examples

So far in this exercise, we've talked about the use of `on:click()`. What about the other functions that feature in the modal-overlay plugin?

Head over to `https://svelte.dev/examples#modal`, which is the basis for this plugin. The three examples I've chosen are `createEventDispatcher()`, the `onDestroy()` method, and `on:keydown()` handler - you can see them at these lines:

- Line 4 - We have `const dispatch = createEventDispatcher()`.
- Line 34 - Contains the `onDestroy` method.
- Line 40 - `on:keydown()` is called in this statement `<svelte:window on:keydown ={handle_keydown}/>`.

For those of you curious about the use of `<svelte:window>`, we can use this to attach event listeners to the window object in the same way we can for DOM elements.

I know the code in the NPM plugin has been formatted a little differently, but that's purely part of packaging the code. All three, though, are good examples of how we can use some of the methods we've discussed in this chapter, and, hopefully, this will give you a flavor of what is possible in your development projects.

Using the Plugin – An Epilogue

I must confess, though, using a plugin here was a little bit of a cheat - while researching this book, I did check the code to make sure it contained examples suited to this chapter, though! That aside, there are a couple of things to be aware of:

- The plugin has styling already built-in - while this is great in a sense, it's also a problem. It means that to use our styling, we have to use the `!important` selector - not ideal! I used the plugin to help illustrate what we *could* do; if we were to use this plugin in anger, I would revert to using code (the plugin is based on a sample from the Svelte website, at `https://svelte.dev/examples#modal`).
- There will be times when we might not want to display the modal immediately, but perhaps after a few seconds delay - to do this isn't going to be practical if we use the plugin. We would have to refactor the code to include a status switch or possibly a timeout to delay its launch - again, another reason for using code rather than the plugin!

- The only way to override any styles is to put them into the `global.css` file – even though we might import the modal component into an existing one, Svelte will ignore any styles added using this route. If we put styles into `global.css`, we will undoubtedly get something displayed, but it means we can't co-locate styling with components which isn't ideal.

Indeed, something to consider! It by no means is a lost cause – it's something we have to allow for during development. It's a perfect excuse to fork the code and create an NPM package to suit our needs.

If you would like to learn more about creating NPM packages, there are plenty of articles online, such as this one: `https://bugfender.com/blog/how-to-create-an-npm-package/`.

Summary

Phew, that was one eventful chapter, and yes, the pun was intended!

Managing events is a vital part of any website – it doesn't matter which framework we use: we need to respond to any interaction from our users. Svelte is no different: the syntax might look slightly different, but the basic principles will be the same. Over this chapter, we've worked through various examples before adding new functionality to our site; let's take a moment to review what we have covered in this chapter.

We kicked off by first reminding ourselves of the theory of reactivity, core to how Svelte works; we then explored some of the different types of events we can use in Svelte.

The first event type we covered was standard events before adding in event modifiers. We then covered the principles of forwarding events into child components before moving on, looking at life cycling events and implementing Actions in Svelte.

We then rounded out the chapter by adding a modal display to our demo site – we saw how easy it was using a plugin, but this wasn't without drawbacks. We then covered some of these drawbacks to understand what changes we might need to fit our requirements better.

Okay, we've come to the end of our tour of events in Svelte and the changes we've made to our site, but there is still more to come! It's time now to get all stylish and smarten up our site (yes, pun very definitely intended there!). Adding styles is very simple for Svelte, but there are several ways to do it – to learn more and see how smart our site will be once we update it. Stay with me, and I will reveal it all in the next chapter.

CHAPTER 6

Binding Elements

A question – how many times have you filled out a form online, only for it to tell you that you can't submit it as there is a problem with a value, but you don't know what format that `value` should take? Sounds familiar, right?

Form filling is an essential part of using any website, particularly an ecommerce one; the exercise is only as good as the validation rules applied to the form. Svelte makes creating forms easy – after all, most of the code required is just plain HTML markup! Constructing forms (using binding principles) is just a tiny part of what Svelte has to offer; we can bind to all kinds of form elements and objects, other DOM elements, and more.

For this chapter, I will focus on the most prominent use of binding, which is building forms. We'll look at some examples before using the techniques to add a new contact us page to our front-end demo store. Let's first look at a fundamental principle of frameworks – and this includes Svelte: data is always top down.

Creating Forms in Svelte

Okay, I confess: that last statement isn't always true – data is usually top down, but this is only a general rule. And rules can be broken. The difference is knowing when to break them and why. Let me explain, using a text input as my example.

We could put an `input` event handler on that text input. This arrangement could get a little clunky, though, particularly as we'd probably need to use an `event.target.value` to reference the triggering element. Instead, there is a simpler way – we use the `bind:` directive, as shown in this example:

```
<script>
  let name = 'Guest';
</script>

<input bind:value={name}>
<h1>Hello {name}!</h1>
```


A. Libby, *Practical Svelte*, https://doi.org/10.1007/978-1-4842-7374-6_6

It's a simple example, but using `bind` here means that if we change the value against the name function in the `<input>` element, it will reflect both in the text within the `<h1>` tags and the variable declared in the script block. Likewise, if we change the value of `name`, this will filter down to both the input value and the text within the `<h1>` tags.

This two-way communication is one thing I love about Svelte – using `bind:` makes our code more straightforward and easier to read. Svelte automatically handles the two-way binding process, leaving us to focus on manipulating the results as suited for our needs. The same principle applies across all form elements – let us look at a few examples before using them later in this chapter.

Catering for Different Form Elements

We've seen how using the bind function makes for cleaner code when setting up two-way interaction with form elements in Svelte – but what about the other elements?

Thankfully, most of them pattern, although there are some subtle differences – this is more down to syntax for a specific element than anything else. I've listed a basic example in Table 6-1 for text inputs.

Table 6-1. *Examples of binding form elements*

Form element	Example of binding element
Text inputs	`<input bind:value={name}>`

Text area inputs are not the only element Svelte can manage – let's take a look at some of the others, starting with numeric inputs.

Working with Numeric Inputs

Numeric inputs work in the same way as text inputs – all we need to do is specify the `bind:value={XXXX}` attribute, where XXXX is the name of the variable to which we assign the value from the numerical input. Examples of standard numeric input and range input are in Table 6-2.

Table 6-2. *Example of binding numeric inputs*

Form element	Example of binding element
Numeric inputs	`<input type=number bind:value={b} min=0 max=10>` `<input type=range bind:value={b} min=0 max=10>`

What would that look like once Svelte has compiled it into the `bundle.js` file you will see on any Svelte-driven website? Well, let's say we had this code as a simple example:

```
<script>
    let a = 1;
    let b = 2;
</script>

<label>
    <input type=number value={a} min=0 max=10>
</label>

<label>
    <input type=number value={b} min=0 max=10>
</label>

<p>{a} + {b} = {a + b}</p>
```

This is what it looks like once compiled by Svelte:

```
/* App.svelte generated by Svelte v3.38.2 */
import { add_attribute, create_ssr_component, escape } from "svelte/internal";

let a = 1;
let b = 2;

const App = create_ssr_component(($$result, $$props, $$bindings, slots) => {
  return `<label><input type="${"number"}"${add_attribute("value", a, 0)}
  min="${"0"}" max="${"10"}"></label>

  <label><input type="${"number"}"${add_attribute("value", b, 0)}
  min="${"0"}" max="${"10"}"></label>
```

```
  <p>${escape(a)} + ${escape(b)} = ${escape(a + b)}</p>`;
});

export default App;
```

It looks like a lot, but bear one thing in mind - unlike frameworks such as React, which compiles on the fly, Svelte compiles it at *build time* into standard JavaScript. It means that even though we may have a fair chunk of code, it will be pre-built, so what we lose in length, we gain in speed (compared to compiling in real time)!

Using Checkbox Inputs

Setting up binding for checkbox-based inputs requires a little more effort - the initial bind is very straightforward, but we need to use a conditional check to determine the result. Table 6-3 shows an example of the `bind` property for a checkbox input; we would then use an `#if` block to determine the result.

***Table 6-3.** Binding checkbox inputs in Svelte*

Form element	Example of binding element
Checkbox inputs	`<input type=checkbox bind:checked={yes}>`

Handling Multiline Text Area Inputs

We can create multiline text areas in one of two ways when using Svelte - we still need to specify the name of the variable to which we bind the text area, but if the value shares the same name, we can use a short-form version, as indicated in Table 6-4.

***Table 6-4.** Handling binding for multiline text area elements*

Form element	Example of binding element

Text area inputs	`<textarea bind:value={value}></textarea>`
	We can also use a short-form version, if the values have the same name:
	`<textarea bind:value></textarea>`

Selecting Choices

This last example can be set up in two ways, depending on whether we permit single or multiple choices. In both cases, we would use an `<option>...</option>` block to iterate through the choices, but the initial syntax will differ, as shown in Table 6-5.

Table 6-5. *Examples of binding with select elements*

Form element	Example of binding element

Single select	`<select bind:value={selected} on:change="{() => answer = ''}">`
	`  {#each questions as question}`
	`    <option value=...`
	`  {/each}`
	`</select>`

Select multiple	`<select multiple bind:value={sizes}>`
	`  {#each menu as flavour}`
	`    <option value=...`
	`  {/each}`
	`</select>`

> The observant among you may spot that I've left one out – and with good reason: it requires more code to handle! I'm talking about group inputs such as checkboxes or radio buttons; I will cover this in our demo shortly.

Dealing with Content Editable Fields

In this example, all we need to do is bind to the HTML content, not the element itself. Table 6-6 shows an example of how to achieve this, specifying `innerHTML` as the variable reference.

Table 6-6. *Example of binding with contenteditable fields*

Form element	Example of binding element
Contenteditable element	`<div contenteditable="true" bind: innerHTML={html}></div>`

Binding and Managing Other Events

Managing form elements is only part of the story when it comes to binding - Svelte also supports binding in some more advanced use cases. Let's take a look at some of these examples in more detail.

The first one is binding in an #each block. This option might seem great initially, but beware - it mutates the array, so if you prefer to work with immutable content, it's better to use event handlers instead. Table 6-7 shows an example of how we might use binding in an #each block.

Table 6-7. *Example of binding in an #each block*

Form element	Example of binding element

Each block	`{#each todos as todo}`
	`<div class:done={todo.done}>`
	`<input type=checkbox bind:checked ={todo.done}>`
	`<input placeholder="What needs to be done?" bind:value={todo.text}>`
	`</div>`
	`{/each}`

This second example is a little more complex - Svelte allows us to bind to a whole component. It doesn't matter if the component is a single element or a complex one made up of multiple objects - binding to it means that if we interact with it, the value property is immediately updated.

For example, if we had an Email Address field with additional validation built into it as a custom component, any time we change the email address entered, this would be reflected in the value property, as shown in Table 6-8.

***Table 6-8.** Example of binding with components*

Form element	Example of binding element
Component-level bindings	<EmailAddress bind:value={email} on:submit={ handleSubmit}/>

For this third and final example, a question – I'm sure you've used properties such as `clientWidth` and `clientHeight`, right? Well, we can use them to get the dimensions of an element. Table 6-9 shows how we might achieve this, with a div that contains a placeholder for text.

***Table 6-9.** Example of binding with dimensions*

Form element	Example of binding element
Dimensions	<div bind:clientWidth={w} bind:clientHeight={h}> <span style="font-size: {size}px">{text}</span> </div>

We've covered some of the basic principles of creating forms, so let's focus our attention on putting some of what we've covered to good use in the form of a quick demo.

Building a Composite Example

For this demo, we're going to build a simple coffee selector to choose the different options we might want when ordering coffee.

We'll keep it simple by focusing on the form elements and not styling; the key here will be to watch how the final statement reacts when we change any of the form options in this demo. With that in mind, let's dive in and take a look at constructing our demo.

BUILDING A COFFEE SELECTOR

To see how easy it is to create and manage form elements in Svelte, follow these steps:

1. First, go ahead and browse to `https://svelte.dev/repl` – don't forget the usual URL redirect that will kick in!

2. Next, in the `App.svelte` tab on the left, add in this script block:

```
<script>
  let cnt = 1;
  let name = 'Guest';
  let grain = 'Coarse';
  let size = ['50g'];

  let coffeeType = [
    'Coarse',
    'Fine',
    'Wholebean'
  ];

  let sizes = [
    '50g',
    '75g',
    '100g'
  ];
</script>
```

3. We have a fair chunk of markup to add in, so we will do it in sections. Leave a line blank, and then add in this code:

```
<p>
  Please enter your name: <input bind:value={name}>
</p>
<h1>Hi {name}!</h1>
<p>
  This is what we have available in stock right now:
</p>
```

4. Next, leave a link blank, and add in this code – it will display a group of radio buttons:

```
<h2>
  Grain
</h2>
<label>
  <input type=radio bind:group={grain} value={'Coarse'}>
  Coarse
</label>

<label>
  <input type=radio bind:group={grain} value={'Fine'}>
  Fine
</label>

<label>
  <input type=radio bind:group={grain} value={'Whole Bean'}>
  Whole Bean
</label>
```

5. Leave a line blank, and then add in this code – this will render a group of checkboxes on-screen:

```
<h2>
  Weight
</h2>
{#each sizes as bagSize}
  <label>
    <input type=checkbox bind:group={size} value={bagSize}>
    {bagSize}
  </label>
{/each}
```

6. Lastly for this portion, go ahead and add in this code too:

```
<p>
  Number of bags required:
</p>
```

```
<label>
  <input type=number bind:value={cnt} min=1 max=10>
</label>

You've chosen {cnt} x {size} {cnt === 1? "bag": "bags"} of {grain}
coffee
```

7. After a few moments, we should see something akin to the screenshot shown in Figure 6-1, shown overleaf.

8. Try changing the selected options or entering a different value into either of the input fields – Svelte will change either the “Hi Guest!” or “You’ve chosen…” statements accordingly.

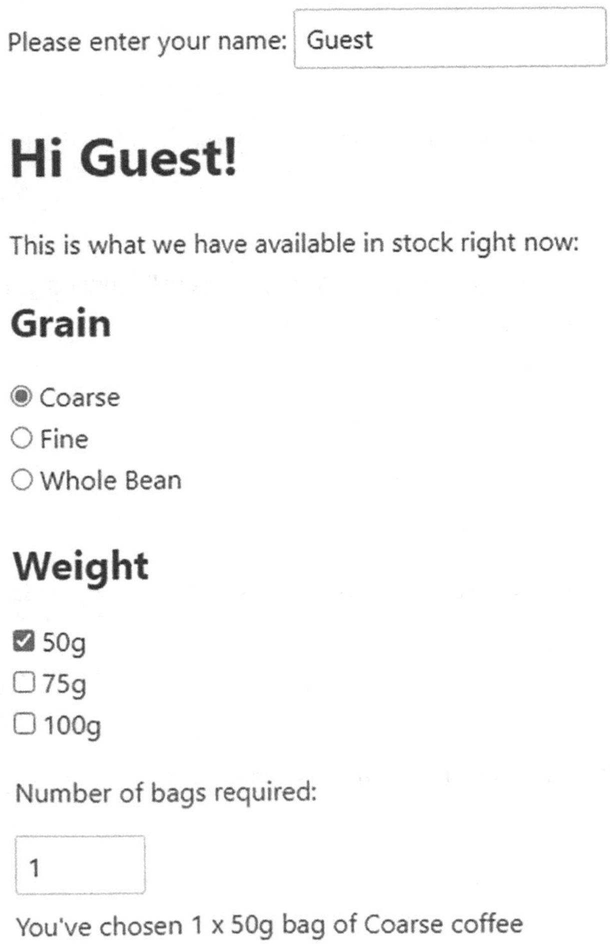

Please enter your name:
Guest
Hi Guest!
This is what we have available in stock right now:
Grain
Coarse
Fine
Whole Bean
Weight
50g
75g
100g
Number of bags required:
1
You've chosen 1 x 50g bag of Coarse coffee

Figure 6-1. *Our coffee selector demo*

It's a simple demo, but it highlights just how we can begin to use form elements in Svelte. We've not included `<form>` tags – or any styling for that matter – but that doesn't matter: it's the principle that counts! We will come back to using form elements later in this chapter when we start to add features to our front-end demo, but for now, let's pause for a moment to review the changes made in this demo in more detail.

Breaking the Code Apart

Take another close look at the demo – notice anything, in particular around the state, or lack thereof?

It is indeed true that our demo doesn't seem to include anything to manage the state (as we might otherwise expect with frameworks such as React or Vue), but then this is the beauty of Svelte: it does much of this automatically for us. It leaves us to focus on the important stuff like setting up the script and HTML markup.

We kicked off by assigning several variables – we will use most of these (such as `name` and `grain`) to store the values derived from the form fields used in our demo. We then created two object arrays to define the coffee type (`coffeeType`) and specify the various bag sizes (`sizes`).

Next up, we added in our markup – the first block took care of rendering a greeting, followed by a group of radio buttons to determine which bean type the customer could select. Notice that we specify `bind:group={grain}` – this is because we have multiple inputs which we need to group as part of the same array. We use the `value` attribute in much the same way as we would typically do with HTML markup for piping out the response.

We could (if needed) use an onChange event handler to get the value of grain separately if we wanted to use it elsewhere in our code.

We then added in several checkboxes – we could have hard-coded these in the same way as the radio buttons, but instead, we've used an `#each` block as this is a more practical alternative (and one we can also use for radio buttons if preferred).

Lastly, we added an input field to allow the customer to choose how many bags they want of a specific option – we've set a `min` of `1` and a `max` of `10`, but we could set these to any value. We then added a statement to display the results of the selected options to the customer. The values are automatically updated as soon as we change any of the options in our demo.

Now that we have that situated, we shall focus on something else: media. Now, let me clarify: we're going to answer one specific question. What happens if we had a page full of, say, music files and tried to play each one?

Managing Context

The obvious answer is that it would sound awful!

But that illustrates a perfect example of how Svelte can help with binding elements – maintaining context. Unless we happen to be a budding DJ, we would only want one tune to play at any one time, right? This is where Svelte comes in – we can declare a `<script context="module">` block in our code; this allows each media element to talk to each other, without the need for us to manage state manually.

I suspect you probably think that this isn't possible – for those of you who work with tools such as React, you would expect to have to initiate some form of state management and update it when triggering a new media element. You'd be right if we were talking about the likes of React. Not so with Svelte. To see what I mean, let's first dive into a demo to see how this all works in practice.

DEMO – "ONE AT A TIME..."

To see Svelte manage context when binding multiple elements, follow these steps:

1. First, go ahead and browse to `https://svelte.dev/repl` – don't forget the by-now-familiar redirection!
2. Next, open a copy of audio player code.txt from the code download that accompanies this book, and copy the contents into the `App.svelte` tab.
3. Click the plus sign next to that tab heading, and rename the new tab to `Audioplayer.svelte`. Go ahead and add in this script block:

```
<script context="module">
  let current;
</script>
```

Don't be tempted to merge the code from step 3 into any existing <script> block. Script modules of this type have to be separate, or this will throw errors.

---

4. Leave a line blank, then add in the following code – this defines several variables and a `stopOthers()` function for our player:

```
<script>
  export let src;
  export let title;
  export let composer;
  export let performer;

  let audio;
  let paused = true;

  function stopOthers() {
    if (current && current !== audio) current.pause();
    current = audio;
  }
</script>
```

5. It's the turn of the markup to be added – leave a line blank, and then add in this code:

```
<article class:playing={!paused}>
  <h2>{title}</h2>
  <p><strong>{composer}</strong> - performed by {performer}</p>
  <audio bind:this={audio} bind:paused on:play={stopOthers} controls {src}>
    <track kind="captions">
  </audio>
</article>
```

6. Last but by no means least, we should add in some styling, so our demo at least looks presentable:

```
<style>
  article { margin: 0 0 1rem 0; max-width: 800px;
padding: 5px; }

  h2, p { margin: 0 0 0.3rem 0; }

  audio { width: 50%; margin: 0.5rem 0 1rem 0; }

  .playing { color: #000; background-color: silver }
</style>
```

You can see my version as a Svelte REPL, at `https://svelte.dev/repl/a1874f8f986b4c719115f3f0035504d0?version=3.38.1` – the demo in this chapter is adapted from the original on the Svelte site, at `https://svelte.dev/tutorial/sharing-code`.

---

7. If all is well, we should see the music players appear, as indicated in Figure 6-2, shown overleaf.

8. Try switching between players – no matter how much you try, you will only see one player operate at a time! As soon as you click the next one, the original will stop, and the new selection kicks in to play.

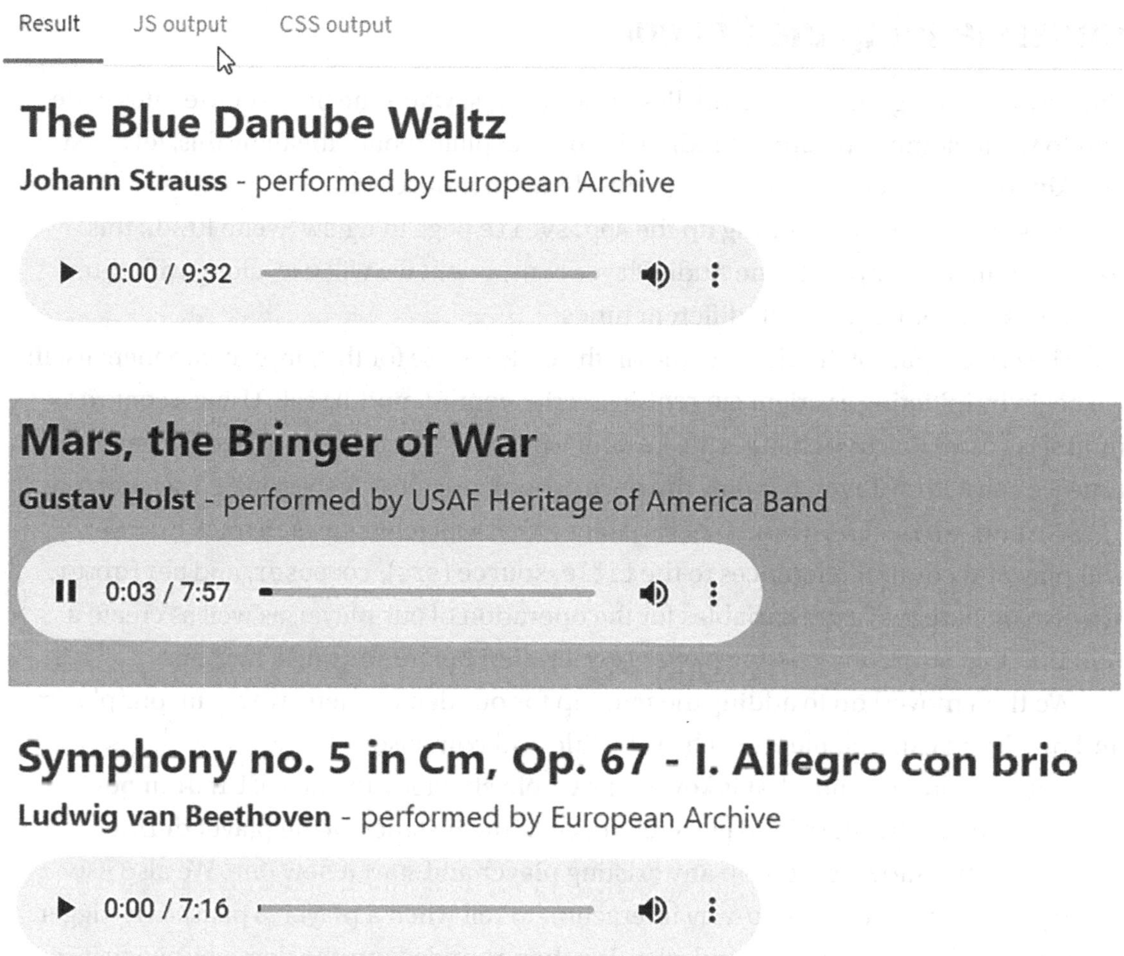

***Figure 6-2.** Managing context with music selection*

I must admit that classical music isn't my typical music of choice, but it's nice to try different things from time to time!

Leaving tastes in music aside, this demo shows off perfectly how we can have multiple media elements on the page yet control which one plays when we want to and don't end up with a cacophony of different sounds. You're probably asking, "How *are* we managing state in this demo, and where does this fit in with element binding?"

Understanding the Changes

The key to making this demo work lies in two things: when the browser executes code and to what element we apply binding. Before I explain what I mean by this, let's first quickly review the code we've used in this demo in more detail.

We kicked off by first setting up the `App.svelte` page in a new Svelte REPL; this page contains an import to the AudioPlayer component we will use, along with three instances, all configured with different tunes.

The critical part of this demo comes in the code we use for the player component itself; we begin by initiating a variant `current` in a script context module call. Using a context module is essential, as it changes the focus of when we run this step; instead of running each time we call `AudioPlayer`, it is only run once, when the code is first evaluated at launch.

Next up, we declare a bunch of variables – these all relate to each track that we will play and contain references to the `title`, `source` (`src`), `composer`, and `performer`. We also declare two extra variables for the operation of our player, as well as create a function that stops any existing player in operation before starting a new one.

We then moved on to adding the markup for our demo – here, we set up our player and displayed extra elements such as the title and composer.

Notice though – and what is key to this whole chapter – the use of `bind:` in our markup? We use `bind:this` to get a reference to the instance of the player during operation; this allows us to stop any existing player and start a new one. We also use `bind:paused` to provide a two-way interaction to tell when a player is paused or trigger an action to pause a player in mid-play. We then rounded out the demo by giving it some basic styling. Moving on, it's time to add functionality to our demo front-end store! For this part, we will focus on adding a "Contact Us" page and provide some basic form validation. That latter part might open up a real can of worms (or trouble, for anyone not familiar with that quote) – let's dive in and see why despite using Svelte to build our form, we still need to be careful when it comes to validating entries from our customers.

Adding a Contact Form to Our Demo

I've lost count of the number of websites I've visited over the years – I can still remember the heady days of 1997 when the Internet became mainstream! There have been some dramatic changes over the years, but most websites have one thing in common: a means to contact a company.

This feature might be anything from a simple email link to a full-blown contact form – whether the company concerned responds and how long it takes is another matter! The important thing is that we should provide some form of contact feature on any site we build: for our next project, we will do just that, using Svelte and the Yup library.

Introducing Svelte-Yup

Yup, I hear you ask what is that? No, it's not someone being lazy when they say yes, but the name of a validation library for forms. Building a form is only part of the picture: we also have to validate the content to ensure it's appropriately formatted before sending it.

Here's where that "can of worms" from earlier comes in: validating forms is not an easy task! Yes, it might be simple to hook up a function to validate an email address, but making sure it's a **valid** address is another matter. It's not just a case of ensuring we have an @ sign, a domain, or TLD suffix – what if the email address contains a subdomain too? This type of check is where it makes sense to use an established validation library rather than trying to reinvent the wheel: trust me, doing the latter is a world of pain.

Let me introduce you to the **Svelte-Yup** library. It is a lightweight wrapper for the Yup validation library and is available from `https://github.com/KamyarLajani/svelte-yup`. It's a schema-based system, so we need to specify a suitably crafted schema, such as this:

```
    let schema = yup.object().shape({
      name: yup.string().required().max(30)
.label("Name"),
      email: yup.string().required().email()
.label("Email address"),
    });
```

The great thing about Svelte-Yup is that its syntax is very similar to jQuery, making it easy to set up. With that in mind, let's dive straight into the following demo to see it in action and explore how it works in more detail.

Laying the Groundwork

Our next demo will come in two parts - we will create a simple contact form for our front-end store, with fields for customer name, their email address, and message.

To keep things simple, we will only focus on the front-end changes - I'm assuming that if we were to push to production, then that system would need an appropriate back-end solution in place to receive and store messages from customers. Let's leave that side alone for now and focus on building that form as part of our next exercise.

BUILDING A CONTACT US FORM

To add in a contact form, follow these steps:

1. First, we need to install the svelte-yup plugin – this is a wrapper for the yup plugin, so we need to install it as well. To do so, fire up a Node.js terminal session, and then change the working folder to our project area.
2. At the prompt, enter `npm i yup svelte-yup --save-dev` and press Enter.
3. Once completed, close the terminal session.
4. Next, go ahead and crack open `App.svelte` from our project folder – add this at the bottom of the `import...` block near the top of the page:

```
import Contact from "./pages/Contact.svelte";
```

5. Scroll down to the `<main>` block – add this entry below the last but one `<Route...>` entry for the Coffee page:

```
<Route path="contact"><Contact /></Route>
```

6. Save the `App.svelte` page and close it – the changes for this file are complete.

At this point, I would recommend taking a break - grab a drink, pause for a bit; the code isn't going anywhere! When you're ready, let's continue with the second part of this demo.

Building the Contact Form

Now that we're rested, let's continue with the second part of this demo - here, we're going to build the contact form and test it:

BUILDING THE FORM

To add the form, follow these steps:

1. Next, go ahead and open a new file, saving it as `Contact.svelte` in the `\src\pages` folder.

2. At the top of the file, add in this script block – there is a good chunk of code to add, so we will do it in sections, beginning with the opening tag and import statements:

```
<script>
  import * as yup from 'yup';
  import {Form, Message, isInvalid} from 'svelte-yup';
```

3. Next comes a function to flag if any fields are not validated:

```
$: invalid = (name)=>{
  if(submitted){
    return isInvalid(schema, name, fields);
  }
  return false;
}
```

4. We need to determine which fields should be validated and how – for this, add in this declaration:

```
  let schema = yup.object().shape({
    name: yup.string().required().max(30)
.label("Name"),
    email: yup.string().required().email()
.label("Email address"),
  });
```

5. We have three additional declarations to add in too:

```
let fields = {
  email: "",
  name: "",
  yourmessage: ""
};

let submitted = false;
let isValid;
```

6. Last but by no means least, we need to add in a function to take care of submitting the responses:

```
  function formSubmit(){
    submitted = true;
    isValid = schema.isValidSync(fields);

    if(isValid){
      alert('Everything is validated!');
      console.log("Validated fields", fields);
    }
  }
</script>
```

7. Next, leave a line blank, and then add in this markup block, which we will do in sections:

```
<section>
  <h2>Contact Us</h2>
  <!-- image from https://www.pexels.com/photo/beans-beverage-black-
  coffee-breakfast-373888/ -->
  <div id="banner">
    <img src="images/banner.jpg" alt="banner" />
  </div>

  <p>Lorem ipsum dolor sit amet, consectetur adipiscing elit. Maecenas
  sed odio id nulla gravida rhoncus. Suspendisse potenti. In volutpat
  nibh non tellus laoreet, vitae faucibus ipsum sollicitudin. Duis
  viverra pulvinar tempus. Phasellus odio nunc, imperdiet vitae diam
  quis, sollicitudin pretium massa. Donec molestie mauris id semper
  sagittis.</p>
```

8. The next block of code takes care of rendering our contact form – we have the opening tags, followed by the name field:

```
<Form class="form" {schema} {fields} submitHandler={formSubmit}
{submitted}>
  <label for="customer"><span class="required">*<span>Name:</span>
  </label>
  <span class="formformat">
    <input type="text" class:invalid={invalid("name")}
    bind:value={fields.name}
placeholder="Name">
    <Message name="name" />
  </span>
```

9. Next comes the email address and message fields:

```
<label for="emailaddress">
  <span class="required">*<span>Email address:</span>
</label>
<span class="formformat">
  <input name="emailaddress" type="text" class:invalid={invalid(
  "email")} bind:value
={fields.email} placeholder="Email address">
  <Message name="email" />
</span>

<label for="yourmessage">Your message:</label>
<textarea name="yourmessage" cols="50" rows="10" bind:value={
fields.yourmessage} placeholder="Enter your message"></textarea>
```

10. Finally, we can add in a submit button and closing tags:

```
    <span class="submitbutton">
      <button type="submit">Submit</button>
    </span>
  </Form>
</section>
```

11. Go ahead and save all of the files, and then close them.

12. Next, make sure you have started your Svelte development server, and browse to `http://localhost:5000/contact` – if all is well, we should see a page with the title, lead-in image, and text; we will see the all-important form further down the page (Figure 6-3), shown overleaf.

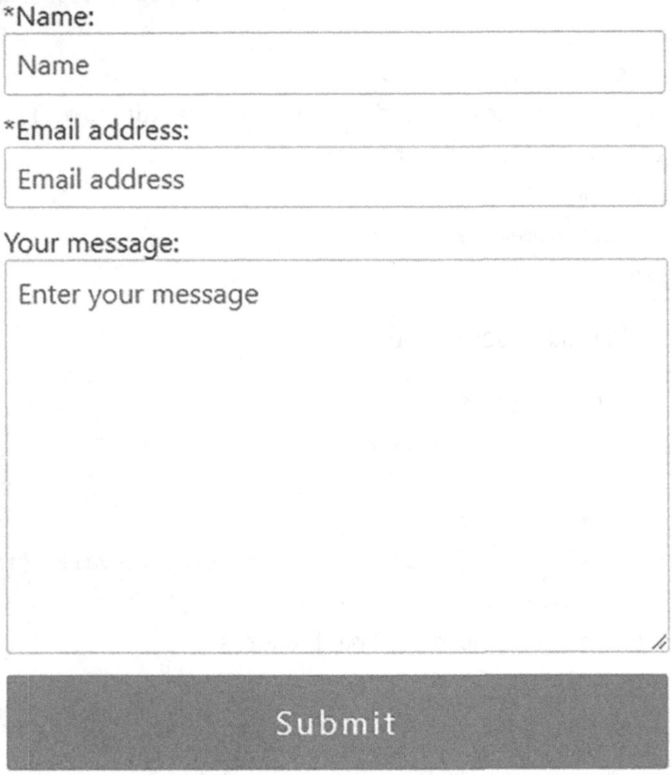

Figure 6-3. *The newly created form*

13. Try hitting Submit now – if all is well, you'll get a message saying there's a problem, and Submit won't let you go any further! If you do enter an email and name, you find all is well when hitting that Submit button.

This was a prolonged, two-part exercise, but worth it! We've covered some valuable techniques while building this demo, so let's rest for a moment and review the changes in more detail.

Understanding the Code in Detail

So, what did we do? In part 1, we started by setting up the groundwork for our contact form – we installed the yup and svelte-yup plugins before updating the navigation in `App.svelte` by adding an additional `<Route...>` for the contact page.

In part 2, things were a little more involved; we started by creating the skeleton for the Contact.svelte page. We added in a script block to handle `functionality`; this first imported the two plugins. Next up came the function `invalid` to determine if we had correctly validated the submitted fields; if not, we flag them as such.

As part of this, we then created a schema to determine how to check and validate our targeted fields. For `name`, we set it to expect a value of type `string()`, made it compulsory (or `required()`), and set it to be no more than 30 characters long, with a field name (highly original, I know!). We did something similar for the `email` field; we set it as a `string()` field, which was of type `email()` and `required()`.

Next up, we then set an object to determine the default values for `name`, `email`, and `yourmessage` fields – note we do not use these for validating! We then set a couple of variables used for determining state before creating a `formSubmit()` function to check our fields are correctly validated.

Last but by no means least, we then added in the markup – most of this is standard HTML, but it's worth noting a couple of extras:

- We add the `{schema}` entry to tie each field back to the validation schema.
- The `{submitted}` value is there to determine if the field has been submitted – it uses the two-way communication we've already talked about.
- It uses the `bind:value={fields.yourmessage}` format to enable two-way communication, so we can use values as and when they are updated in the form.

Otherwise, the form is made up of standard HTML markup that you will find for each type of field we've used – hopefully, this shows that we don't need to add too much extra code to our markup when creating forms using Svelte.

Note the presence of `class:invalid={invalid("email")}` – it looks odd, but this is purely to add a styling class. We will cover this more in the next chapter.

Summary

Forms, forms... who loves filling them out? I certainly don't, and I'm sure many of you would agree!

Form filling is one essential part of any website – while they serve a purpose, the whole design can be a real hit-and-miss affair, with some companies getting it spot on and others leaving you feeling frustrated. Leaving the subject of frustrations aside, form creation is just one part of what Svelte has to offer when binding elements using this framework. We've covered several useful principles, so let's take a moment to review what we have learned in this chapter.

We started with a look at the core principle of data being driven from top to bottom and how this doesn't apply to forms; we understood that frequently we need two-way communication when it comes to binding form elements. We then reviewed examples of how to bind different types of form elements, such as numeric inputs or multiline text boxes, before covering some of the other ways we can bind elements using Svelte.

Next up, we then moved onto the subject of context – when binding to certain elements such as media, we explored how it was helpful to maintain a direct reference to the correct element using context. It means that if we have multiple elements, such as videos, we can target the right element.

We then turned our attention to adding a new feature to our front-end store – this took the format of a new contact us page, with the beginnings of form validation. We covered how validating form elements can be an absolute minefield. We mentioned that in most cases, it is often more effective to use an existing validation library rather than create one from scratch!

In this chapter, we've added all of the core features for our website. It's time to make it look a little more stylish and presentable for our customers! At this point, things will get more interesting, as this opens up some real possibilities for us; it should be no surprise that I'm of course talking about adding styles. We have a lot to cover, so without further ado, let's crack on and get our website looking presentable in the next chapter.

CHAPTER 7

Adding Styles

We come to the point in the book where we add one of the most critical parts – styling! For some frameworks, this involves using lots of extra code to manage styling in-line, not so with Svelte.

One of the great things about applying styles is that Svelte doesn't expect anything complicated – just plain CSS added to the top of each file will do just fine. Of course, you can use techniques more associated with the likes of React and Vue, but it's entirely optional.

In previous chapters, we began exploring some of the techniques we would use in our demo, followed by applying a selection of those techniques to our demo front-end site. This time around, I'm going to flip things on their head and jump straight into styling the site! Don't worry – there is a good reason for this: we will come to this shortly. First, though, there are some minor changes we need to make to the markup of our site, primarily around links; let's dive in and take a look.

Making Some Small Adjustments

Ordinarily, I would say that making changes to markup as a result of styling a site is not necessarily best practice: it feels like we're using styling to dictate how our content should appear when it should be the other way round.

That said, if we were to run the site now, we would see two errors appear:

- So far, we've used standard link tags – while there is nothing technically wrong in doing so, they do cause an issue with using stores. If, for example, we navigate from a product page back to the products listing, this can reset a Svelte store. It forces a complete full re-render of the page, which loses anything held in the Svelte store.
- If we click a link from the front page, we might see this error appear in the console log (Figure 7-1).

A. Libby, *Practical Svelte*, https://doi.org/10.1007/978-1-4842-7374-6_7

```
▸<Product> was created with unknown prop 'location'   Product.svelte:28
▸<Product> was created with unknown prop 'id'         Product.svelte:28
>
```

Figure 7-1. *Example of an unknown prop error*

Don't worry though, the fixes for both are easy - we need to replace the `href` tags with `<Link to="">` tags and reconfigure the routing block in `App.svelte` to use a different tag. Let's dive in and take a look at how in more detail.

FIXING THE ERRORS

We have two key changes to make, so let's make a start:

1. First, go ahead and open `App.svelte`, and then replace the <Route...> block with this:

```
<Route path="/"><Home/></Route>
<Route path="products"><Products /></Route>
<Route path="about"><About /></Route>
<Route path="coffee"><Coffee /></Route>
<Route path="contact"><Contact /></Route>
<Route path="/product/:id"><Product/></Route>
```

2. Save the file and close it.

As an alternative to the Route option we've used, we could use something akin to this syntax: `<Route ... let:location let:navigate let:params> ... </Route>`. Both work equally well; it's a matter of preference!

---

3. Next, open `Product.svelte`, and replace any instance of `<a href=` with `<Link to=` – there should only be one present in the code. Save and close the file.
4. Repeat step 3, but this time with `Products.svelte` – we use the `<a href...` tag to link to the individual product page. Save that file and close it.

5. Fire up your browser, and then browse to `http://localhost:5000/` and click the Shop link and then the name of any product. If all is well, we should not see any difference visually; updating the links to use the Link component prevents the page from re-rendering completely.

Okay, now that we've fixed our code, let's move on and take a look at how we can style elements in Svelte.

Understanding Styling in Svelte

One of the features where Svelte excels is in its approach to styling – unlike other frameworks, where you often have to style elements in-line or perhaps use CSS-in-JS, Svelte keeps things very simple. It uses the basic premise of why reinvent the wheel when you already have an excellent mechanism for styling content?

Sure, you can use libraries such as "Emotion," but it's not necessary – it just adds an overhead that will ultimately make your site slower! Often you will find code has been divided into individual components, rather than by file type – you might discover JavaScript in the main component, but with CSS written in-line or defined as constants in a separate JavaScript file. It works, but Svelte takes this one step further – we include everything in one file per component: this includes markup, CSS, and JavaScript.

Taking this approach has some real benefits – everything in a component file is scoped to that component only. There's no need to bring in other files, and it makes for much cleaner, easier-to-understand code when reviewing later. We will come back to this concept in greater detail, but for now, let's move on with adding the styling to our front-end demo.

Adding Styling to the Front-End Demo

Over the following few pages, we have a lot of styles to add in for our demo, which we will do in a series of exercises – before we can do that, there are a few housekeeping steps we need to complete:

- We will check the results of our work after each demo, so make sure you have your Svelte development server started in a Node.js terminal and that you can browse to `http://localhost:5000/` without issue.

- Go and find `global.css`, which should be in the \public folder - delete everything except for the rules for `html` and `body{}`.
- Leave a blank line after the last rule, and then add in `/** ADDED FOR DEMO **/` - this isn't obligatory but will be a helpful marker to indicate where original styles end and our changes start.

Once those two changes have been made, we should be left with this:

```
html,body { position: relative; width:100%; height: 100%; }

body { color: #333; margin: 0; box-sizing: border-box; font-family: -apple-
system, BlinkMacSystemFont, "Segoe UI", Roboto, Oxygen-Sans, Ubuntu,
Cantarell, "Helvetica Neue", sans-serif; }
```

I've compressed the styles for space reasons; the styles will be correctly formatted in the code download that accompanies this book.

With those housekeeping tasks completed, we can now add styles to our site, beginning with some that will apply across the entire site.

Updating the Global Stylesheet

For this first exercise, we will focus on adding styles into Svelte's default `global.css` file - changes made in this style sheet will apply across the entire site, so it is perfect for elements such as navigation and general body layout. We need to add a few styles, so let's start with updating the body tag first.

STYLING – PART 1: GLOBAL

To update the global styles, follow these steps:

1. First, open `App.svelte` – we can remove the reference to `CartLength` in the first import, as this is no longer required. Save the file, and close it.

2. Next, open `global.css` from the `\public` folder – below the comment we added just now, add in these styles:

```
body { display: flex; flex-direction: column; min-height: 100vh; }

a { text-decoration: none; font-weight: bold; }
```

3. We still have a few more styles to add – this next bunch will take care of the navigation bar at the top of the page:

```
nav { background-color: #c59747; }
nav>a,nav>a:visited { display: inline-flex; padding: 10px 15px;
text-decoration: none; font-weight: bold;  color: #552200; }
nav>a:hover { color: #552200; text-decoration: none;  border-bottom:
5px solid #552200; position: relative;}

a[aria-current="page"] { border-bottom: 5px solid #552200;
position: relative; color: #ffffff; }
```

4. We need to position the main content and banner image on the page – this is covered by these two next style rules:

```
section {  max-width: 60rem; }
#banner { margin: 20px auto; width: 50%; display: table; }
```

5. The last handful of changes are for the modal dialog we added earlier in the book – go ahead and add in this code:

```
.modal-background { background-color: rgba(0, 0, 0, .7) !important; }

div.modal>div { display: flex; justify-content: center; }

div.modal>div:nth-child(1) { justify-content: flex-end; }

div.modal>div>button { background-color: #ffffff;
border: 1px solid #c4c4c4; font-weight: bold; font-size: 18px; }
```

6. Save the changes and close the file – we will preview the results later, once more styles have been added.

Although we didn't add that much in the way of code, the changes we've made in this exercise are still significant – we started by getting rid of what would be a lot of extraneous and redundant styles. We then removed a reference to `CartLength`, which was no longer required, before adding new styles to cover links, navigation, general placement on the page, and some overriding styles for the modal on the home page. Nothing too outrageous, as I'm sure you will agree!

We still have a lot of styles to add, so let's swiftly move onto the next part of this mega exercise: styling the pages in our demo.

Styling the Pages

For this next exercise, we need to make changes to two of the four files in our demo – let's take a look at the changes in more detail.

STYLING – PART 2: PAGES

To update the styling for the two pages concerned, follow these steps:

1. The first change we will make is in `Contact.svelte` – we're going to add in some additional markup that was missing from the original version. The code uses a standard HTML button element – go ahead and add in this reference at the start of the script block:

```
import Button from '../components/Button.svelte'
```

2. With this in place, we can now switch out the standard button element for a custom component. Scroll down to almost near the end, and then replace the instance of `button` with `Button`.

3. Next, scroll back up to `<div id="banner">`, and then leave a blank line after its closing tag (two lines down). Add in `<div id="content">`. Scroll down to the end, and then just before the closing `</section>` tag, add a closing `</div>` tag.

4. With the updated markup now in place, scroll back up to just before the opening <section> tag, and add in this block:

```
<style>
  #content { display: flex; column-gap: 80px; }
  .form, label { display: flex; flex-direction: column; }
  label { padding-top: 10px; }
  input { width: 380px; margin-right: 10px; }
  textarea { width: 380px; }
  .formformat { display: flex; }
  .invalid { border-color: red !important; }
  .submitbutton { display: flex; }
</style>
```

5. The next change we need to make is in the Home.svelte file. Open the file in your text editor, and then scroll down to the closing </script> tag. Go ahead and leave a blank line, and then add in this block:

```
<style>
  @font-face { font-family: 'black_jackregular';
  src: url('/fonts/blackjack.woff') format('woff');
  font-weight: normal; font-style: normal; }

  .welcome { font-family: 'black_jackregular', sans-serif;
  font-size: 30px; width: 50%; }
</style>
```

6. Make sure you save both files, then switch to your browser, and head over to http://localhost:5000. If all is well, we should see something akin to the extract shown in Figure 7-2 (taken from the Contact page).

Contact Us
Lorem ipsum dolor sit amet, consectetur adipiscing elit. Maecenas sed odio id nulla gravida rhoncus. Suspendisse potenti. In volutpat
*Name:
Name

Figure 7-2. *An extract of the completed Contact Us page*

7. Browse to Home – once there, you will see similar styling that uses the same rules we've applied in `global.css`.

As in the previous exercise, nothing we added was unusual – everything was standard HTML markup or CSS styling.

Adding standard markup or styling is what is so appealing about Svelte. It keeps things very simple, allowing us to focus on what is essential and reduce code bloat to a minimum. As you will see, this is a recurrent theme throughout the styling code for this site; to prove it, let's continue with the following demo, which is styling the header and footer for our site.

Use of `class:` in markup

Notice how we used `class:invalid={invalid("email")}` in our code? It might look a little odd, but this is purely to add a styling class. It's effectively saying, "apply the class `.invalid` to this element, if the `invalid("email")` parameter is true, and not if it is false."

Styling the Header and Footer

This next exercise will be the largest of all four parts - we need to style all of the components! It will be a long one, but we will break it down into three sections; let's begin styling the header and footer for our site.

STYLING – PART 3A: HEADER, FOOTER

To style the header, we need to make several changes, so follow these steps:

1. First, open `header - markup.txt` from a copy of the code download accompanying this book. Copy and paste the contents directly over the `<header>...</header>` block within the component.

2. Next, just before the `<header>` tag, go ahead and add this code:

```
<style>
  header { background-color: black; color: #fff; display: flex;
  justify-content: space-around; }

  header > div { min-height: 100px; display: flex;
  align-items: center; }
  header > div > span:nth-child(2) { font-size: 30px;
  padding-left: 10px; }

  div.basket { display: flex; }
  div.basket > div:nth-child(1) {margin-right: 10px;}
  div.basketcount { background-color: #c59747;  padding: 5px 10px;
  border-radius: 50px; margin: 0 0 15px 0px; }
</style>
```

3. Go ahead and close this file – we've finished making changes to it.

4. Next, open the Footer.svelte file in your editor, and as per before, scroll to just before the opening <footer> tag, and then insert this block of styling:

```
<style>
  footer { background: linear-gradient(360deg, #594c59 0%, #343334
  100%); color: #fff; display: flex; justify-content: space-around; }
  footer > div { min-height: 100px; display: flex;
  justify-content: center; flex-direction: column; }
  footer div span a { margin-right: 5px; }
</style>
```

5. Save the file and close it – we will preview the results later in this chapter.

Parts 1, 2, and 3A complete: have a breather! Our demo didn't cover anything unusual or complex; we added appropriate styling to make our header and footer look more presentable. Right, once you're ready to continue, let's move on with styling the next part, which is the call-to-action buttons for our site.

Styling the Buttons

Adding call-to-action (or CTA) buttons to any site is an essential task - after all, how will customers be able to order any products, or submit feedback, for example? It would be a little awkward if they couldn't; to remedy that, let's cover the two button types we need for our site as part of the next exercise.

STYLING – PART 3B: BUTTONS

To get the buttons styled, work through these steps:

1. First, open CTAButton.svelte, and then add this code in on the first line:

```
<style>
  button { background-color: #c59747; border: none; color: white;
  padding: 10px 16px; text-align: center; text-decoration: none;
  display: inline-block; font-size: 18px; width: 380px; letter-
  spacing: 2.4px; width: 175px; margin-top: 10px; }
```

```
  button:hover, button:active { background-color: #000000; color:
  #ffffff; box-shadow: 1px 1px 6px rgba(0, 0, 0, 0.26); }
</style>
```

2. Go ahead and leave a line blank after the closing `</style>` tag; it's not obligatory, but it will make the code easier to read!

3. Next, open `Button.svelte`, and add the same code as per steps 1 and 2, but this time, we need to make one change – change `width: 380px` to `width: 175px`.

4. Save and close both files – we will preview the results when we complete the styling changes for the product pages and cart component.

Phew, that was a straightforward exercise, in comparison to the others! It does bring up one important question, though: why two buttons? Well, the honest answer is probably due to laziness - yes, I know, not ideal!

But it highlights one important point and something we could improve on later: we should reconfigure the Button component to accept a parameter value as its width and potentially a button type. This way, we can pass in that value, set it in CSS, and potentially deprecate one of the components. We can then use the button type to specify a priority - we might use `primary` for `call-to-action` buttons such as add to cart, with `secondary` for informational purposes only, such as submitting feedback.

Okay, let's move on. We have one set of changes left to do: the product pages (product gallery and individual product) and the cart component. Let's move on with these as part of our final exercise.

Styling the Product Pages and Cart

We reach the most critical point in this chapter: adding styles to our product pages and shopping cart!

There is a fair bit of work to do, but we will also (in the spirit of continuous improvement) make a few changes to the markup at the same time. Okay, leaving that aside, let's move on with making those changes, beginning with `Product.svelte`.

STYLING – PART 3C: PRODUCTS AND PRODUCT PAGES, CART

We have a few changes to make to the product, products, and cart files, so let's make a start:

1. First, go ahead and open `product.svelte in your` file editor, and then wrap the entire HTML block with `<section></section>` tags.
2. Next, add a couple of blank lines before that opening `<section>` tag, and then add the styling code from `styling - product page.txt`, in the code download accompanying this book.

Although we have a Back to Shop element on the page, we're not going to style it here. We already have styles in the `global.css` file that will be sufficient.

---

3. Next, we need to add in a hack for the navigation – I will explain why later, but for now, go ahead and add this before the closing `</script>` tag:

```
let getShopMenuItem = document.querySelector("nav > a:nth-child(2)");
if (individualURL.indexOf("/product") != -1) {
  getShopMenuItem.style.borderBottom = "5px solid #552200";
} else {
  getShopMenuItem.style.borderBottom = "none";
}
```

4. At the same time, we can also improve on the markup – I know this isn't strictly related to styling, but in the spirit of continuous improvement, we shouldn't let that stop us! Scroll up to the start of the `<script>` block, and then comment out the highlighted lines as indicated:

```
const addToCart = (product) => {
//    for (let item of $cart) {
  //      if(item.id === product.id) {
  product.quantity = 1
  $cart = $cart;
  //        return;
  //      }
  // }
  $cart = [...$cart, product]
}
```

5. At this point, we've finished making changes in `Product.svelte`, so go ahead and save the file and close it.

6. We can now turn our attention to `Products.svelte` – leave a line blank after the closing `</script>` tag, and then add the code from `styling - products page.txt` in the code download for this book.

As before, I've compressed the styles for space reasons – the code download for this book shows the styles in an uncompressed format.

---

7. We need to make a couple of changes to the markup. Look for the start of the `#each` block, and then replace it with the code from the code download that accompanies this book.

8. Save the changes to `Products.svelte`, and then close the file.

   We have a couple more changes to make – this time they are in `Cart.svelte`.

9. Go ahead and open this file, and then scroll down to the closing `</style>` tag.

10. Leave a line blank, and then add in the styling code from `styling - cart.txt` in the code download accompanying this book.

11. Save the file and close it – we've completed the changes required in this exercise.

12. Go ahead and browse to `http://localhost:5000`, assuming, of course, you have your Svelte development server running! Click Shop | any product name, and you should see something akin to the extract shown in Figure 7-3, with that product added to the cart, in Figure 7-4.

<<Back to Shop
Indian Monsoon
SKU: 3
Lorem ipsum dolor sit amet, consectetur adipiscing elit. Etiam ac tellus finibus, molestie purus id, placerat augue. Sed in arcu placerat, ultricies nibh et, auctor dolor.
$18
Add to cart
FRESH ROASTED

***Figure 7-3.** An extract of the product page*

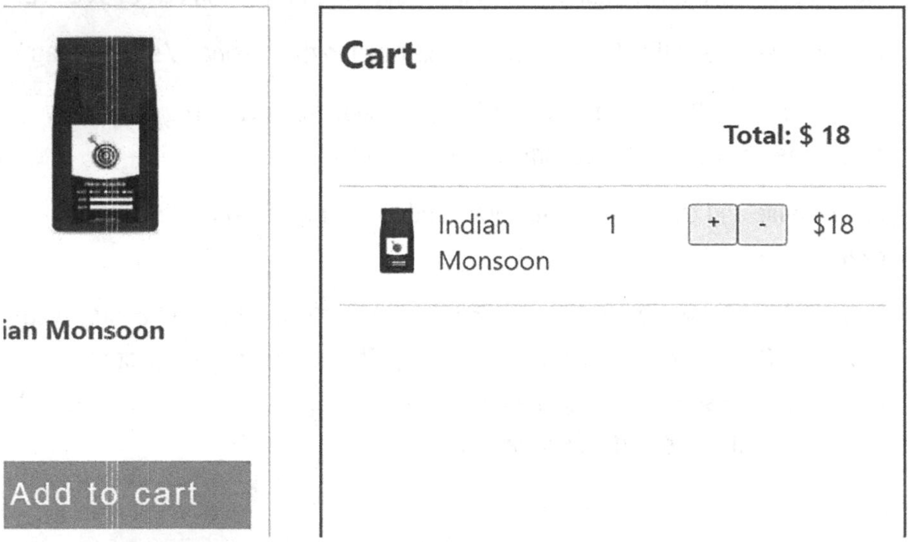

***Figure 7-4.** Our basket with a product added*

That was a lengthy exercise, but we can now celebrate: our site is pretty much now done! Although we've focused on styling (which should be pretty straightforward in itself), there are a few things we should cover off; let's pause for a bit to review the changes made in more detail.

Breaking Apart the Code Changes

Over the last few pages, we've made a fair few changes to our code – most of it has been styling, but we've also taken the opportunity to tidy up some of the markup at the same time.

This last exercise may have only covered three elements of our site. Still, it was the largest by far – we started by adding all of the relevant styling for the product page, including `borders`, `font-weight`, and general alignment.

We then added a hack for our navigation to get around an issue with displaying the product page. If you take a look back at `App.svelte`, you will see that we put a `<Route...>` element to help route requests to this page. The problem is that there isn't a corresponding entry for it in the `<Link to="...">` block just above; it means without this hack, we end up with a navigation bar that resizes each time we click a product link. Not a good experience!

Next up came some changes to the `<script>` block – we commented out some of the condition checks in the `addToCart` event handler. We lifted and shifted the code from the products page, but as was discovered while writing this book, it meant the items had to exist in the basket first, which wouldn't always be the case! This way, products will be added, whether they already exist or not, in the basket. It does mean that we would have to implement some better checking to ensure we add valid items, but that would be for another day.

We then turned our attention to the products page – this time, we added styling and updated the `#each` block in the markup to improve the overall appearance. To round out the demo as our last step, we applied styling for the `Cart.svelte` component before previewing the results in our browser.

Using a Style Preprocessor

A question – hands up if you've used or are familiar with the terms "preprocessing," "Sass," or potentially "superset." Sounds familiar?

Some of you will recognize these terms as being associated with preprocessing CSS. For the uninitiated, it's about applying a dash of JavaScript-esque variables, simple math calculations, and a few other tricks to create well… valid CSS!

Okay, that's probably a little glib, but Sass is an excellent tool for writing CSS styles more effectively. Imagine the person who asks you to change the color of every single button on your website, and you know full well that the styles used on the said site are well, shall we say, not the most efficient. To add insult to injury, it's also 5 pm on a Friday, and you know there is a pint of beer with your name all over it, getting slowly warmer and warmer. If you've not had that at some point, you're not a web developer!

Sass allows us to use a mix of variables and other tricks to avoid the need for multiple updates, so you no longer need to do a tiresome search and replace. You set up variables, so a simple change means **every** button has the change applied to it. A 30-second change and 5-minute rebuild later, et voilà! Button styling changed.

Okay, I digress - back to reality. As a concept, preprocessing CSS works perfectly with Svelte; we use the svelte-themes-preprocess plugin, available from `https://github.com/NikolayMakhonin/svelte-themes-preprocess`. It uses "Dart Sass" as a dependency in the background, so we will need to install that too. To see how it works, let's make a start on our next exercise.

SETTING UP POSTCSS

To set up preprocessing, follow these steps:

1. First, open a Node.js terminal session, and set the working directory as our project area (if it isn't already).

2. At the prompt, enter `npm install svelte-preprocess sass` and press Enter.

3. Next, go ahead and open `rollup.config.js`, and then add this line after the last import statement:

   ```
   import { scss } from 'svelte-preprocess'
   ```

4. Scroll down a little further, until you see this in the `export` block:

   ```
   Plugins: [
     svelte({
       compilerOptions: { dev: !production },
   ```

5. Immediately after that last line (and before the closing `}),`), go ahead and add in this block:

```
  preprocess: [ scss() ]
}),
```

6. Save the file and close it – the changes for this file are complete.

7. We have one more chance to make – for this, open a new file and add this code, saving it as `svelte.config.js`:

```
// svelte.config.js
const preprocess = require('svelte-preprocess');

module.exports = {
  preprocess: preprocess(),
  // ...other svelte options could go here
};
```

8. It's time to test the process – we will adapt the existing code for this purpose. Open this file in your editor, and change the opening `<style>` tag to this:

```
<style type="text/scss">
```

9. Next, change the last few lines of the style block to match this:

```
  margin-top: 10px;

  &:hover,
  &:active { background-color: #000000;  color: #ffffff;  box-shadow:
  1px 1px 6px rgba(0, 0, 0, 0.26);  }
}
```

10. Go ahead and save the file, then switch back to a `Node.js` terminal session. At the prompt (and make sure it's in the project folder!), enter npm run dev and press Enter.

11. If all is well, we should still see the button on the product page, as indicated in Figure 7-5 – it won't look any different, but we will serve it from a Sass stylesheet.

FRESH ROASTED
Cuban Altura Lavado
SKU: 2
Lorem ipsum dolor sit amet, consectetur adipiscing elit. Etiam ac tellus finibus, molestie purus id, placerat augue. Sed in arcu placerat, ultricies nibh et, auctor dolor.
$18
Add to cart

***Figure 7-5.** Displaying the Button component using Sass*

If you've made it this far, then congratulations – you now have a working system for Sass!

Granted, we had to make a few changes to accommodate this feature, but the good thing to note is that they are all pretty much a one-off; we can now focus on just adding styles as we see fit with the changes in place. This demo was a valuable exercise for those familiar with Sass or interested in knowing more about how we can incorporate it when using Svelte – let's take a more in-depth look at the changes we made to see how it all hangs together.

Breaking the Code Apart

So, what did we achieve? This exercise raises an important point – it doesn't look like we've achieved anything!

In reality, this isn't entirely true: setting up a preprocessing facility is more about setting up a tool to help facilitate writing CSS more effectively. It means we can do this:

```
// generate variables to store values
$background: #fff;
$primary-type-size: 1em;
$heading_type: "helvetica";
$mainType: "georgia";
```

```
// use variables in Sass code
body {background: $background;}
h1 {font-family: $heading_type;}
p {
  font-family: $mainType;
  font-size: $primary-type-size;
}
```

Just imagine that replicated across your site, multiple times - when we compile the Sass file into a style sheet, all of those entries will be updated automatically, which is a great time-saver!

But back to reality. We started by installing the `svelte-themes-preprocess` plugin and Sass (as a dependency). It is a good start, but we needed to configure the `rollup.config.js` file to accept the new plugin to get it working.

For this, we imported the `scss` option from the plugin, which we used as part of adding the `preprocess` option to our Svelte configuration. We added a configuration option under `preprocess` (as part of the svelte `compilerOptions` attribute) and a new `svelte.config.js` file to tell Svelte about the new plugin. We then updated some of the code for the button and tested it by refreshing the browser - it showed the same effect as before, which means it wasn't any worse!

Note - if Sass is working correctly, then it's essential to understand that you won't see any visual difference compared to vanilla CSS. This exercise was about updating how we generate that CSS and not changing the styles used to decorate our site.

If you would like to learn more about using Sass, please refer to my book, *Practical Dart Sass*, published by Apress.

Taking Things Further

Over these last few pages, we've focused all of our efforts on styling our site, but it does raise a few questions, of which one is - once we finish adding our initial styling, how could we take things further if we wanted to?

We can do a few things, such as use CSS-in-JS options like styled components (`www.styled-components.com/`) or a preprocessor such as Sass. We should also consider how we architect our CSS – should we in-line it or run it from external files? Or is that even an option? These are all interesting questions; we will take a look shortly at how we might use a preprocessor such as Sass as our next exercise, but for now, let's explore answers to the other two: should we in-line or run externally? And what about using CSS-in-JS solutions?

I would say that the answer is really "it depends"! Yes, I know you've probably seen that answer given for dozens of different questions in all manner of contexts, but there is good reason here.

It all has to do with Svelte's architecture, which uses the **single-file component** (SFC) principle. In a nutshell, it means that we can co-locate styling, script, and markup in the same file – this reduces the number and different types of files that we have to work with when using Svelte:

- Styles generated in Svelte components are scoped to that component by default (although we can make them global if needed).
- Svelte will flag any styles that are unused automatically (which might not happen if we use third-party libraries).
- We can make conditional classes very terse if desired, as long as names are the same for variables and classes.
- We get the benefits of using CSS-in-JS conventions (such as naming classes automatically) but without the need for any runtime libraries.
- Svelte doesn't require any form of runtime libraries to manage CSS – it compiles it into a format that looks like static BEM styling.

There are a few limitations, particularly around optimization and sharing code, but these the developers hope to address in future versions of Svelte.

Here's where things get controversial – I would strongly recommend not using CSS-in-JS solutions unless necessary!

With increasing emphasis on speed, CSS-in-JS solutions will add extra weight to the page; we can achieve pretty much all with standard CSS, without the excess baggage that comes with CSS-in-JS options. It doesn't preclude us from importing styles from libraries such as styled components (`www.styled-components.com`) or even from third-party

NPM modules. Still, we should give serious consideration to whether we can achieve better results with pure CSS, or circumstances are such that we must use third-party libraries in our code.

There are a couple of interesting articles on writing CSS in Svelte that might be of interest at this point – take a look at `https://css-tricks.com/what-i-like-about-writing-styles-with-svelte/` and `https://svelte.dev/blog/the-zen-of-just-writing-css`.

Summary

In the late 1990s/early 2000s, the general theme was to build a website as one giant monolith, with styling coming last. It seemed a long time ago, but the styling stage was (at least for me) a good indicator that we're coming to the end of a build process and that it won't be long before we see the results of our work, out in the wild.

We may use a more modular, component-based approach, but the basic principle is still the same – once we reach the styling stage, it won't be long before we see the results of our work. We've taken the same approach in this chapter by focusing on styling each component or page in turn – let's look back at what we've achieved in this chapter.

We started by making a few adjustments to our markup – we talked about this being something of a less conventional approach, but still important if we consider it a form of continuous improvement.

Next up came a quick look at the basic premise of how we should style components in Svelte; we revisited this at the end, with a brief discussion on the merits of why this approach is preferable when using Svelte over alternatives such as CSS-in-JS or external files.

We then moved onto the crux of this chapter, which is styling the individual elements of our site – we started with global changes before focusing on pages, header, footer, buttons, shopping cart, and pages in that order. We rounded out with a quick discussion on some of the ways we could develop styling further but equally considering that many of these ways will mean losing some of the benefits when using single-file components in Svelte.

We've covered a lot, but we're almost done! We still have plenty to explore – next up is probably one of the more essential tasks. It's time to get testing and finally deploy our website.

CHAPTER 8

Unit Testing and Svelte

So far, we've covered Svelte's different elements as a framework and have steadily been creating our ecommerce front-end project. It's now time to put it to the test – this is the scary part: does it all work as expected?

If we've done our homework correctly, then yes, but I'm sure there will be something there that will trip us up! Over these pages, we will explore how to perform unit testing for Svelte; we'll understand how to set up a unit testing library specifically for Svelte and begin to test our site's various elements and features.

As with all good things in life, one must start somewhere, so there is no better place than with deciding our strategy – how will we approach testing our site?

Deciding Our Strategy

We could use a host of different testing tools when it comes to testing – do we do unit testing, end-to-end testing, acceptance testing, or something else? So which package do we use – Jest, Mocha, Chai, Cypress, WebDriver, or something completely different? Heck, where does one start?

Well, one might hope things should be straightforward, but based on my research, it would seem not! Several packages are available, such as Svelte Testing Library or Jest (both with additional support for Svelte), but I struggled to get either to work – not a good sign. In the end, I decided to go with Cypress as it has worked very well for me in the past. Of course, there are some limitations, but for this chapter, they are not an issue.

So, with that in mind, this is the strategy I've decided to use: we will use Cypress 6.8.0 and the NPM package cypress-svelte-unit-test. It's not the latest version, as support for Cypress 7 in cypress-svelte-unit-test isn't available yet.

A. Libby, *Practical Svelte*, https://doi.org/10.1007/978-1-4842-7374-6_8

Cypress is available from `www.cypress.io`, with documentation at `https://docs.cypress.io/`. The cypress-svelte-unit-test package is available at `https://github.com/bahmutov/cypress-svelte-unit-test`.

With this in mind, here is the strategy we will use:

- We're testing a simple site, so no need to overcomplicate matters – Cypress uses a clean, easy-to-understand syntax that is quick to learn.
- We will focus on unit testing examples of components, but not all – I will focus on providing code for the key ones and point out how we can adapt them for others.
- The unit testing approach is a better fit also for the state of the code – ours isn't production-ready yet, so unit testing seems more appropriate.
- There are two ways to create tests for Svelte in Cypress – we'll use the `mount()` method, but I will also show you an example of an alternative approach.
- Cypress-svelte-unit-test also includes support for code coverage too so that we will add this later in the chapter.

Out of curiosity, what other packages exist that offer support for testing elements of Svelte?

Well, there are indeed a few; I've touched on a couple of names just now, with Svelte Testing Library (from `https://github.com/testing-library/svelte-testing-library`) and Jest. Here are a few more to consider:

- Svelte-jsx (available from `github.com/kenoxa/svelte-jsx`) – This allows you to write tests using JSX/Babel.
- Svelte-jsx (`https://github.com/kenoxa/svelte-htm`) – it works in the same way as Svelte-jsx but uses HTML markup instead.
- Jest-svelte-events (`https://github.com/mihar-22/jest-svelte-events`) – it offers custom Jest matchers for Svelte, using the Jest testing framework.

Okay, now we have our strategy in place. So let's crack on with the first step: to set up Cypress and the cypress-svelte-unit-test plugin.

Browser Support

Before we do so, I want to consider one critical question, which I am sure will be on your mind when it comes to unit testing: what browsers do we use?

We touched on what is an important point there – some might think we have to test in multiple different browsers, ideally in ones that match those that our customers use. However, at face value, this could present an issue when using Cypress; Cypress does not support IE browsers, for example!

It is less of a concern if we focus on testing just functionality; acceptance testing should come later once we have completed the initial development. With that in mind, it's worth noting that Cypress supports recent versions of Chrome, Edge, Firefox, Brave (a Chromium derivative), and its in-built browser, Electron.

We can switch between different browsers from within the Cypress GUI (top-right corner); it will display options for any it can find installed and supports, along with an option for Electron.

Focusing on just testing features will, of course, place greater emphasis on testing the site thoroughly when it comes to performing acceptance testing – but I'm sure you would do that as a matter of course, right?

Setting Up the Test Environment

One of the great things I love about Cypress is that it is a single install, but it incorporates a host of different toolsets into a unified GUI. Before Cypress came along, we would have to install several tools such as Mocha, Chai/Expect.js, and Webdriver; Cypress includes all of the necessary tools as standard.

Cypress itself is easy to set up: we can download a version to install, but it's simpler to install it using NPM. However, to get it installed and set up to support Svelte components requires a few steps – let's look at what's involved in the next exercise.

INSTALLING AND CONFIGURING CYPRESS

To get Cypress set up and configured to work with Svelte components, follow these steps:

1. First, we need to install Cypress – for this, fire up a Node.js terminal, and change the working folder to our project area.
2. At the prompt, enter `npm install cypress @6.8.0 cypress-svelte-unit-test` and press Enter.
3. Cypress takes a few minutes to install, so while that's happening, crack open the `cypress\plugins\index.js` file, and then replace the code with this – we use it to tell Svelte to bundle spec files:

```
files:module.exports = (on) => {
  const filePreprocessor = require('@bahmutov/cy-rollup')
  on('file:preprocessor', filePreprocessor())
}
```

4. Please save the file and close it. We now need to turn the (experimental) component support on in `cypress.json` (located at the root of the project folder). So go ahead and replace the contents of that file with this:

```
{
  "experimentalComponentTesting": true,
  "componentFolder": "./src/components",
  "testFiles": "**/*spec.js"
}
```

5. Save that file, and then switch to `package.json` in your editor – go ahead and modify the scripts block to include this extra line:

```
"scripts": {
  "build": "rollup -c",
  "dev": "rollup -c -w",
```

```
    "start": "sirv public -s",
    "start:dev": "sirv public --dev -s",
    "cypress:open": "node_modules\\.bin\\cypress open"
},
```

This last (highlighted) line is written for Windows – please adjust to suit your operating system if you are not using Windows.

---

6. We have one more change to make – fire up your file manager, and then browse to the `\cypress\integration` folder in your project area. Move all of the files to another location outside your project folder for safekeeping.

This step is voluntary but recommended – it makes for a cleaner view when we open the Cypress GUI, as we will only have our tests visible, not a bunch of examples! However, if you're new to Cypress, then it's worth taking a look at the examples separately to get a feel for how to write Cypress tests.

---

7. At this point, all changes are now complete – save the files, and then close them. We can now open Cypress by entering `npm run cypress:open` at the prompt and pressing Enter.
8. If all is well, we should see something akin to the screenshot shown in Figure 8-1.

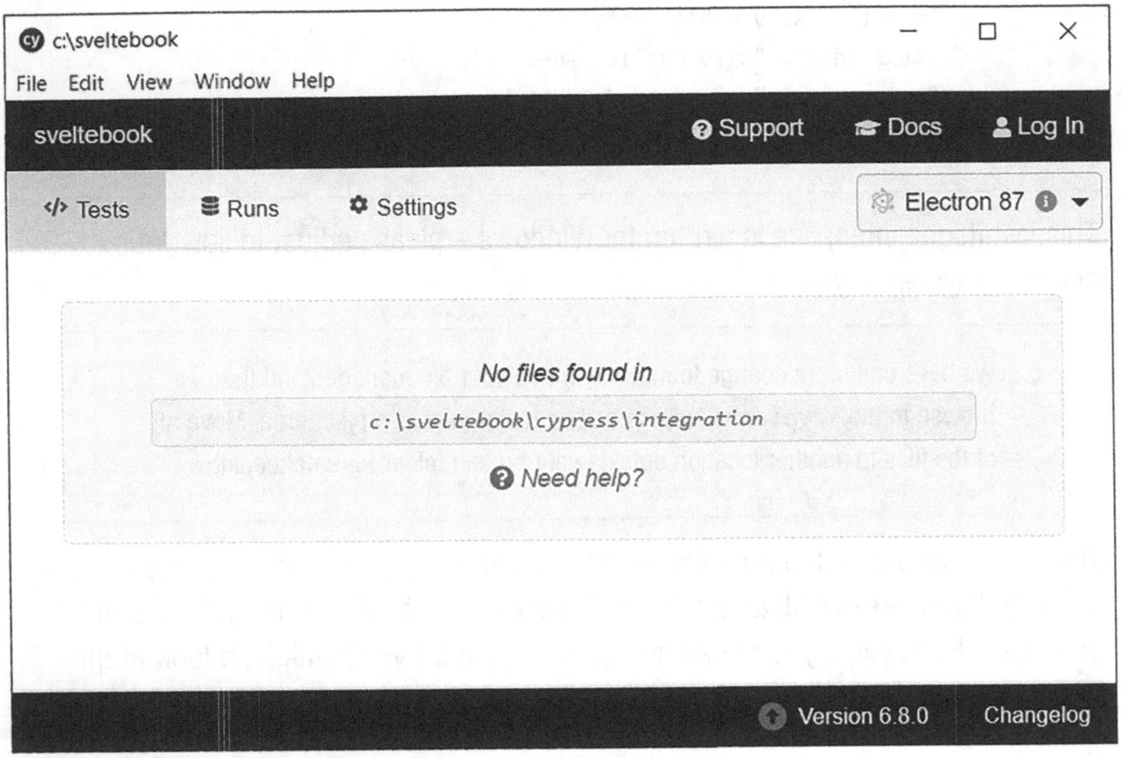

***Figure 8-1.** The Cypress GUI*

Getting our testing environment set up is a big step forward and arguably the most complex part – we can now start testing! The message we see when firing up Cypress for the first time might seem a little scary, but something we should expect to see: we've not yet written any tests, which will come later in this chapter. In the meantime, we've covered some essential points in the approach and setup of our testing tool, so let's spend a few moments going through what we've covered in the last exercise in more detail.

Understanding the Changes Made

When it comes to unit testing our website components, we could have picked any one of several different testing suites. However, I've decided to use Cypress as it (a) has a very natural syntax, which is supereasy to learn, and (b) allows me to write tests for different situations using one unified syntax. I could have picked suites such as Jest, Mocha, WebDriver, or any of the dozens available, but somehow Cypress just seems to fit the bill for me!

Okay, coming back to reality, what did we achieve in this demo? We started by installing Cypress and the extra plugin, `cypress-svelte-unit-test`, using NPM. While that took place, we updated the `index.js` file in the Cypress plugins folder to tell Cypress about using the `cy-rollup` plugin that is part of the `cypress-svelte-unit-test` plugin. This update overrides the rollup plugin already used to allow `cypress-svelte-unit-test` to bundle Svelte components correctly during testing.

We then moved onto updating the `cypress.json` file – this is effectively a configuration file, where we specified settings to enable Svelte component testing, locating the components, and identifying the test spec files. At the same time, we added an option into the `package.json`, to make it easier to fire up the Cypress GUI.

To round out the demo, we then moved the example tests that come with Cypress by default into an area for safekeeping (and out of the GUI – it makes for a clearer view). We then fired up Cypress to confirm it opens successfully, ready for us to add tests for our demo website.

Note – you may, after a while, get prompted to update your version of Cypress: beware! The cypress-svelte-unit-test plugin does not (at the time of writing) support version 7.x of Cypress. This lack of support may be addressed by the time this book comes into print; it is worth checking before you make any changes.

Okay, let's crack on. With our testing suite in place, it's time for us to get coding! But, before we get stuck into the minutiae of writing tests for our demo front end, let's quickly knock out a couple of example tests – this will help familiarize you with the UI and confirm that Cypress is operating correctly.

Creating an Example Test

Over the following few pages, we're going to use our new setup to test that Cypress works, so we can get a feel for what to expect. First, I will focus on using an example that is not part of our project; we will switch to adding tests for our demo front end later in this chapter.

We will choose an easy target for this test – I can't think of a more appropriate one than Svelte's website itself! As this is a public website, we will keep the test simple to keep demand low; we will test for the three colored boxes on the page and that they all have different colors.

TESTING SVELTE WEBSITE

Writing tests in Cypress is easy, thanks (at least in part) to the natural language syntax. To see how easy, go ahead with these steps to create our first test:

1. Fire up your text editor, and then create a new document – save it as `example1.spec.js` in the `\cypress\integration\` folder.

2. In that document, go ahead and add this block first:

```
beforeEach(() => {
  cy.visit("https://svelte.dev");
})
```

3. Leave a line blank, and then add in the first part of our tests – this takes care of counting the right number of boxes present on the page:

```
describe('Testing Svelte website front page', () => {
  it('shows 3 boxes', () => {
    cy.get('.box').should('have.length', 3);
  })
```

4. This next text checks the background color of each box as expected:

```
  it('each box is of a different color', () => {
    cy.get('.box:nth-child(1)').should(
      'have.css',
      'background-color',
      'rgb(255, 62, 0)'
    )
    cy.get('.box:nth-child(2)').should(
      'have.css',
      'background-color',
      'rgb(64, 179, 255)'
    )
    cy.get('.box:nth-child(3)').should(
      'have.css',
      'background-color',
```

```
        'rgb(103, 103, 120)'
      )
    });
  })
```

5. Save the file, and then switch to a Node.js terminal session – make sure that the working folder is our project area.
6. At the prompt, enter `npm run cypress:open` – give it a couple of minutes to allow the Cypress GUI to appear.
7. Go ahead and click the name of the test – it will fire up a new window, and then load and run the test.
8. If all is well, we should see something akin to the screenshot shown in Figure 8-2, where the results show a successful test.

***Figure 8-2.** The first of two example tests*

A simple test, but one that shows the power of Cypress - I will bet that if you read the code carefully, you could probably work out what each step does without too much prompting! That said, it's worth taking a few minutes to work our way through each step in more detail; let's break down the code before moving onto the second of two of our demo tests.

We started by creating our test file - Cypress can work with different file extensions for writing tests, but the usual convention is to end each file with `.spec.js` as the preferred format. Next up, we added a `before` statement, which acts as a precondition where we visit the site first before running the tests. We then added tests: the first checked that the box count has a `length` of `3`. In the second test, we checked the CSS property of `background color` for each to confirm what colors they had (in effect, making sure all are different).

We then rounded out the demo by running that test in the Cypress GUI - we confirmed it completed successfully, which means our testing installation works as expected.

One thing to point out, though - our test uses the URL route to verify the state of each box; this works perfectly well but isn't always ideal. A better approach allows us to test a component in isolation: it requires a change to our file structure, so let's dive in and explore what this means for us in more detail.

A Note About File Structure

At this point, you might be wondering why I'm making particular reference to the file structure - there is a good reason for this, though: it has to do with *how* we are testing our components.

In these two demos, we've tested using the URL for the page - you will see that in subsequent tests, we will test by mounting the component directly and test it in isolation.

The usual convention is for tests using the URL method usually go in the `\cypress\integration` folder, although we can change this setting in the `cypress.json` file. However, when we create tests that mount components directly, we will put these inside a subfolder that sits in the `\src\components` folder, which is a prerequisite for the cypress-svelte-unit-test plugin.

Applying Principles to Our Project

The time has come for us to finally commit (figurative) pen to paper and write the tests for our demo front-end site! Over the following few pages, we will tackle what will be a lengthy exercise; by the end, we should have tests in place that cover a range of features in our site.

With that in mind, I've split this section into three distinct parts:

- Part 1 - This will cover the home page.
- Part 2 - This covers the "Our Coffee," "Contact," and "Our Story" pages.
- Part 3 - This takes care of the products gallery page, the individual product page, and the shopping cart.

It sounds like a lot, but it will be easier than it first might seem! Let's start with part 1, where we will test different elements on the home page of our site.

Writing Tests for the Home Page

Remember how I mentioned that we could test Svelte code using one of two different ways – by URL or by component? In this first test, we will use a mix of both: it allows us to mix up our approach a little! There is a more serious point to this, though, which I will discuss later when we review the code; let's for now set up the test as part of the next exercise.

WRITING TESTS – PART 1: HOME PAGE

To test the home page, follow these steps:

1. First, fire up your text editor, and then create a new file called Homepage.spec.js, and save it to a new folder called `__tests__` under `\src\components`.
2. We have a few lines to cover, so I will go through it block by block – first, let's add in some import statements for various components we will use in this test, plus the mount function from the cypress-svelte-unit-test plugin:

```
import Disclaimer from '../../components/Disclaimer.svelte'
import Header from '../../components/Header.svelte'
import Homepage from '../../pages/Home.svelte'
import Footer from '../../components/Footer.svelte'

import { mount } from 'cypress-svelte-unit-test'
```

3. We can now add in the tests for the home page – the first one uses the mount option to test the Disclaimer component:

```
describe('Run tests for Homepage', () => {
  it('shows disclaimer at top of site', () => {
    mount(Disclaimer, {
      props: {name: 'World',},
    })

    cy.contains('span', 'This is a test site only')
  })
```

4. Go ahead and leave a line blank, and then add in this next test – this confirms the site has the correct site title:

```
it('header contains correct title', () => {
  cy.reload()
  cy.visit('http://localhost:5000')
  cy.get('div.modal > div:nth-child(1)
> button').click()

  cy.get('header > div > span:nth-child(2)')
.should('have.length', 1)
  cy.contains('header > div > span:nth-child(2)',
 'Small Coffee Company')
  })
```

5. As per before, leave a line blank, and then drop in this function – this takes care of checking we have three new arrival items, plus the title is correct:

```
it('homepage should show 3 new arrivals', () => {
  mount(Homepage, {
    props: { title: 'New Arrivals', },
  })

  cy.get('button').click()
  cy.get('#newarrivals img').should('have.length', 3)
  cy.get('span.welcome').contains('New Arrivals')
})
```

6. We've almost finished, but not quite – this penultimate test will confirm we have three social media icons present in the footer and that each has the correct name against it:

```
it('footer should have 3 social media icons', () => {
  mount(Footer, { props: { name: 'World', }, })

  let reference = 'footer > div:nth-child(2) > span > a'

  cy.get(reference).should('have.length', 3)
  cy.get(reference + ':nth-child(1)')
```

```
    .should('have.attr', 'href')
    .and('include', 'https://facebook.com
/smallcoffeecompany')

  cy.get(reference + ':nth-child(2)')
    .should('have.attr', 'href')
    .and('include', 'https://instagram.com/
smallcoffeecompany')
  cy.get(reference + ':nth-child(2)')
    .should('have.attr', 'href')
    .and('include', 'https://twitter.com/
smallcoffeecompany')
  })
```

7. Last but by no means least, we can test that the footer exists and has the correct copyright text present:

```
  it('copyright exists and has correct text', () => {
    mount(Footer, { props: { name: 'World', },
    })

    cy.get('footer > div > span').should.exist
    cy.get('footer > div > span').contains('© Small Coffee Company
    2021')
  })
})
```

8. Go ahead and save the file, and then close it – the changes are complete.

9. Next, revert to a Node.js terminal session, and make sure the prompt shows our project folder as the working directory.

10. Go ahead and enter this command at the prompt and press Enter:

```
npm run cypress:open
```

11. Once the Cypress GUI is open, click the `Homepage.spec.js` name on the left – let the test run. If all is well, we should see the screenshot in Figure 8-3 to indicate successful completion of the test.

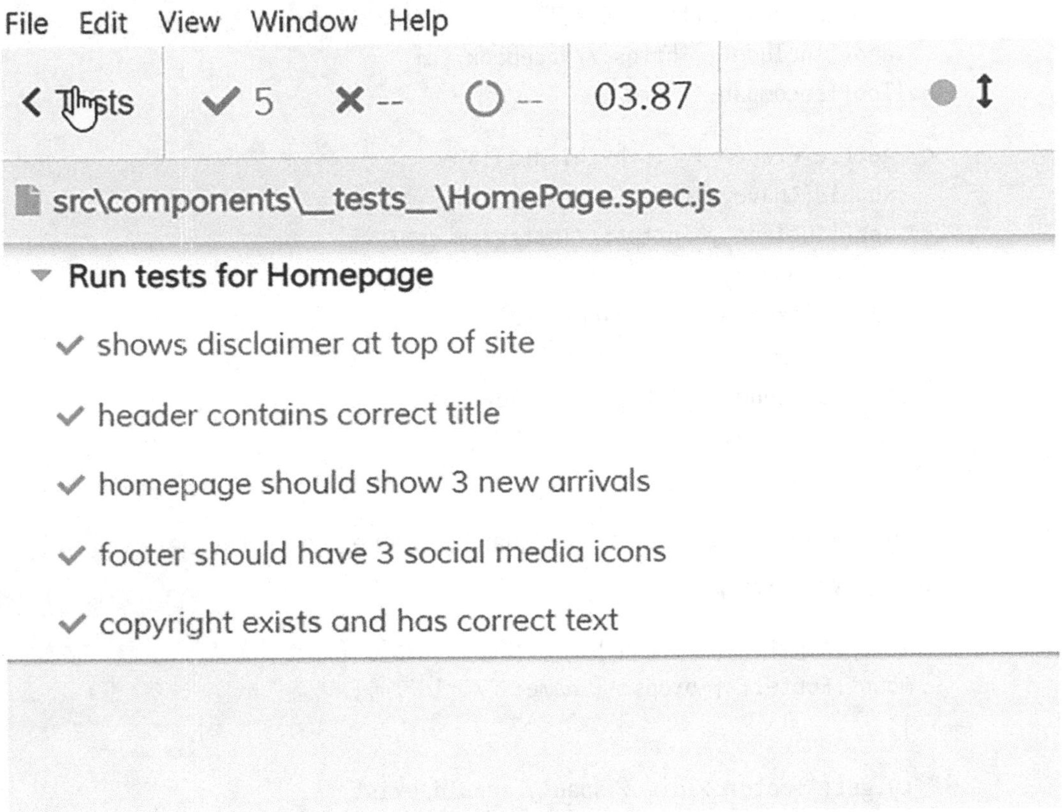

Figure 8-3. *The results of the Homepage tests*

This last exercise might seem to have a lot of steps, but in reality, not all of it is code; some of it relates to the execution of the test in Cypress (and with which you will become more familiar as we progress through this chapter). Leaving this aside, we've covered some valuable points in this test – including the use of both testing methods! So let's take a moment to review the code in more detail before moving onto our next test.

Breaking Apart the Changes Made

Ouch, that was one exercise that didn't go quite according to plan!

The main culprit for me was step 4 – I had planned to use the `mount()` method but could not overcome an issue with assigning and using context. Remember how we wrote code to determine if we were logged in or out? That's right – that was what I wanted to use here, but I couldn't get it to work.

That aside, we used a mix of both `mount()` and URL when testing the home page. We started by adding imports for all of the components, the home page, and the `mount` method from the `cypress-svelte-unit-test` plugin. We then added the first test to check and validate that we had the correct text in the Disclaimer component.

Next up came the proverbial problem child – testing the site title. Yes, problem child might well seem apt here, given how much grief it gave me! It's for that reason we're using the URL method and not `mount()`. While that wasn't the intention, I see it as one reason we have to be flexible sometimes and adapt our approach.

The following three tests all use the `mount()` method – we checked that three images exist under the New Arrivals block (`cy.get('span.welcome').contains('New Arrivals')`) plus that the three social media icons at the bottom of the footer all have the correct links. The last test asserted that we had a `<span>` element present, which contained the right text for the copyright message at the foot of our site.

There is one thing I want to point out – and that is the use of `cy.reload()` in step 4. Yes, that step again: but with good reason! We're using a mix of methods to test the page, so you should know that Cypress will execute all actions one after another without stopping or refreshing the page.

The switch to using the URL method in step 4 meant that we would get two instances of the test running (and would fail - we have six images, not three). Adding `cy.reload()` has the effect of clearing the previous test (once validated correctly) **before** executing the next test. It means we would correctly get three images, and not ones doubled up from two different test steps in our code.

Okay, let's move on to our next test. The next one will cover the remaining content pages, with the last test taking care of the shop and product pages, later in this chapter.

Testing the Remaining Content Pages

For the second of our three-part demo, let's focus our attention on the remaining pages – I'm referring specifically to "Our Coffee," "Contact," and "Our Story." I like to term them as the content pages – in real life, they would contain helpful content about the company but aren't the most important in the pecking order, below the home page and shop pages.

In the previous exercise, we focused on using the `mount()` method for most of the testing; this time around, we will switch to using the URL method. There is a good reason for doing this, which I will cover shortly – let's take a look first at testing the pages.

WRITING TESTS – PART 2: OUR COFFEE, CONTACT, OUR STORY

To test the various content pages on our site, follow these steps:

1. First, fire up your text editor, and then create a new file called `ContentPages.spec.js`, and save it to the `__tests__` folder we created earlier, under `\src\components`.

2. We have a few lines to cover, so I will go through it block by block – first, let's test that the Coffee page has the correct content present:

```
describe('Testing Svelte website content pages', () => {
  it('Coffee page has correct content', () => {
    cy.visit("http://localhost:5000/coffee");

    cy.get('#banner > img').should('have.length', 1
    cy.get('h2').should('have.length', 1);
    cy.get('h2').contains('Our Coffee');  // title exists, and has
    correct text
  })
```

3. Next, we will perform a similar test for the About page – go ahead and add these lines:

```
it('About page has correct content', () => {
  cy.visit("http://localhost:5000/about");

  cy.get('#banner > img').should('have.length', 1
  cy.get('h2').should('have.length', 1);
  cy.get('h2').contains('About Us');  // title exists, and has
                                         correct text
})
```

4. We have one more test – this is for the Contact Us Page. Add these lines:

```
it('can submit form from contact us page', () => {
  cy.visit("http://localhost:5000/contact");

  cy.get('#banner > img').should('have.length', 1);
  cy.get('h2').should('have.length', 1);
  cy.get('h2').contains('Contact Us');
```

```
    cy.get("form > span:nth-child(2) > input").type("Joe Customer")
    cy.get("form > span:nth-child(4) > input").type("joe.customer
    @example.com")

    cy.get("form > textarea").type("This is a test message")
    cy.get("button").click()
    cy.on('window:alert', (txt) => {
      //Mocha assertions
      expect(txt)
.to.contains('Everything is validated!');
   })
  })
})
```

5. Go ahead and save the file, and then close it – the changes are complete. Next, revert to a Node.js terminal session, and make sure the prompt shows our project folder as the working directory.

6. Go ahead and enter this command at the prompt and press Enter:

```
npm run cypress:open
```

7. Once the Cypress GUI is open, click the `Homepage.spec.js` name on the left – let the test run. If all is well, we should see the screenshot in Figure 8-4 to indicate successful completion of the test.

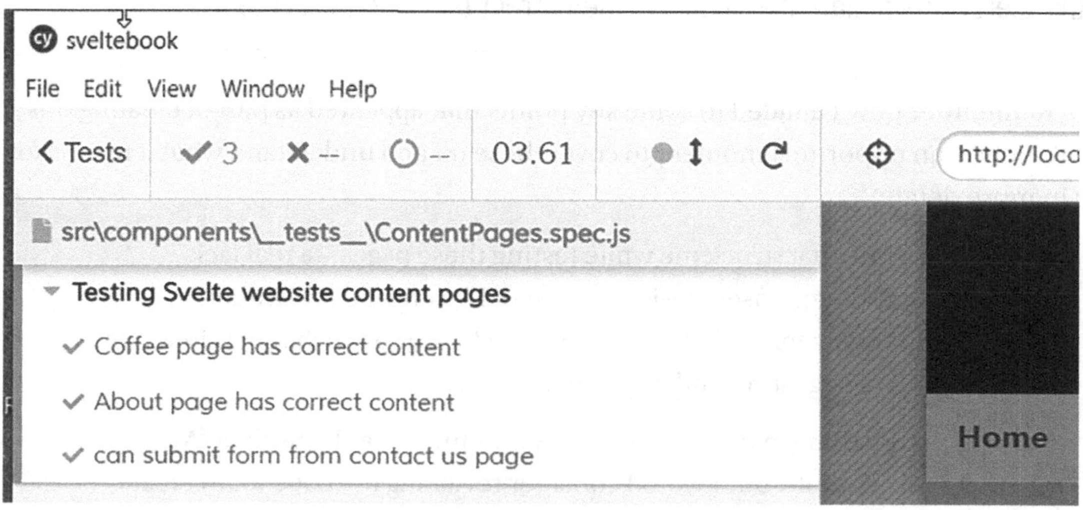

***Figure 8-4.** The completed tests for content pages in Cypress*

We're making good progress in testing our site. As a result of that last exercise, we will have tested the home page and content pages; this leaves the shop, cart, and product pages left to test. This previous exercise has raised some key points worth exploring in more detail – let's dive into the code and break down some of these points in more detail.

Reviewing the Code in Detail

In this last exercise, we started by creating a `describe()` block – this is a typical format for testing in Cypress (and other frameworks that support a similar arrangement). Inside this, we created a number of `it()` assertions – the first one was to validate that we had the correct content on the Coffee page.

In this instance, we first visited the page before asserting that we had a banner image, a title encased in H2 tags, and that the latter contained the words "Our Coffee." We then repeated the same steps, but this time with the About page – we first checked that we had the expected banner text ("`... should('have.length', 1)"`) before asserting that the title has the correct text as well.

The last stage was a little more complex – here, we first performed the same checks as before, but this time we entered fake details into each form field. Then, as the final step, we submitted the form and used the `cy.on()` function to spy on `window.alert` and validate that it would return the appropriate text on submission of the form.

These two methods are a great way to spy on an event in our code – we intercept the alert and validate that it shows the correct text when executed.

Remember how I alluded to some key points that appeared as part of creating this test? Now is an opportune moment to cover these off and understand what it means for us in more detail:

- One thing that struck me while testing these pages – a real lack of component-based design! Granted, I've created individual components for each page, but we still have too much repetition, both at a page level and in testing.
- It's something to think about – as a minimum viable product (MVP), it is acceptable. But I would consider revisiting the code to (a) create more reusable components and (b) adapt the tests to loop through arrays/objects of items such as the social media links instead.

- While testing the code, I hit some issues with tests failing – it turns out I had been a little careless and used <h1> tags in some instances, rather than <h2> tags! However, leaving aside the perils of not checking code, testing has served its purpose: I was able to identify the errant tags, update them, and rerun the tests to confirm they passed without issue.

Okay, let's crack on. It's time to attack the most crucial part of our site! I'm, of course, talking about testing the product gallery, pages, and cart. Let's dive into our next exercise to see what is involved in more detail.

Testing the Product Pages and Cart

For this next test, I've elected to use the URL format throughout our code. It is partly to keep things simple, but also because the site's design is such that testing using the `mount()` method has been my preferred method, but not one I could get working satisfactorily with the code as it stands.

While some may see this as a downside, I would say it's a good reason to refactor the code as a second iteration. It all boils down to the fact that we should consider a site as finished when we have no further need for the site, not when we've finished designing it! Leaving that problem aside for now, let's dive in and take a look at the code in more detail.

WRITING TESTS – PART 3: PRODUCTS PAGE, PRODUCT PAGE, CART

To test that the shop, product pages, and product gallery all work as expected, follow these steps:

1. First, fire up your text editor, and then create a new file called `Shop.spec.js`, and save it to the `__tests__` folder under `\src\components`.
2. We have a few lines to cover, so I will go through it block by block – we will test by URL (for which reasons will become clearer, later in this demo). Let's first add in the initial test to confirm we have six items in our product gallery:

```
describe('Products gallery page should display items', () => {
  it('product gallery displays six items', () => {
```

```
    cy.visit("http://localhost:5000/products")
    cy.get('main > div.product-list > div').should('have.length', 6)
  });
```

3. To finish that first test, we will confirm that product 1 ("Italian House Blend") has the right product details present:

```
  // product 1
it('product 1 should have the right details', () => {
  cy.get('div.product-list > div:nth-child(1) > h4').contains('Italian
  House Blend')
  cy.get('div.product-list > div:nth-child(1) > p').contains('$18')
  cy.get('div.product-list > div:nth-child(1) > div.image').
  should('have.css','background-image', 'url("http://localhost:5000/
  images/1.png")' )
    cy.get('div.product-list > div:nth-child(1) > div.cta > button').
    contains('Add to cart')
    cy.get('div.product-list > div:nth-child(1) > h4 > a').
    should('have.attr', 'href').and('include', '/product/1')
  })
});
```

4. This next test will validate that we can click through to our chosen product and pause the test until we have reached that product page, before validating that the product details are correct:

```
describe('Product page should display correct information', () => {
  it('product page should have the right details', () => {
    cy.visit("http://localhost:5000/products")
    cy.get('div.product-list > div:nth-child(1) > h4 > a').click()
    cy.wait(5000)

    cy.get('#productdetails > div:nth-child(2) > p:nth-child(1)').
    contains("Italian House Blend")
    cy.get('#productdetails > div:nth-child(2) > p:nth-child(2)').
    contains("SKU: 1")
    cy.get('#productdetails > div:nth-child(2) > h2').contains("$18")
```

```
    cy.get('#productdetails > div:nth-child(2) > p:nth-child(3)').
    contains("Lorem ipsum dolor sit amet")
  });
});
```

5. With the product added, we need to validate that it shows the correct count in the header:

```
describe("Clicking add to cart adds correct number of items to
basket", () => {
  it('Cart should display X items when requested', () => {
    cy.visit("http://localhost:5000/products")
    cy.get('div.product-list > div:nth-child(1) > h4 > a').click()
    cy.wait(5000)

    cy.get("button").click()
    cy.wait(5000)
    cy.get(".basketcount").contains("1 items: $18")

    cy.get("body > main > section > a").click()
    cy.wait(2000)
    cy.get("div.basketcount").contains("1 items: $18")
  });
})
```

6. This next test will add another item to the basket from the gallery page and validate that we have an increased count displayed:

```
describe('clicking add to cart on two products shows correct number in
basket', () => {
  it('adding to basket shows 2 items in basket', () => {
    cy.visit("http://localhost:5000/products")

    cy.get("div.product-list > div:nth-child(1) > div.cta > button").
    click()
    cy.get("div.product-list > div:nth-child(2) > div.cta > button").
    click()
    cy.get("div.cart-list > div.cart-item").should('have.length', 2);
  })
})
```

7. Go ahead and save the file, and then close it – the changes are complete.
8. Next, revert to a Node.js terminal session, and make sure the prompt shows our project folder as the working directory.
9. Go ahead and enter this command at the prompt and press Enter:

```
npm run cypress:open
```

10. Once the Cypress GUI is open, click the `Homepage.spec.js` name on the left – let the test run. If all is well, we should see the screenshot in Figure 8-5 to indicate successful completion of the test.

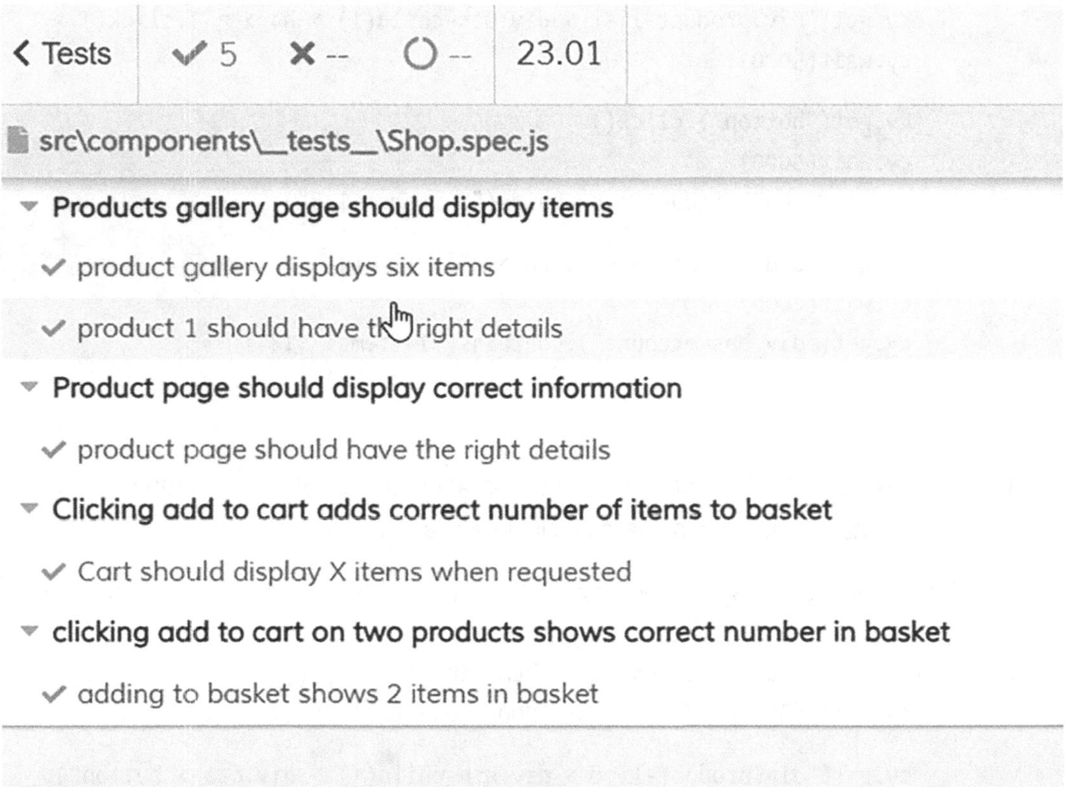
Tests
5
--
--
23.01
src\components_tests_\Shop.spec.js
Products gallery page should display items
product gallery displays six items
product 1 should have the right details
Product page should display correct information
product page should have the right details
Clicking add to cart adds correct number of items to basket
Cart should display X items when requested
clicking add to cart on two products shows correct number in basket
adding to basket shows 2 items in basket

***Figure 8-5.** The results of the shop test*

This last demo was somewhat more lengthy and involved - it might have seemed a lot of code, but in reality, we're still using the same techniques as before. This time, though, many of the methods have been forced on us due to the site's design - this is something we need to consider!

Now is an excellent opportunity to review why and other critical points raised by this code. Let's pause for a moment to digest what we've covered in this demo in more detail.

Exploring the Changes

We began with creating two tests for our products gallery page (a.k.a. the shop) – we first visited the shop page before asserting that we had six items in the gallery. We then picked the first product (I could have picked any – it was a random choice!) and tested that we are displaying the correct product details such as description, SKU, and price.

In the second `describe()` block, we focused our attention on testing the individual product page – we first had to visit the products gallery before clicking the first product ("Italian House Blend"). Then, we inserted a `cy.wait(5000)` step to stop the test while it switched from products gallery to individual product page, before checking individual details of the product such as SKU, price, and product name.

We should note that at this point, I would have preferred to use the mount() option to test the product detail page. However, it seems this wasn't possible – the page technically doesn't exist! Svelte generates this page on the fly, using a page template and not a dedicated page such as About or Coffee. One could argue that we're using template pages throughout, but it's the reuse of the product page for all products that makes it different.

There is a second catch that prevents the use of `mount()`: we generate the product page based on what ID value is in the page URL, using `document.pathname.location` (in the website, not the test). Unfortunately, the browser renders this as null in our test, which means Cypress can't tell which product to test – we could work around it, but I like to keep things simple, hence using the dedicated URL for our test.

In the next test, we focus on testing the add-to-cart feature; we navigate to the product page as before, but this time click the add-to-cart button and wait to confirm that the correct amount and total are displayed in the header. To help test it, though, we then navigate back to the product gallery using the Back to Shop link ("`body > main > section > a`") before adding a new product and confirming the totals are not reset to zero (i.e., maintained state).

For the last test, we come back to the product gallery again, but this time we add two products; we confirm that the basket contains two separate items ("`....should('have.length', 2);`") and not just two of the same item (where have.length would equal 1, not 2).

Phew, we've completed our testing, at least within Cypress! But, of course, this isn't the only testing we could do; if we were developing our site further, we might want to do acceptance testing, penetration testing (for security), and the like.

We could even do something toward testing code coverage – the cypress-svelte-unit-test plugin works well with a plugin called code-coverage (available from `https://github.com/cypress-io/code-coverage`). It is an excellent way to develop further and refine our code – I will leave doing it for another day, though!

If you are keen on finding out how, then the preceding link has step-by-step instructions. Alternatively, you can look at the bonus PDF that comes with this book.

Okay, let's move on. We've completed testing for now, but there are two more areas I would like to cover that are related to testing. The first is what might happen if we discover an issue and need to debug the root cause. We might typically use something like `console.log()` – nothing wrong with that, but Svelte has another trick up its sleeve that is worth investigating. It might not be a big tip, but it will be worth exploring!

Debugging Svelte

Until now, we've focused on testing our site – we've used a mix of approaches, with tests running on a specified URL or by mounting components as we see fit. But, of course, all tests would pass in an ideal world, and we would then proceed to push our code into production, right?

Well, we don't live in an ideal world, and there will be a point where reality bites us! By reality, I mean a need to debug an issue – it could come at any point, but there's a good chance it will likely come while testing.

A typical action would be to use the likes of console.log to help narrow down that problem before fixing it – it's a perfectly adequate solution, but what if we could take it a step further? For example, Svelte has a tag we can use to inspect our code – step up @debug.

It takes the format `{@debug <value1>, <value2>...}` where we provide the tag with a comma-separated list of values we want to examine. To see what I mean, let's dive into a quick exercise, where we can explore the user object using the `@debug` tag.

DEBUGGING IN SVELTE

To examine one or more elements using @debug, follow these steps:

1. First, go ahead and browse to `www.svelte.dev/repl`.
2. In the tab marked `App.svelte` on the left, add this code:

```
<script>
  let user = {
    firstname: 'Alex',
    lastname: 'Libby'
  };
</script>

<input bind:value={user.firstname}>
<input bind:value={user.lastname}>

{@debug user}

<h1>Hello, {user.firstname}!</h1>
```

3. Take a look in the console section on the right, at the bottom of the page – you might need to expand it by dragging the divider up. If all is well, we should see something similar to this:

```
Object {
  user: Object {
    firstname: "Alex"
    lastname: "Libby"
  }
}
```

4. Now try swapping out the `{@debug user}` line with this:

```
{(console.log(user), '')}
```

5. We still get the same values, but not in quite the same format – not only is this solution more verbose, but we don't get the complete structure of the user object:

```
Object {
  firstname: "Alex"
  lastname: "Libby"
}
```

Debugging is, of course, an essential part of developing any website - I've lost count of the number of times I've used statements such as `console.log()` in my code over the years. Of course, if I'd had a dollar for each time I've used one, I would have retired long ago, but, hey, I digress!

Back to reality - this might have been a simple exercise, and yes, we did it in a Svelte REPL: that was purely for simplicity. We can, of course, get similar results using `console.log()`, but @debug allows us also to get the structure (i.e., it's the user object in this example), as well as the values - and both can be just as important. As an aside, we included input fields in this demo, purely so you can see the interaction - if we change the values in them, not only do the results change on screen but the console area updates automatically too.

> As a test, try running the code in app.svelte.txt from debugging svelte folder in the code download, in a Svelte REPL. Notice how it renders both objects in the code?

Okay, let's crack on. There is one more tool we can use when testing (and analyzing) Svelte. It's not a dedicated tool, but it's free: why not use it? I'm talking about Lighthouse - it's perfect for getting a feel for how our site rates against several aspects, such as performance and accessibility. Let's take a closer look at what this might throw up - who knows? It might be a pleasant surprise or a complete shocker. Anything can happen!

Using Lighthouse

> *Spoiler alert – the results I got back when I ran it locally were better than I expected...!*

As a tool, Lighthouse has been around for several years; we can run it in several different ways, from using the command line to an NPM package or directly in a browser. So it's perfect for getting a feel for how a site performs – it won't give you acres of detail, but for a free tool, it's a good starting point.

If you download it as a plugin, it may appear in a separate tab on its own.

For this tool, you will need to run it in Chrome – it comes as part of the browser and is available in the DevTools area under the Audit tab. It gives us an option to select Desktop or Mobile – I chose Desktop and let it run. You can see the results I had back in Figure 8-6.

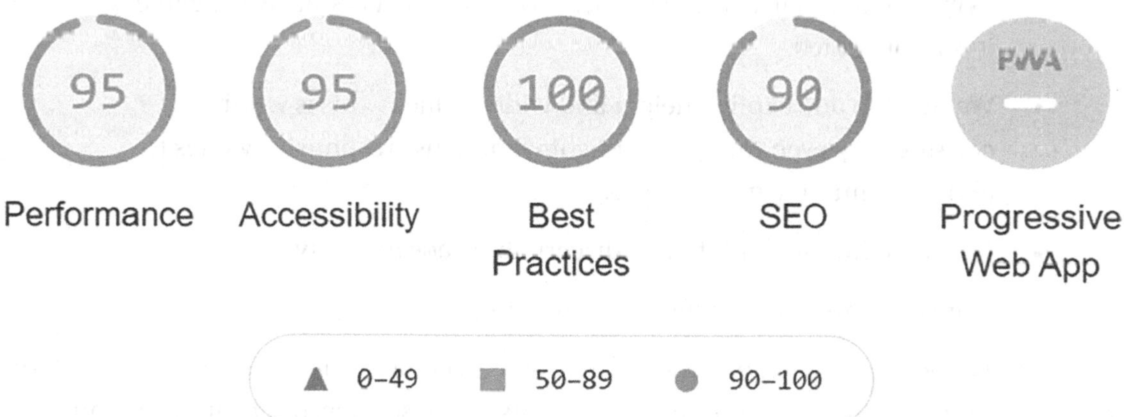

Figure 8-6. *The results of running a Lighthouse audit*

The vital thing to note here is that while it's great to get to 100%, it is more about what Chrome highlights as potential issues we should address. With that in mind, I should set some expectations:

- I've only run this test once on my machine – you might not get the same results if you run it on your hardware, as they tend to vary from device to device.

- Running it a second time may give better or worse results – yes, this can happen!
- We ran this test using development code – while the results are pretty good at this level, they will be even better if we were to run a production-ready version.

Lighthouse highlighted several changes that we should consider making – some were more complex than others; some we can change very quickly:

- Lighthouse reported a sizeable chunk of JavaScript that was unused – this included live reload. Of course, a lot of this will go once we move to production, but we should still consider analyzing the code to see if we can improve coverage.
- Lighthouse highlighted an issue around CSS – it suggested we should inline some of it and defer the rest. Of course, we already do the latter by default, but could/should we have critical CSS inline?
- Lighthouse complained of an issue with hidden text that we style using the blackjack font – we need to make sure it is still visible while it is reformatted.
- We need to add explicit height and width values – this is worth considering, even though we might want to use responsive values to allow for multiple device types.
- Links on the site don't have a discernable `name` property.
- Our site is missing a meta description tag.

There is a good selection of issues there – we can certainly address most (if not all) of those very quickly! Sure, more complex problems might surface, but bear this in mind: using Lighthouse is free of charge, so why not use it? Sure, we can do more complex things later once the site takes off, but for now, any improvement we can make for free has to be worth the effort and resources required to implement the change.

Summary

Testing, testing, 1...2...3...

Okay, yes, we're not on a set of some movie or trying to wire up some fiendishly complex communications system: that was my poor attempt at some testing-related humor! However, it does raise an important point, in that testing can feel frustrating if it is not done well; it might reveal all manner of different issues that make us think we should head back to the drawing board. But that wouldn't be testing if we didn't highlight and rectify any problems that appeared, right?

Back to reality – what did we achieve in this chapter? We kicked off with a brief discussion around our strategy – the key point being the choice of testing suite and the approach we would take to testing the relevant areas of our demo website.

We then moved onto setting up the testing environment using Cypress; this included installing support for the `mount()` option to allow us to test components in a more Svelte-like manner. We then switched to creating a simple test to confirm that Cypress was operating as expected before quickly exploring the file structure and how this would affect where we would store our tests.

Next up came the most crucial part – we turned our attention to writing the various tests for the main areas of the website. It included the home page, content pages (a.k.a. Coffee, Our Story, and About) before tackling the shop, and product pages. We then rounded out the chapter with a quick look at how we might use Svelte's debugging tool to help with narrowing down any issues that might crop up and use Lighthouse to help further perfect our code.

We've now completed testing, so the next major milestone is... shock horror... releasing our code! Yes, we are technically at that point where we would release, but the reality is that our project would need further development before we could class it as *true* production-ready code. That said, it's essential to see how we might perform a release – for this example, I will use my good friend GitHub Pages to assist; to see how, stay with me, and I will reveal all in the next chapter.

CHAPTER 9

Deploying Svelte

Yikes, we're coming ever closer to releasing our project into the wild! Although we've performed unit testing, in reality, our project would need more development work before we can class it as production ready.

Irrespective of what might be left to develop or test, the principles of deployment of a Svelte site are still the same. This chapter will examine how to prepare and deploy our site onto the Internet. We'll cover off some of the options available for hosting, as well as how we might automate the deployment process. As a bonus, we'll even tack on a custom domain name to boot!

Okay, let's start with some simple checks: we've done a lot of this in the previous chapter, but it's an excellent way to do a final sign-off before we commit to pushing code live.

Doing Final Checks

Ladies and gentlemen – it is time...

Yes, indeed, it's where we hit reality and unleash our site onto our customers!

Okay, perhaps that was a little too dramatic, but the reality is that we've created our development site, tested it, and now it's time to make it ready for release. Sure, there will be a lot more work we would need to do if we were to release it for real, but a release is still a release – we still need to decide how this will happen.

I am sure that you will be familiar with the kind of steps we might take when it comes to releasing code – we should test it, perform checks to ensure nothing obvious stands out that shouldn't be there, and make sure it performs as expected. As a developer, I know this is something you will have done dozens of times – it's still a little bit of an anxious time, as we can never be sure if everything will work as expected!

A. Libby, *Practical Svelte*, https://doi.org/10.1007/978-1-4842-7374-6_9

We've already covered the unit testing process in the previous chapter (and in a more real-world environment, we would also execute stages such as pen testing or acceptance testing). Once we've completed this step, we can also do some preparatory checks to ensure everything is present and that we didn't miss anything in one of the testing procedures. Yes, I'm probably supercautious at this time, but the more checks we do, the less likely something will slip through!

We need to add one more component – this is not an essential part of the shop, though, but more for our sanity. What is this component, I hear you ask?

It's a disclaimer – we're about to release something into the wild, and you can be sure someone will try to purchase from the store. It is just to let them know that this is a dummy store, and if they are foolish enough to try to buy something, well, we can at least say that we did warn them! It's a simple component to set up and add to our store, so without further ado, let's dive in and take a look at the code in more detail in the next exercise.

ADDING DISCLAIMER

To set up the Disclaimer component, follow these steps:

1. First, crack open a new file in your editor, and then add this styling block:

```
<style>
  span {
    background-color: #ff0000;
    color: #ffffff;
    text-align: center;
    padding: 5px 0;
    font-weight: bold;
    letter-spacing: 1px;
  }
</style>
```

2. Leave a line blank, and then add in this <span> element:

```
<span>
  This is a test site only - please note that no orders will be
accepted
</span>
```

3. Go ahead and save the file as `Disclaimer.svelte`, in the `\src\components` folder.

4. Next, crack open `App.svelte`, and then alter the first import statement to show this:

```
import {
  Products,
  Footer,
  Header,
  Product,
  Cart,
  Disclaimer
} from "./components";
```

5. Scroll down to the closing `</nav>` element, and then add in a call to the Disclaimer component, as indicated:

```
  <Link to="/coffee">Our Coffee</Link>
  <Link to="/contact">Contact</Link>
</nav>
<Disclaimer />
<main>
```

6. Crack open `index.js` from the `\src\components` folder, and then add this line immediately below the last import statement:

```
import Disclaimer from "./Disclaimer.svelte";
```

7. At the end of the file, you will see an export statement – add the reference to `Disclaimer`, as indicated:

```
export { Products, Footer, Header, Product, CartLength, Cart,
Disclaimer }
```

8. Save and close all open files – we have completed the changes.

9. Switch to your browser, and then head over to `http://localhost:5000/`. If all is well, we should see a red banner appear, with the warning (Figure 9-1).

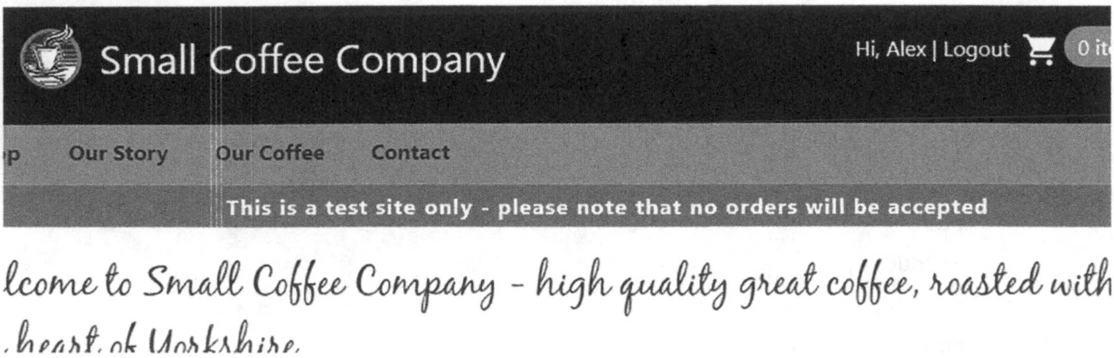

***Figure 9-1.** The newly added disclaimer on our site*

That may have been an easy exercise, but an important one – you can be sure that someone will try to buy something from the site, thinking it should be a real one! We can't stop them from trying, but we can make it more transparent that they won't receive anything they try to order from the shop.

Okay, let's move on. It's time for us to start breaking apart the deployment process. We have a few steps to cover; let's start with choosing our hosting provider.

Understanding the Deployment Process

We now have a working site for which we've done our final checks: it's time to make it live!

Okay, in reality, we probably wouldn't want to publish our site as it stands; it's still very much a development project and needs a lot more work before we could put it in front of paying customers. Nevertheless, it's still important to consider the *principles* of how we might go about publishing our site, ready for when we can indeed make it live.

There are several different ways to publish our site, depending on whether you might want to use a provider such as AWS, Netlify, Surge, Now, or Vercel. We have to consider several factors such as resilience, compatibility with technologies we use, costs, security, and so on – clearly something we should not rush! For this book, I'm going to use GitHub Pages – there are several reasons for this:

- It includes native support for SSL, which is easy to enable – it's something Google looks for by default for SEO purposes.
- GitHub Pages is free, as long as you use an open repo – this is fine for our needs (but see the comments shortly).

- It doesn't limit the number of build minutes available (as other hosts such as Netlify do) – as long as you don't need to use GitHub Actions, which we don't.
- I already have a good handful of GitHub repos, so I don't want to introduce another hosting facility into my collection!

I will say that choosing GitHub is purely my preference – please feel free to use an alternative host if you prefer. The focus of this chapter is about seeing our site available in the wild and not the specifics of how we host it.

With our host provider chosen, let's turn our attention to setting it up – this does require a fair few steps, but thankfully most of them will be a one-off, assuming all goes well! In a nutshell, we have to

- Set up a GitHub Pages account
- Create a working area for cloning the repository
- Upload content

As a bonus, I will also tack on a custom domain name to see how our site will look in real life. Yes, it won't be ready for **actual** production use, but it will at least give us a flavor of what to expect.

Okay, let's crack on with setting up a GitHub site as the first part of this multistage exercise.

Setting Up the Hosting Provider

The first stage in our multipart demo is to set up a GitHub account – you can, of course, use an existing one, but it will make configuring a little trickier! Creating a new one from scratch means keeping the setup nice and clean and not worrying about affecting any existing code or configuration.

Before we crack on with setting up our repository, there are a couple of assumptions you need to bear in mind:

- For this exercise, I will assume we are using the username `smallcoffeecompany`; you will need to think of a suitable name and swap this in as appropriate.
- I'm also assuming that you will create a new account and repository for this exercise; you can use an existing one, but it will make things more complicated!

With this in mind, let's make a start with setting up our GitHub space.

PREPARING THE HOST

To set up a new repository, please follow these steps:

1. We'll start by creating a new repository – for this, browse to `https://github.com`, and click Sign Up in the top right.
2. Go ahead and follow the instructions provided on-screen, including adding an email account (it's worth it!) – make sure you take note of the details you use for your account. Once done, sign in with your new account, and make sure it is validated.
3. Next, we need to create our repository – click the + sign in the top right and then New repository.
4. On the next screen, the Owner field will be your account name. Enter a repository name in the format `username.github.io`, where the username is your chosen username on GitHub.
5. If you want to fill in a description, then go ahead and do so – it is not compulsory for this exercise.
6. Next, choose Public as the repository type, and click the checkbox against Add a README file to initialize the repository with a readme file.
7. For the Add `.gitignore` option, choose Node, and set the Add a license to MIT.

8. Click Create repository – if all is working as expected, we should have an empty repository, similar to the screenshot shown in Figure 9-2.

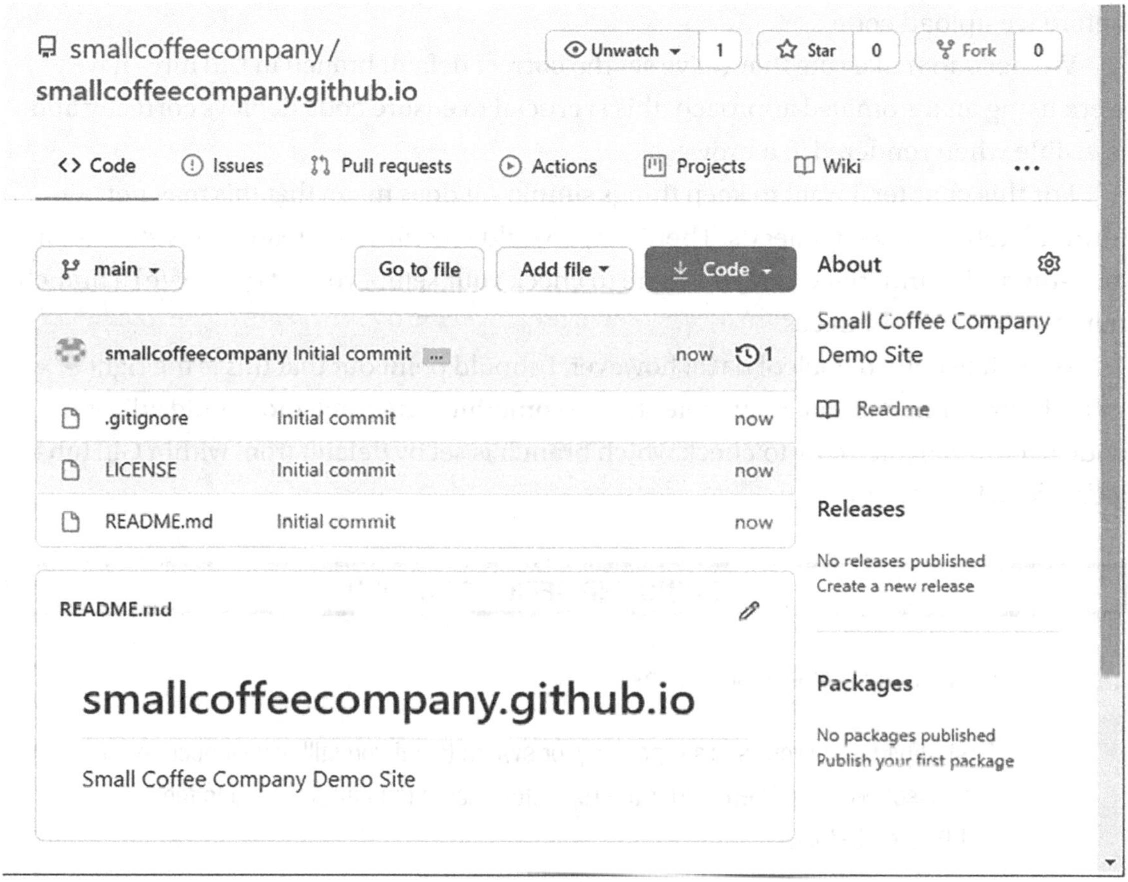

Figure 9-2. *Our new repository on GitHub*

Excellent - at this point, we should now have a working repository, ready to accept our uploaded code. The upload process is very straightforward - we could automate it, but I will use the manual format for this book. Let's look at what's involved in more detail, beginning with a simple but all-important check.

Checking the Default Branch

Although we have our repository in place, there is a straightforward check we should do before we upload code.

We need to make sure that we've set the correct default branch in GitHub - if we were using an automated approach, this is crucial to ensure code deploys correctly and is visible when rendered in a browser.

For this chapter, I want to keep things simple - it does mean that this may not immediately match your needs. Therefore, I would recommend treating this step as an aide-memoire and that when you come to check your setup, you set (or create) a branch name that suits your needs.

We will use the default of `main`; however, I should point out that this is the right branch for our needs. You may prefer to use something different and should adjust the code accordingly. It's easy to check which branch is set by default from within GitHub - let's take a look at how.

CHANGING THE DEFAULT BRANCH

To change the branch, follow these steps:

1. First, navigate to your site's repository, or switch to it if you still have it open in a browser window. Then, under the repository name (and in the menu to the right), click Settings.
2. In the GitHub Pages section, click the link to go to the Pages configuration.
3. Ensure the value set in the Source drop-down list is `main` – as indicated in Figure 9-3.

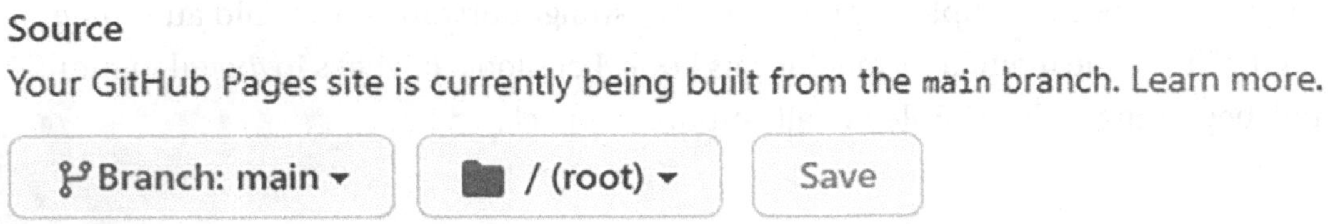
Source
Your GitHub Pages site is currently being built from the main branch. Learn more.
Branch: main
/ (root)
Save

Figure 9-3. *Checking the branch settings in our repository*

4. Click Save – the site is ready to host content.

It might seem as if we're a little too cautious, but not checking could mean the difference between us having a working site and potentially a blank page or errors showing on screen! In our case, we shouldn't have had to make any changes, but your needs might be different, and that you should adjust accordingly.

Okay, let's crack on. The next step is where things start to happen. It's time for us to upload our code to GitHub, so we see the finished site on screen.

Deploying Content to Production

One of the great things about Svelte is the deployment process – when it comes to uploading code into GitHub Pages, we might typically use a package called gh-pages. It was designed to simplify the uploading process; the weird thing is that it is overkill for our needs!

Why? There is a straightforward reason – Svelte sites, when built, compile down to standard JavaScript, CSS, and HTML markup. It means that we can use the usual `git add` and `commit` commands to upload content; we don't have to use any other package! As anyone who knows me personally, I'm very much a fan of keeping things simple – after all, the more complex it gets, the more likely it will go wrong, right?

Before we get stuck into uploading code, there are a couple of housekeeping points you need to be aware of:

- I'm assuming that you have Git already installed for your platform, along with Git Bash; if you don't, then please go ahead and get it installed before you continue with the exercise.
- I've already set up a GitHub repository under `https://github.com/smallcoffeecompany` – the steps in the demo will use this as an example. Please substitute `smallcoffeecompany` with your GitHub repository username when completing the exercise.

If you need any help with installing Git, then please refer to `https://git-scm.com/book/en/v2/Getting-Started-Installing-Git`, which details the process for most popular platforms.

Okay, with that bit of housekeeping out of the way, let's move on to the exercise. Figure 9-4 gives you a flavor of what to expect once we've uploaded all of the code and configured the custom domain.

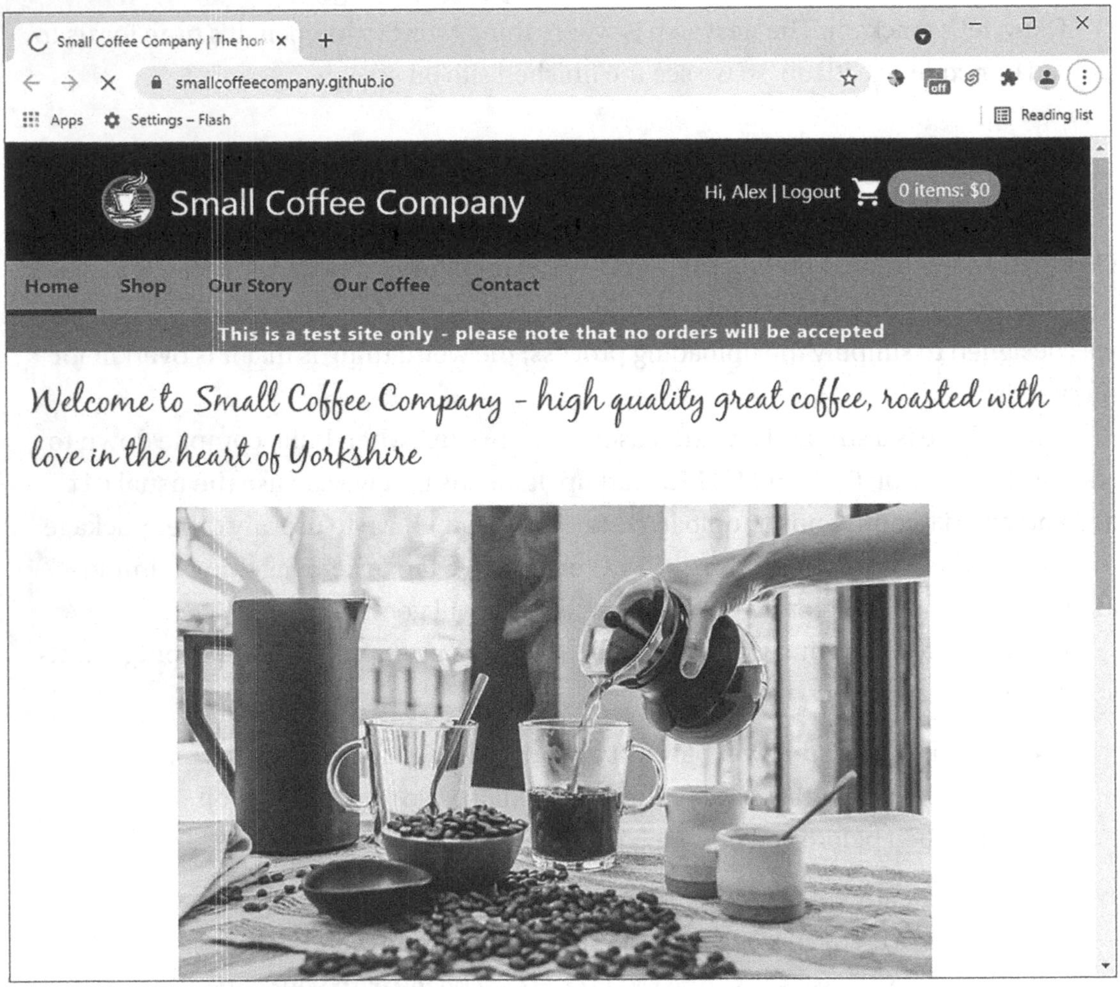

Figure 9-4. *The completed site, hosted in GitHub Pages*

Now that we know what it should look like, let's get stuck into setting up Git ready for us to upload code to the new site.

SETTING UP GIT

To upload our code to GitHub, please follow these steps:

1. First, fire up a Git Bash terminal session (and **not** a regular Node.js terminal), then change the working folder to our project area.
2. Once changed, enter this command and press Enter – this will build a production-ready version of our site:

   ```
   npm run build
   ```

3. Switch to your GitHub repository area in your browser, and then go to the main page. Click the green Code button, and then copy the URL in the HTTPS tab. Revert to the Git Bash prompt, and then enter this command:

   ```
   git clone << YOUR GITHUB URL >>
   ```

4. Once cloned, go ahead and copy the contents of the `public` folder from our project area into this new Git folder.
5. Next, enter git status at the Git Bash prompt to verify that Git has marked the new files for tracking.
6. At the prompt, enter these commands one after another, pressing Enter after each one:

   ```
   git add .
   git commit -m "initial commit"
   git push
   ```

7. Once committed, go ahead and browse to the site in your browser – if all is well, you should see it published. You can see an example of how it should look with my version, available at `https://smallcoffeecompany.github.io`, as shown at the start of this section.

Our site is now finally live! Yes, okay, it's not ready for production use, but it's the principle that matters here: we can go back and develop the site further, safe knowing that we have a mechanism to publish it.

That aside, we've covered some essential points as part of this process – let's take a moment to review the changes we made before cracking on with adding the bonus domain name.

Breaking Apart the Changes

Although we could have automated the upload process, I've deliberately kept things simple, using techniques that I'm sure you will already be familiar with as a developer. Nothing should stop you from automating the process, though – how will depend on your own environmental needs. The fundamental principle here was to show that we don't need any extra tools to achieve this process.

Talking of process, how *did* we upload the code? We started by running `npm run build` in the project folder; this creates a production-ready version of our site as static HTML, CSS, and JavaScript. I say "production-ready" because our site does need extra work to get it there; it's the process that counts at present.

Next up, we then used Git to clone a copy of our GitHub Pages site before transferring a copy of the contents of the `/public` folder from our project area into the upload space. Of course, we would have created the GitHub site first in an ideal world, but that might add a little extra complexity; having a separate area means we don't risk uploading code that isn't ready.

We used standard Git commands to create the merge request for the last stage before using `git commit` to push it up to our site. The code is visible straight away; this isn't an issue for us as we're working in a development capacity. You might want to create a separate branch first so that the master branch can still operate. At this point, we checked the site – assuming we encounter no issues, we successfully viewed the site in our browser at the new GitHub Pages address.

Okay, here comes the proverbial icing on the cake: adding a domain name! Svelte doesn't have to run with one: Svelte will run quite happily without one. I like to add one in, though, to give the site an extra sense of realism. To learn how to, let's take a look at the steps involved in more detail.

Adding a Custom Domain Name

Adding a custom domain is easy when using GitHub Pages, although we may have to factor in a 24-hour delay in the process. There are several benefits, though, in doing this process, irrespective of what tooling or framework we use:

- Using a short domain name is more memorable to customers, rather than what is effectively a custom subdomain – it inspires more confidence and is better for SEO purposes.
- An external domain name can be purchased cheaply, which makes for no excuse when it comes to creating a site.
- Having a subdomain doesn't suit every purpose – after all, why would you have a domain name such as `coffee.github.com` if you owned a coffee shop? GitHub Pages domains may serve technical people such as developers, but not your average Joe in the street!

Let's take a look at the steps we need to run through to get our site set up with a custom domain in more detail.

Before we start with the exercise, please make sure you have the means to update DNS; you might need to get assistance if you don't have access. Also, references to SSL in this text are generic: GitHub Pages uses the more secure TLS version for encrypting your website.

ADDING A DOMAIN NAME

I will assume you have a registered domain name for this exercise – it can be an existing one or one registered anew. If it is a new registration, you may want to wait 24–48 hours to allow it to propagate around DNS before working through these steps:

1. First, browse to your GitHub site using the format `https://github.com/<name of site>`.
2. On the main page, click Settings, and then scroll down to Custom domain.
3. In the Custom domain name field, enter the name of your chosen custom domain (in my case, I used `smallcoffeecompany.co.uk` - see Figure 9-5), and then hit Save.

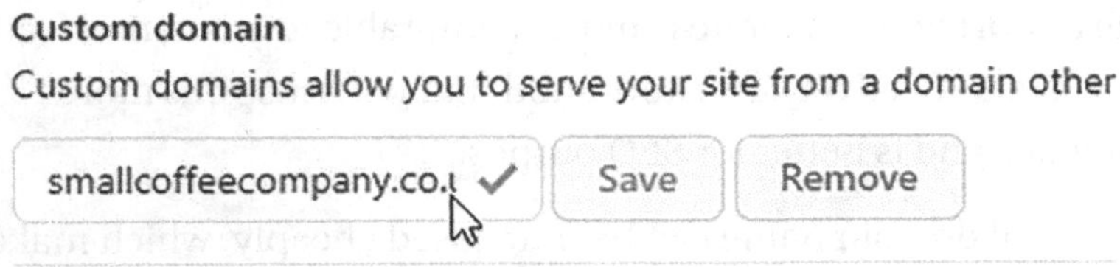
Custom domain
Custom domains allow you to serve your site from a domain other
smallcoffeecompany.co.
Save
Remove

Figure 9-5. *Confirmation that GitHub Pages has saved our custom domain*

This action will create a commit that adds a CNAME file in the root of your repository.

---

4. Next, navigate to your DNS provider and create an A record – use these IP addresses; you may find you need to create four separate A name records for each of these IP addresses:

```
185.199.108.153
185.199.109.153
185.199.110.153
185.199.111.153
```

We're using A records here, as the IP addresses are known and stable; CNAME entries are name aliases that map to other names.

---

5. To confirm that your DNS record configured correctly, use the `nslookup` command – enter this in a terminal session:

```
nslookup <your domain name>
```

If you are using Linux (or potentially Mac), then you can use this: `dig EXAMPLE.COM +noall +answer`, where `EXAMPLE.COM` is your domain name.

---

6. It will display something similar to the responses shown here:

```
Non-authoritative answer:
Name:    smallcoffeecompany.co.uk
Addresses:  185.199.108.153
            185.199.111.153
            185.199.109.153
            185.199.110.153
```

7. We have one more change to make, but when you can do it will depend on how quickly GitHub Pages completes a step. This step should be completed relatively quickly but can take time to update (Figure 9-6).

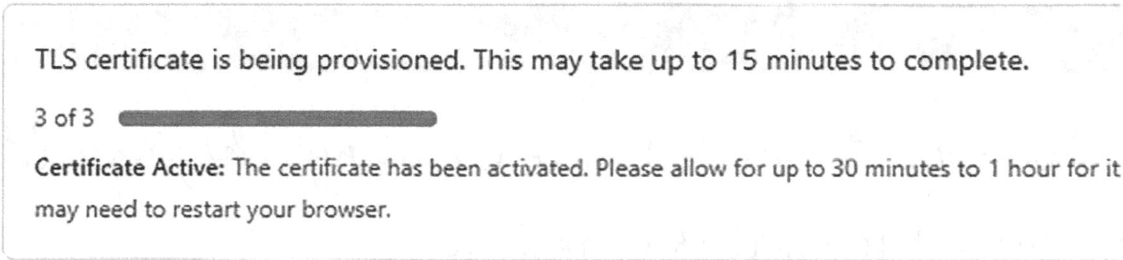

TLS certificate is being provisioned. This may take up to 15 minutes to complete.
3 of 3
Certificate Active: The certificate has been activated. Please allow for up to 30 minutes to 1 hour for it
may need to restart your browser.

Figure 9-6. *SSL certificate provisioning in progress*

You might want to refresh the page to check the status: the next step can be completed once GitHub enables the checkbox.

---

8. Once prompted, scroll a little further, and you will see an Enforce HTTPS box, similar to Figure 9-7. Go ahead and tick it to force access to be HTTPS.

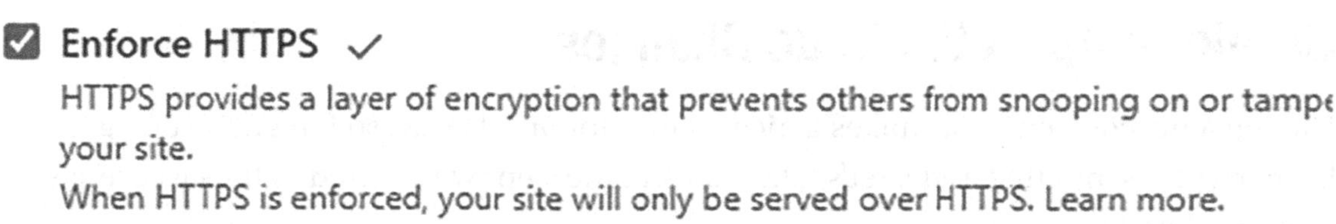

Enforce HTTPS
HTTPS provides a layer of encryption that prevents others from snooping on or tamp
your site.
When HTTPS is enforced, your site will only be served over HTTPS. Learn more.

Figure 9-7. *HTTPS access is now set*

9. In a separate tab, go ahead and browse to your new site – as an example, Figure 9-8 shows how my version looks, under the new URL of `www.smallcoffeecompany.co.uk`.

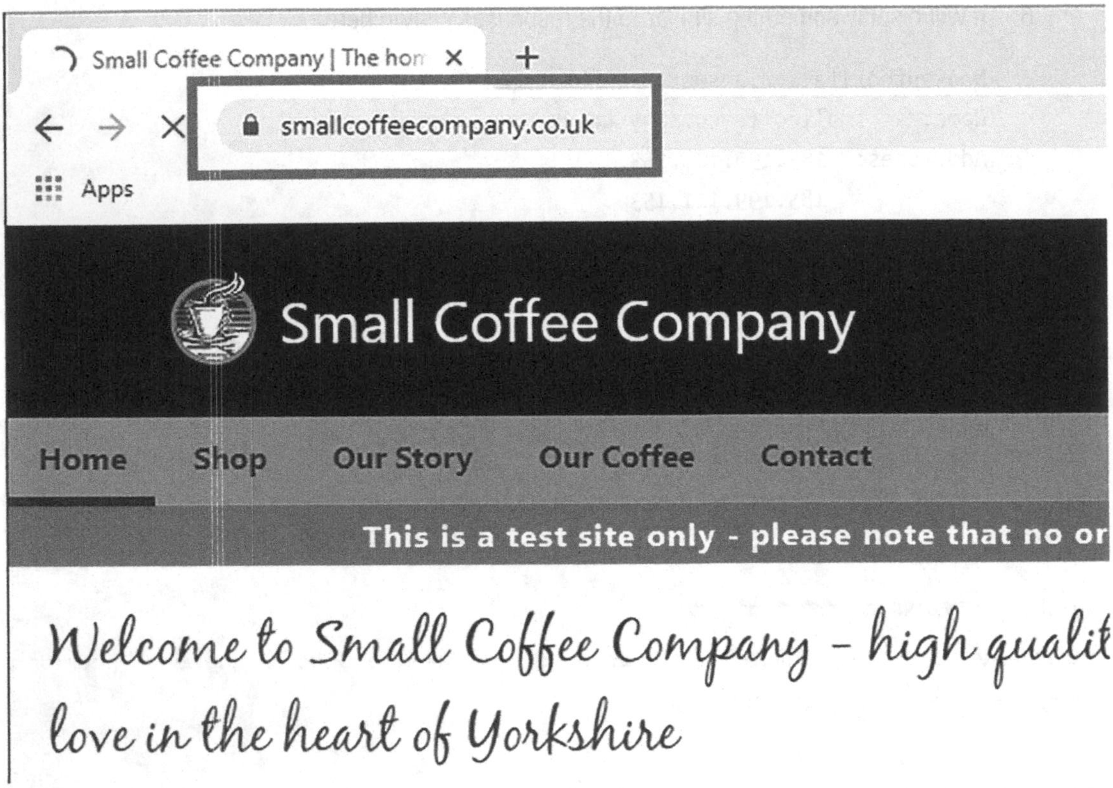

Figure 9-8. *The completed site with the new custom domain name (highlighted)*

Yay! Our site is now complete! This simplicity is one reason why I love using GitHub Pages – it takes a lot of the hassle out of tasks such as setting up SSL certificates for us.

This step marks the final part of getting our core site live, but by no means the end of the project: we have more to cover in future chapters. In the meantime, though, let's pause for a moment to review the changes made in this chapter.

Breaking Apart the Code Changes

Having a no-code exercise makes a nice change for once! Okay, so I might be being a little frivolous, but that aside, let's take a look at the steps we covered in the last exercise in more detail.

We kicked off by browsing to our GitHub Pages site settings before adding in the custom domain and allowing the change to take effect. At the same time, we noted that this would create a CNAME record in our site automatically – this is required to redirect content correctly with our domain name and not display it as a GitHub Pages URL.

We then added the DNS entries that point to GitHub Pages into our DNS – you will notice that we use four entries to provide redundancy, which is standard practice with any GitHub Pages site. However, the preference is to use A records for this, as the IP addresses are known and stable. We then did a quick `nslookup` to verify that DNS had been updated (it's not noted in the exercise, but you might find this takes a few minutes to complete before you get the expected result).

We rounded out the exercise by enabling SSL support – GitHub uses TLS for this purpose which is more secure but does precisely the same thing. Once we provisioned the certificate, we switched the site over to use HTTPS by default – it means that the site is only available via a secure URL which is standard practice nowadays, particularly for SEO purposes!

Taking It Further

We've now reached the point where our site has been deployed and is available for all to see – the question is, what next, I wonder?

Well, we have a couple of projects still to come in future chapters, but there are a few more immediate questions we can answer:

- Automation – can we improve on the deployment process?
- Is the folder structure we've used sufficient for our needs, or can we improve on it?
- We elected to use the main branch in our repo – is this the best option?
- We've deployed code to our GitHub repo, but what about tidying up the front page of the repo, so others can see how to install and run our (test) site?

Hopefully, you can start to see a theme of continuous improvement running here – I'm a firm believer in the principle that a site is only finished when it no longer serves a need, not when we've finished writing code.

To see what I mean, let's take the first point as an example – how *could* we automate the deployment process? Let's work through a potential answer to that question as part of our next exercise.

This walkthrough is a purely theoretical exercise designed to show how we might automate the process; it will likely need tweaking before using it in anger.

WALKTHROUGH: AUTOMATING THE DEPLOYMENT PROCESS

To understand how we might start to automate the deployment process, let's walk through some example steps using code from the DevSamples website:

1. We briefly mentioned using gh-pages earlier in this chapter – if we were to automate deployment, then the first step would be to install it via a Node.js terminal session:

   ```
   npm i gh-pages
   ```

2. To upload content requires we provide certain details, such as the URL of our repository, username, and email address. We can achieve this by creating a script that might look like this (and which would live at the root of our project area):

   ```
   var ghpages = require('gh-pages');

   ghpages.publish(
     'public', // path to public directory
     {
       branch: 'gh-pages',
       repo: 'https://github.com/username/
   yourproject.git',
       user: {
         name: '<ADD YOUR NAME HERE>',
         email: '<ADD YOUR EMAIL ADDRESS HERE>'
       }
     },
     () => {
       console.log('Deploy Complete!')
     }
   )
   ```

It's worth noting that we must provide both of these details. Otherwise, you might end up with some weird results, such as other GitHub accounts appearing to add commits when they should be!

3. We need to make sure that links in the `index.html` file at the root of `\public` contain relative paths; otherwise, links might not work correctly:

```
<!DOCTYPE html>
<html lang="en">

<head>
  <meta charset='utf-8'>
  <meta name='viewport' content='width=device-width,initial-scale=1'>
  <title>Small Coffee Company | The home of great coffee</title>
  <link rel='icon' type='image/png' href='/favicon.png'>
  <link rel='stylesheet' lang="css" href='/global.css'>
  <link rel='stylesheet' href='/build/bundle.css'>
  <script defer src='/build/bundle.js'></script>
</head>

<body>
</body>

</html>
```

The links are relative by default – this step is to catch any changes made to the default markup since we provisioned the initial site.

4. We've already done this next step in our manual deployment, but the same needs to happen if we automate it:

```
/node_modules/
# /public/build/

.DS_Store
```

5. This final step would be to run through commands similar to these to first build a production version of our site before committing it to our repo:

```
npm run build

git add .
git commit -m "initial gh-pages commit"
git push origin gh-pages

node ./gh-pages.js
```

6. If all is well, we would see our site updated at https://github.io/<yoursite name>.

Seems pretty straightforward, right? We first install the gh-pages library to aid with uploading content and then create a script that takes care of the upload process. At the same time, we make minor changes to ensure we're not pushing up irrelevant content. Other than this, we can use standard commands to create a merge request and push it to our repo.

The critical point here is the use of the ghpages script – the ghpages library takes what we push up to the repo and then creates a temporary copy of the repo. Next, it creates a temporary copy of the target branch (in this case, ghpages) before pushing any changes to the branch.

You can learn more about this library at https://github.com/tschaub/gh-pages.

Creating a ghpages script is only the tip of the proverbial iceberg, though; these changes would allow us to go further. We could, for example, add a step in the package.json that runs most (if not all) of the steps automatically – it would rely on us passing suitable parameters for the commit message and hard-coding the default branch into the script.

We might even go as far as uploading the source code (or at least the relevant folders) and then using a process such as GitHub Actions and a YAML configuration file to build the site for us. Much of what we could do will, of course, depend on your circumstances – suffice to say it's something to think about for future development!

To get a flavor of how GitHub Actions *could* work (in a general context), take a look at this article by Frontend Weekly on Medium: `https://medium.com/front-end-weekly/ci-cd-with-github-actions-to-deploy-on-github-pages-73e225f8f131`.

Summary

The publishing of any site can be a tense moment – we know that site development is finished (at least for this iteration). Still, equally, there is a certain amount of nervousness about how our customers might take to our newly published site.

Customers are fickle beasts at the best of times; we can't dictate what we want them to do (despite trying!), but we can make sure that the publishing process is painless. We've covered several valuable tips in this chapter to that effect – let's take a moment to review what we have learned.

We kicked off by exploring one final check step to ensure we haven't missed anything obvious. We talked about the fact that this is probably me being supercautious, but a last check is equally an excellent way to sign off before final publication.

We then went through the deployment process, beginning with understanding the critical steps before setting up our base site with GitHub Pages. We then moved onto creating the deployment steps and pushing our code up before checking to ensure we can display our site as expected on screen. As a final step, we added a custom domain name to give our site a little extra realism. We then finally rounded out the chapter with a brief look at some of the "next steps" we might take, principally around refining the deployment process to make it even smoother for future development.

At this point, we can breathe a sigh of relief – our site is up and running! The bad news is that we still have more we can do: we've created a shop front, but how will people pay for our products? We can't let them go for free, so clearly we need to do something: we need a payment process! I've got the perfect candidate that can help here, as well as show off how well Svelte works with third-party libraries – stay with me, and I will reveal all in the next chapter.

CHAPTER 10

Working with External Libraries

One of the key benefits of using Svelte is that we can use it in conjunction with other libraries or frameworks – Svelte can work with any library, including using components created for other frameworks, such as React.

That's a bold statement to make, so in this chapter, we will put this theory to the test and work with some external libraries to see how Svelte can interact with them. First, we'll create demos using some Svelte third-party libraries before finishing up using an external library to supplement our ecommerce front-end project. At the same time, we'll explore how we might live up to that theory – can we import a component from another framework into Svelte?

Before we get to answer that, we must start somewhere – let's begin with a look at how we can import external libraries into Svelte.

Importing Libraries into Svelte

By now, I'm sure you will be familiar with the process of importing NPM packages, such as Svelte – we'd use a typical import such as `import { setContext } from "svelte"`, right? I won't dwell on the subject for fear of teaching something we already know!

However, we have a few more options open to us when importing external libraries (such as the Tailwinds CSS library, from `www.tailwindscss.com`). The great thing about them is that we can make them as straightforward or as complex as we like – let's take a look at them in order of complexity, as shown in Table 10-1.

A. Libby, *Practical Svelte*, https://doi.org/10.1007/978-1-4842-7374-6_10

***Table 10-1.** Options available to import third-party libraries*

Method	Example
Importing a library using script tags	Usually into `\src\public\index.html`, and not into the component. It works, but take note that we can't maintain a clean separation of concerns. So, the imported library will be in the `index.html` while you work in a component – a neater arrangement is to use `svelte:head` to import the library directly into the component

`svelte:head`	A typical example looks like this:
	`<svelte:head>`
	`   <link rel="stylesheet"`
	`   href= "tutorial/dark-theme.css`
	`  ">`
	`</svelte:head>`

`onMount()`	Using `onMount()` is more complex and better suited to occasions where you need a callback – it also doesn't work if you are using Svelte in a server-side capacity:
	`onMount(() => {`
	`  const interval = setInterval(() => {`
	`  console.log('beep');`
	`}, 1000);`
	`    return () => clearInterval(interval);`
	`  });`
	`</script>`

Using an action	Svelte actions allow us to set up any third-party library or framework and make it reusable with the `use:` attribute:
	`<script>`
	`  import { typewriter } from "./typewriter.js";`
	`</script>`
	`<h1 use:typewriter={['Hello from our action!']}>Hello from our action!</h1>`

So, how does one choose which to use? A lot of this will depend on your requirements; if you need to provide a callback, then `onMount()` is best. Alternatively, if you need to use the library in multiple places, I suggest using a Svelte action. In many cases, though, I suspect that simply importing the library into the head of your code (either directly in `\public\index.html`) or using `svelte:head` will work fine.

Let's put some of this newfound knowledge to good use and create a few demos – they will be simple but are designed to show some of the ways we can import third-party libraries into Svelte.

Testing Compatibility with Svelte

Over the following few pages, we will put together some simple demos that show the various ways to import or reference third-party libraries or frameworks within Svelte. We will build all of them in Svelte's REPL playground for convenience – let's take a look at each of them in turn, starting with importing CSS.

DEMO 1: IMPORTING CSS WITH HEAD

To set up our mini photo album, follow these steps:

1. First, head over to `www.svelte.dev/repl` – go ahead and copy this code into the `App.svelte` tab on the left:

```
<script>
  import Flat from './Flat.svelte'
</script>

<svelte:head>
  <link href="https://unpkg.com/tailwindcss
@^1.0/dist/tailwind.min.css" rel="stylesheet">
</svelte:head>

<Flat/>
```

2. Next, go ahead and add a new tab to the right of `App.svelte` – rename this to `flat.svelte`.

3. Go ahead and extract a copy of `flat.svelte.txt` from the code download for this book (which you can access by clicking the Download Source Code link located at `www.apress.com/9781484273739`), and then copy the contents into the tab created in the previous step.

4. If all is well, we should see a date box appear on the right in the Results tab – click the icon to the right to show a date picker, as indicated in Figure 10-1.

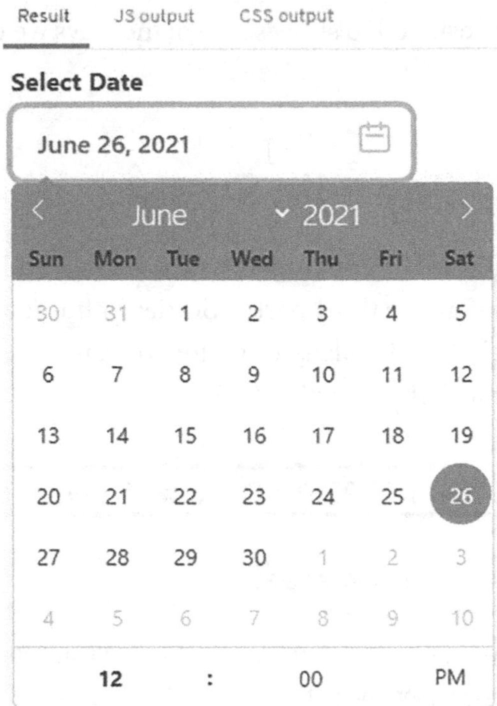

***Figure 10-1.** A date picker component using the svelte: head directive*

I don't know if it's me, but there's something about this demo that evokes memories of using jQuery UI from years ago – anyone remembers using that library? So now there's a blast from the past!

If we leave aside trips down memory lane for the moment, this demo shows a great way to import content such as the Tailwind CSS library while still keeping it within the component. We could have added the `<link...>` statements in the head within the `\src\public\index.html` file, but that means it's spread over multiple locations, making for a less clean approach.

Okay, let's crack on with the second demo. This one references the `onMount()` event handler to allow us to import content as before, but this time provides the opportunity to add in a callback as part of the process.

DEMO 2: USING ONMOUNT

To set up our mini photo album, follow these steps:

1. First, head over to `www.svelte.dev/repl` – go ahead and copy this code into the `App.svelte` tab on the left:

```
<script>
  import { onMount } from 'svelte';

  let photos = [];

  onMount(async () => {
    const res = await fetch(`https://jsonplaceholder
.typicode.com/photos?_limit=20`);
    photos = await res.json();
  });
</script>
```

2. Leave a line blank, and then go ahead and add in this styling block:

```
<style>
  .photos { width: 100%; display: grid; grid-template-columns:
  repeat(5, 1fr); grid-gap: 8px; }

  figure, img { width: 100%; margin: 0; }
</style>
```

3. Last but by no means least, we need our markup – miss a line, and then add in this code:

```
<h1>Photo album</h1>

<div class="photos">
  {#each photos as photo}
    <figure>
      <img src={photo.thumbnailUrl} alt={photo .title}>
      <figcaption>{photo.title}</figcaption>
    </figure>
```

```
  {:else}
    <!-- render if photos.length === 0 -->
    <p>loading...</p>
  {/each}
</div>
```

4. If all is well, we should see our photo gallery appear on the right after a few moments (Figure 10-2).

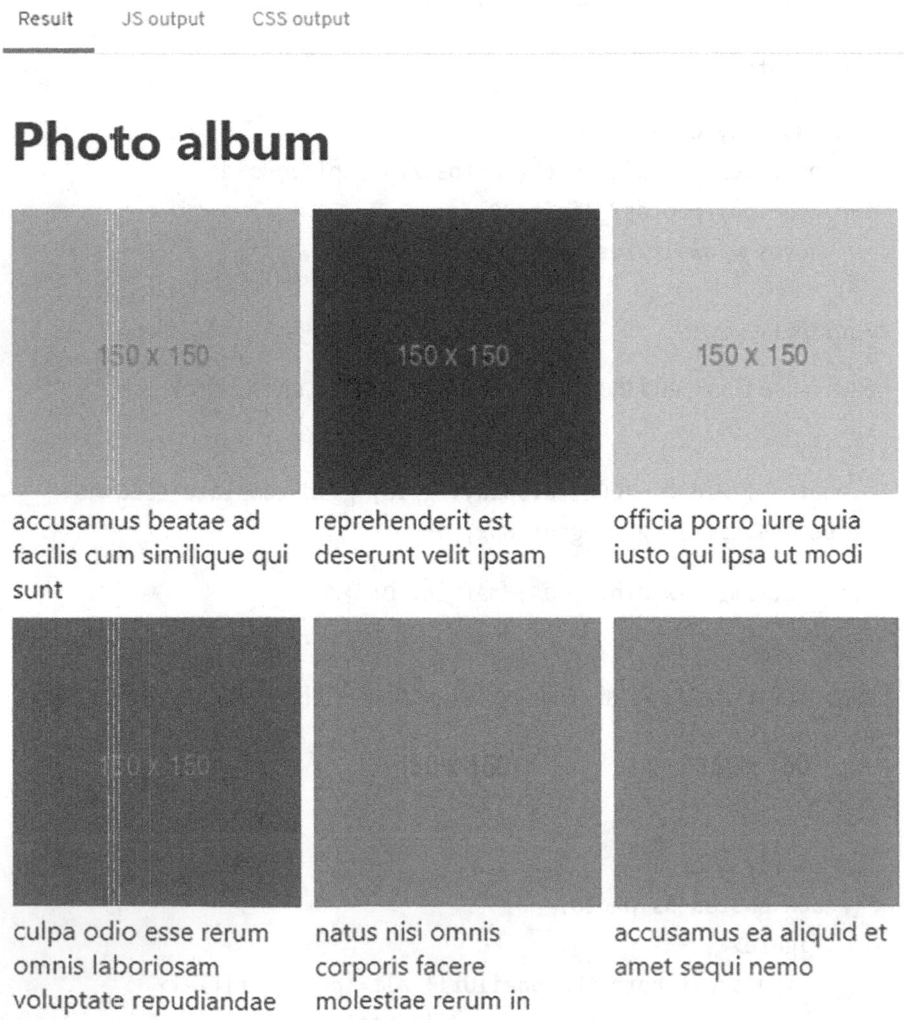

***Figure 10-2.** The demo photo album created using onMount()*

This demo shows off a great way to source third-party information or content and effectively import it into our Svelte code. It's suited for those occasions where you might want to execute that callback function we talked about earlier while still maintaining a mechanism that degrades gracefully if the external content is unavailable.

Moving on, this next demo provides an excellent effect we can use on websites and online applications - remember the days when we had to use typewriters? Yes, it might seem a long time ago, but old-school apparatus often works better and more reliably than modern-day technology! That aside, let's take a look at how we can replicate the typewriter effect as part of the next exercise.

DEMO 3: CREATING A TYPEWRITING EFFECT

To set up a typewriter effect, follow these steps:

1. First, head over to `www.svelte.dev/repl` – go ahead and copy this code into the `App.svelte` tab on the left:

```
<script>
  import { typewriter } from "./typewriter.js";
</script>

<h1 use:typewriter={['This is our typewriter action!']}>This is our
typewriter action</h1>
```

2. Next, click the plus sign to the right of this tab and add one called `typewriter.js`:

```
import Typewriter from 'typewriter-effect/dist/core';

export function typewriter(node, text) {
  var typewriter = new Typewriter(node, {
    strings: text,
    autoStart: true,
    loop: true
  });
}
```

3. If all is well, we should see this effect in the Result tab, as shown in Figure 10-3.

***Figure 10-3.** Creating a typewriter effect*

Over the years, I've always maintained there is more than one way to crack a nut – this is no different with Svelte and importing third-party content; we've seen a few ways to achieve this in the last few demos. So let's take a moment to review the code we've set up to see how each works in more detail.

Exploring the Code in Detail

So, what did we create? We started using the `svelte:head` function to import the Tailwind CSS library and create a simple date picker component in the first of our three demos. We could have built this by linking to the same CSS file from within `\src\public\index.html`, but this gets messy if we wanted to reuse this component elsewhere.

Inside `flat.svelte`, we first import the Flatpickr component from `svelte-flatpickr`, before setting up the `flatpickrOptions` configuration object with some appropriate values (such as the host element, `#flatpickr`). We then linked in the Tailwind CSS library using `svelte:head`, before setting up the relevant markup for our picker component. If you look closely, you will see that TailwindCSS uses a similar approach to Bootstrap. It works well, but you have to be careful; otherwise, you can overload content with too many classes!

Moving on to demo number two, and this time we use the JSONPlaceholder feed to create a dummy photo library. This time, we've used `onMount()`, as the content won't already be available (unlike TailwindCSS). Instead, we're `fetch`ing the content and assigning it initially to the variable `res`, before converting it into valid JSON once the `fetch` is completed. The rest of the demo is standard markup and styling, but note that we use the Svelte `#each` command to iterate through each photo, importing each `thumbnailUrl` and `title` into the markup.

In the last demo, we go back to the good old days of hardware! This time, we replicate the typewriter effect when rendering text on-screen. We first import a typewriter script file that imports the Typewriter library before exporting a new instance with appropriate settings. In `App.svelte`, we then create an `H1` tag, to which we apply the `use:` statement; Svelte looks for the same name in the exported file as is provided in the `use` clause. If it finds it, it will reuse the code from the exported file - this allows us to create a one-time setup, which we can reuse as many times as we want in our code.

Before we go any further, there is one crucial point I want to cover off - server-side rendering (or SSR) and how this might affect the use of external libraries. SSR has an impact since `onMount()` is not available; it also opens a broader question about whether we need to use SSR when working with Svelte.

Working Client Side vs. Server Side

If you've spent any time working with frameworks such as React, then I suspect you will have come across the term server-side rendering at some point. In a nutshell, it's the difference between building the code client side and server side. We can defer many more expensive tasks such as JavaScript rendering when running client side, whereas server side will build everything but come at a higher cost in terms of resources.

So, how does this affect us, particularly when we're using third-party libraries? There are several reasons why we might use SSR generally, but the biggest one is SEO. If we rendered our code server side, then the crawler can download our site as fully constructed HTML (including some JavaScript - not all); it means we don't need to execute JavaScript client side to render the code.

In theory, we could build a Svelte application entirely server side, but it would almost certainly render as 100% pure static code; users expect a certain amount of interactivity, making this approach impractical!

To get around this, we would need to perform dynamic rendering - effectively a mix of server and client side. The former is perfect for the content which can remain static while using the client side to create the interactive content. This approach does have some limits, though. For example, SSR code cannot interact with client-side code and vice versa; each must execute independently.

Why Is Svelte Different?

Remember how, back in Chapter 1, I said Svelte is different? Unlike other frameworks such as React, Svelte works by compiling code at *build* time, not runtime.

It means that (in a sense) you get the best of both worlds – Svelte compiles our code into static markup where possible at build time while still allowing those elements that need to remain dynamic to operate. In most cases, this will be enough; given that we don't need to use a runtime library like React, this should lead to a pretty fast site!

There is something to be aware of, though – it's possible to create and use client-side components if you decide to work server side with Svelte. It does require changes to how you factor your code; working in a server-side environment will help give better SEO (we can compile more on the server, compared to client side). The downside is that any changes made will force a re-render on the server, which can get expensive in terms of resources. Nevertheless, it's something to think about – if your site isn't that technically complex, you might get better performance working client side!

If you would like to delve into the world of server-side rendering with Svelte, then take a look at these two articles as a starting point. One is by Nathan Kessler at `www.base2.io/2020/12/12/svelte-ssr`, and the second is the main API docs for SSR and Svelte, at `https://svelte.dev/docs#Server-side_component_API`.

Okay, let's move on. It's time we got stuck back into our demo front end, methinks! So, over the following few pages, we will turn our attention to incorporating an external library into our demo front-end site. There are dozens we might want to use, but I have the perfect task for us: why not incorporate a payment processor feature into our website?

Adding a Payment Processor

Yes, the sharp-eyed among you will have spotted that we've built everything else but not provided a way to pay for our goods.

In the hope that we wouldn't want to give things away for free, we need a way to pay for goods. Adding a payment processor is where things get interesting: there are dozens of different tools we might use, but, surprisingly, there seems to be a shortage of documentation available on how to incorporate them into Svelte.

Huh? I hear you ask, surely we don't need anything, right? Wrong – this is one occasion where it pays to have the proper documentation! If we didn't, there is every possibility we might miss something, and that could mean the difference between accepting and rejecting a card. Not a good start, particularly if we reject what might be a perfectly valid card.

But I digress. Fortunately, there is one payment provider that has created a library to support Svelte: it's our good friend, PayPal.

In some respects, this is a good choice: we have a small site, and PayPal makes it supereasy to start on something small. Yes, we could go to the extremes of setting up catalogs in tools such as Shopify or Stripe, but for a small site, this is overkill! So instead, using a tool such as PayPal means we can get set up quickly; if we start adding more products, we can then consider moving up the scale to tools such as Shopify.

Okay, enough chitchat. Let's crack on with our demo. We will get to coding momentarily, but we do need to complete some basic housekeeping admin first. I know it's not everyone's favorite topic, but we would have to do the same for any payment provider, so let's get it out of the way before moving onto the fun stuff.

Getting Prepared

Before we get started, please make sure you have signed up for a personal account with PayPal or can use one you already have. PayPal comes with a sandbox option for developers; it's this option we will use through the rest of this chapter. We will not submit any actual orders or charge anything to your account; everything will happen in a sandbox environment, away from any real account settings.

You may need to set any settings for your own country to satisfy PayPal's security requirements; please adapt any steps where needed for your country.

DEMO – PAYPAL HOUSEKEEPING

Assuming you have access to a PayPal account, follow these steps to get the details we need for integrating into our demo:

1. Once complete, we need to get our API credentials, so we can begin to use PayPal – log into your developer dashboard at `https://developer.paypal.com/home`, and then under Dashboard, click My Apps & Credentials.
2. Make sure you select the Sandbox tab at this point – this is important: it will show the proper credentials to use in a test environment.
3. Click Default Application under the App Name column – PayPal will create a new developer dashboard account for you.
4. Next, take a copy of the long Client ID value, and save it for safekeeping – we will use it in the following two exercises.

You will also see a sandbox account email address – this isn't a real one! It's there to act as the recipient's email address when receiving orders.

---

5. Once copied, head over to `https://developer.paypal.com/developer/creditCardGenerator/`. Go ahead and choose your country, and then note the details provided; this we can use to test our integration later in the following two demos.

Excellent, we now have the details we need for the next part of our demo. I know it might seem a bit of a mixed bag of steps, but it will all become clear as we move to use the values in our demo.

At this point, we could skip ahead and try to incorporate the PayPal code directly into our site. However, we won't have the opportunity to see how it runs; if it doesn't go according to plan, we may make changes to our site that are unnecessary. To reduce the risk of that happening, let's run the code as a stand-alone demo first to get a feel for how it works before making changes to our front-end demo.

Taking a First Look at the PayPal Demo

The payment stage is the most critical part of our site – yes, we need pages with information about our products, but we're not going to give anything away for free, no matter what state those pages are!

Before we go hammer and tongs to change our demo, let's quickly run the vanilla example provided by PayPal to get a feel for how it works. As it so happens, we will need to make a small change to get it to work.

I will assume you install to the root of C: for convenience – please adjust if you wish to use a different area.

RUNNING THE SVELTE DEMO

To try out the initial PayPal demo for Svelte, work through these steps:

1. First, browse to `https://github.com/paypal-examples/svelte-paypal-js` – go ahead and click the Code button toward the top right and then Download Zip to download the demo.
2. Go ahead and open the archive file you've just downloaded, and then extract the contents and save to the root of your C: drive. Rename the extracted folder to `svelte-integration`.

The rename option isn't obligatory – it's just to make it easier to reference in the next step.

---

3. Go ahead and open `Checkout.svelte` from the `\src` folder, and then look for `const CLIENT_ID = 'your-client-id'`. Change the `'your-client-id'` text to the ID you saved in step 4 of the previous exercise. Save and close the file.
4. Fire up a Node.js terminal session, and then change the working folder to the svelte-integration folder.

At this point, we would typically run `npm install` to download dependencies, but if we do, you may hit a small error in the code! It's irritating but easily fixed and relates to a slightly out-of-date package – let's fix it before continuing with the remaining steps.

5. Switch to your text editor, then crack open `package.json`, and look for this line:

```
"rollup-plugin-css-only": "^3.0.0",
```

6. Change the value to this: "^3.**1**.0". The newer version of this package fixes the issue.

7. With the updated package in place, switch to a Node.js terminal session, and make sure the working folder is pointing to our project area. At the prompt, enter `npm install` to download and install all of the dependencies for this test.

8. The install will take a few minutes – once complete, enter `npm run dev` at the prompt.

9. If all is well, we should see the screenshot shown in Figure 10-4. Go ahead and click Debit or Credit Card at the foot of the demo.

Figure 10-4. *The starting screen for the PayPal demo*

10. Fill out the details shown in the form that appears – make sure you enter something in every field where it **doesn't** show the word Optional!

11. Once filled out, leave the Deliver to billing address field ticked, and then click Buy Now.

12. You will see a spinner kick in while the browser sends the data to PayPal – if all is well, we should see the response shown in Figure 10-5.

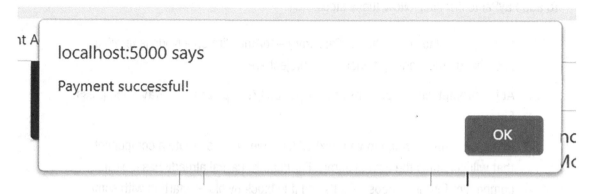

***Figure 10-5.** Confirming that the initial PayPal demo works as expected*

Yes, that's a relief: we have something that works! But, while it is a big step forward, it does raise some questions about what we might do if we wanted to upgrade to a payment provider that offered more features. But – as they say – that's for another day: instead, now that we've seen it working, let's crack on and get PayPal integrated into our site.

Adding PayPal to Our Front-End Site

Okay, it's time to bite that bullet and add PayPal to our site!

Although this might seem a little scary, don't worry, PayPal has done most of the hard work for us already. We simply need to drop in the extra component and wire it up as part of our existing Cart component. That said, we will still have a few steps to work through – let's get to it and see what is involved in more detail in the first part, where we add the PayPal code to our site.

DEMO – ADDING PAYPAL

To add PayPal to our site, follow these steps:

1. First, we need to install the PayPal library – for this, fire up a Node.js terminal, and change the working folder to our project area.
2. At the prompt, enter `npm install @paypal/paypal-js --save` and press Enter.
3. In the meantime, switch to your text editor – we need to create a component that will consume the PayPal library. Fortunately, PayPal already has a perfect component for this purpose – let's add it in block by block, starting with some declarations:

```
<script>
  import { loadScript } from "@paypal/paypal-js";
  import { cart } from "../stores.js";

  $: total = $cart.reduce((sum, item) => sum + item.price * item.
  quantity, 0)
  const CLIENT_ID = "<<<INSERT YOUR ID HERE>>>";
```

4. Next, we call `loadScript()` to create two buttons in our cart – one for PayPal itself and the other to pay by card using PayPal:

```
  loadScript({ "client-id": CLIENT_ID })
.then((paypal) => {
    paypal
      .Buttons({
        style: {
          color: "blue",
          shape: "pill",
        },
```

5. This next block sets up the payment object, with the cart total – leave a line blank after the previous step, and then add in this:

```
createOrder: function (data, actions) {
  // Set up the transaction
  return actions.order.create({
```

```
      purchase_units: [
        {
          amount: {
            value: total,
          },
        },
      ],
    });
  },
```

6. When PayPal has approved the sale, we capture details of the order and then post an alert to say it has been successful:

```
        onApprove: function (data, actions) {
          // Capture order after payment approved
          return actions.order.capture()
.then(function (details) {
            alert("Payment successful!");
          });
        },
```

7. This (almost) last block takes care of any issue that crops up – for now, we're piping out a message on-screen and to the console log:

```
  onError: function (err) {
    // Log error if something goes wrong during approval
    alert("Something went wrong");
    console.log("Something went wrong", err);
  },
})
```

8. This last section renders the payment buttons on-screen, using a predefined container:

```
      .render("#paypal-button-container");
  });
</script>

<div id="paypal-button-container" />
```

9. This last step is to add in a tweak for styling, to make sure that the PayPal button container is suitably positioned on-screen:

```
<style>
  #paypal-button-container { margin: 30px 0; }
</style>
```

10. Save the component as `Checkout.svelte`, at the root of the `\src\component` folder.

11. We have a couple more steps to do – the first is to add a reference to the Checkout component at the head of the `Cart.svelte` file. Crack that file open, and then amend the code as highlighted:

```
<script>
  import Checkout from './Checkout.svelte';
  import { cart } from "../stores.js";
```

12. Scroll down to the foot of the Cart component, and then amend the last few lines as indicated:

```
  {/each}
  <Checkout />
</div>
```

13. Save the file and close it – the changes are complete.

14. Switch to your Node.js terminal session from earlier, and then enter npm run dev at the prompt and press Enter.

15. Go ahead and browse to `http://localhost:5000/products`, and then add a product to the basket. If all is well, we should see something akin to that shown in Figure 10-6.

Figure 10-6. *Paypal added to our cart*

16 **Don't close anything down in your browser** – we will need it as is for the final part of this demo.

See, that was easy, right? There is nothing to fear when using PayPal: they like to make things easy, and for a small site like ours, it's perfect. The real crunch comes, though, when we test it - does it all work as expected on our site? There's only one way to find out, so let's crack on and try out our integration in part 2 of this exercise.

Testing the Result

Testing, testing, 1...2...3...

Okay, it's a little running joke, but it does have a serious point - we need to test our code! I know it's not going in front of customers just yet, but it's still worth testing; we can always return and add changes to it, which is more manageable while still developing the site.

Fortunately, the second part of this demo is substantially shorter than the first - I should point out that we're purely testing functionality at this stage. I'm assuming you would use some of the techniques from Chapter 8 to test our code! In the meantime, let's take a closer look at the steps needed to validate that our site is working in more detail.

TESTING THE RESULT

Assuming we have one or more products added, follow these steps to test it works as expected:

1. First, hit the Debit or Credit Card button, and then wait for it to display the credit card information form.
2. We need to enter in some dummy credit card information – for this, log into your PayPal dashboard in a separate tab, and then browse to `https://developer.paypal.com/developer/creditCardGenerator/`.
3. Go ahead and choose a preferred card type and country – it doesn't matter which for this demo!
4. You will see details appear in the Generated Credit Card Details block below it – we will use these details.
5. Switch back to our demo site, and then enter the chosen details into the card number, expires, and security code fields.
6. We need to add in a billing address – please enter in something fake, but **make sure it is appropriate for your country**. For example, there is no point in adding a French credit card but putting in an address for somewhere such as South Africa! (I know, it's only a test, but it's not realistic.)

Make sure you enter text to all fields that are **not** marked Optional; otherwise, the test will not proceed.

---

7. At the bottom, make sure the Deliver to billing address field is ticked.
8. Hit the Buy Now button and be patient – you will see a spinner for a few moments before this should appear (Figure 10-7).

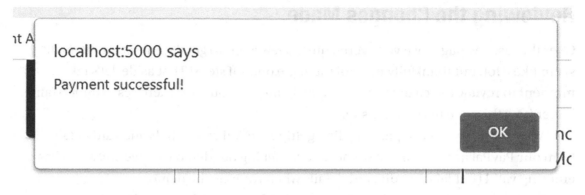

***Figure 10-7.** Confirming our Paypal integration works*

9. The real test comes in PayPal – if you browse to `https://developer.paypal.com/developer/notifications/` in your account, you should see something akin to the screenshot shown in Figure 10-8.

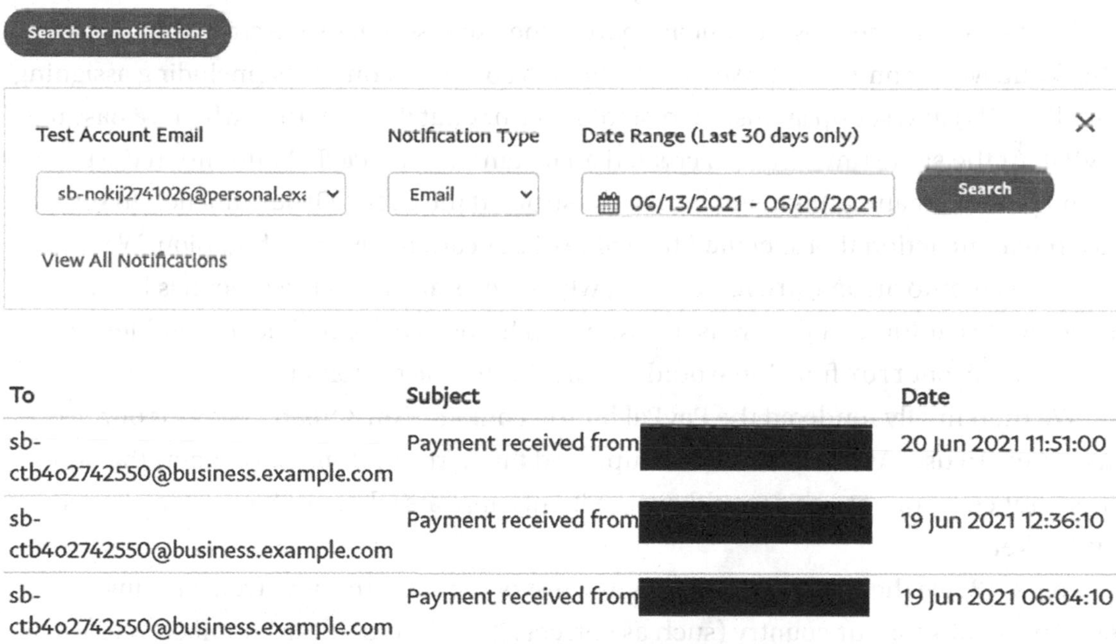

***Figure 10-8.** Notifications of (fake) payments received by Paypal*

That said, the component exposes a few important points we should explore in more detail, so first – and in this order! – get a drink, then take a breather, and when you're ready, let's take a look at the code in greater detail.

Reviewing the Changes Made

Over the last few pages, we've covered quite a few steps to get PayPal set up – it might seem like a lot, but thankfully most of them are one-off steps! That aside, let's take a moment to review the changes we've made in the previous two exercises to understand better how the code fits into our site.

We started way back in part 1 by first getting the API credentials and card details from our PayPal account; these we needed for telling our demo who we are, as well as entering valid (but fake) credit card details when running the demo.

We then updated the vanilla demo provided from PayPal – we had to adjust the `CLIENT_ID` value (using the value we retrieved just now) and fix a minor bug from a (now) out-of-date dependency. When running up the demo, we were able to test it by selecting the plant, choosing credit or debit card, and providing relevant details. Assuming all was successful, we had an alert message to confirm the same, and that (had we done it) we could also verify the payment was successfully received in our account.

Next up came the most significant part of the exercise – here, we created our Checkout.svelte component. We first declared a couple of constants (including assigning our client ID) and set up an instance of total to work out the final total when we pass it to PayPal. At the same time, we also created an instance of the PayPal buttons on the page.

As part of creating this instance, we constructed the `CreateOrder` function to set up a payment action that specified the value of our cart, ready for submission. We then moved onto an `onApprove` function, which posts an alert if the order has been successfully captured and there is no issue with funds. If there had been a problem with the latter, the `onError` function would handle this for the customer.

We then finally rendered the PayPal button container on-screen, ready for our customers to use. As the final step, we updated the Cart component to import the new Checkout component – this would ensure it only appears when we have added items to our basket.

In part 3, we then ran through an initial test of the site – this involved entering relevant details for our country (such as correct zip code, credit card numbers, etc.) before hitting Submit and verifying that the test had been completed successfully.

Okay, let's move on. Remember how I mentioned at the start of this chapter that question around importing components into Svelte? In this instance, I don't mean Svelte ones, but I'm referring to others, such as React or even Vue. Sounds crazy, right? After all, why would you want to import something into a Svelte application that isn't even written in Svelte, I wonder?

What About React?

Well, at first, it might seem crazy to import a React component into Svelte, but let's consider that for a moment: both are JavaScript based and use relatively similar principles, so it might not be as crazy as it seems! Let me explain.

Sure, having a React runtime library will cancel out the benefit of not having one in Svelte. Yes, the speed might not be as fast nor the code as clean as Svelte. But there is one benefit to all of this: migration.

If you happen to be part of a team migrating a complex React application to a Svelte equivalent, this will take a lot of time and resources. Building a complete site from scratch in one go isn't practical, so we use the principle of MVP, or minimum viable product - what can we do to begin the conversion while still maintaining service for customers?

One way to do that - and to show off the flexibility of Svelte - is consuming a React component in Svelte code. We can use `onMount()` to load in that component and then render it on-screen. There are some limitations around how we might call or use prop values, but as long as we take a considered approach, it will help reduce the immediate work required to migrate to Svelte.

Okay, enough talk. Let's see this in action! For this demo, we will use a CodeSandbox app instead of Svelte's REPL - this is purely because the REPL playground doesn't support React. With that in mind, let's dive in and take a look at what's involved in more detail.

CONSUMING A REACT COMPONENT

To see how we can consume a React component in a Svelte application, follow these steps:

1. First, head over to `www.codesandbox.io/`, and then hit Create Sandbox in the top-right corner.
2. From the list of Official Templates, scroll down to and click Svelte.
3. On the left, add in `react` and `react-dom` to the dependencies list; enter the name and press Enter after each one to add it to the list.

4. In the App.svelte file, we have a fair amount of code to add, so let's do it in sections, starting with the requisite Svelte and React imports:

```
<script>
  import { onMount } from "svelte";

  // React component
  import React from "react";
  import ReactDOM from "react-dom";
```

5. Next comes the React component – leave a line blank, and then add in this code:

```
  const e = React.createElement;
  class LikeButton extends React.Component {
    constructor(props) {
      super(props);
      this.state = { liked: false };
    }
    render() {
      if (this.state.liked) {
        return "You liked this.";
      }
      return e(
        "button",
        {
          style: {
            color: "red",
            width: "200px",
            height: "50px",
            fontSize: "16px",
            fontWeight: "bold"
          },
          onClick: () => this.setState({ liked: true })
        },
        "Like"
      );
    }
  }
```

6. We need to finish it off by mounting the code – for this, go ahead and add in this last block:

```
  // Svelte mounting
  let container;
  onMount(function() {
    ReactDOM.render(e(LikeButton), container);
  });
</script>
<div bind:this={container}/>
```

7. Press Ctrl+S (or Cmd+S) to save the code, and then hit the Refresh button next to the URL in the tab on the right – if all is well, we should see a new button appear (Figure 10-9).

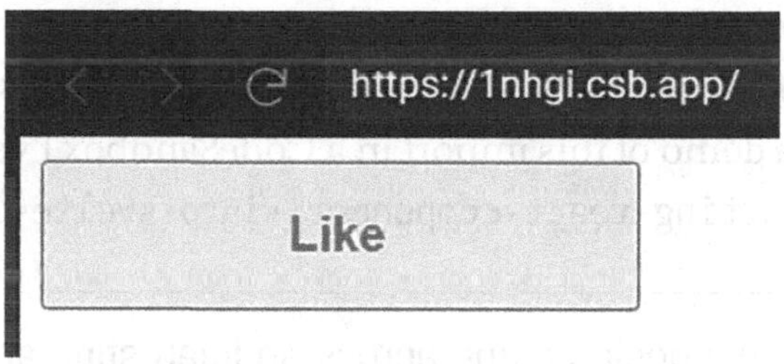

***Figure 10-9.** A React button in a Svelte application*

And voilà, we have a working React component running inside a Svelte application! Granted, it was a simple React component and probably not using techniques that reflect current development practices, but - it's a React component.

I'm sure we could refactor the code to make it more reusable (such as moving the React component into a separate file). Still, it illustrates how we might consume existing React components in the interim until native replacements can be sourced or written in Svelte. In the meantime, this technique exposes a couple of valuable points, so without further ado, let's take a closer look at how the demo works in more detail.

Breaking Apart the Changes

Combining React and Svelte seems like a bit of a paradox! After all, both operate differently (although there are some similarities, at least in code). Nevertheless, it can be helpful on occasion to consume existing React components in Svelte code, particularly if we're migrating from the former to the latter.

To achieve this, we first imported three functions - `onMount()` for Svelte and the two React libraries for React. We then created our React component - in this instance, I kept it simple by using `React.createElement` to create a `LikeButton`, but we could have chosen to build something more complex.

We've defined the initial state inside this component and then rendered the `LikeButton` and its `onClick` event handler, along with some basic styling. I know the styling isn't great, but the key is the import, not how we make it look aesthetically pleasing!

For the last step, we used Svelte's `onMount()` to render the `ReactDOM` object that contains the instance of our `LikeButton`, which we display on the screen in the specified container. You can see a demo of this import in a CodeSandbox I've created at `https://codesandbox.io/s/importing-react-components-into-svelte-1nhgi`.

While researching for this book, I came across an interesting article by Chris Coyier on understanding the differences between React and Svelte and how one can refactor code from React to Svelte to cover most circumstances very quickly. The article is at `https://css-tricks.com/svelte-for-the-experienced-react-dev/` – it's worth a read, particularly if you're moving from React to Svelte!

Summary

Although Svelte is a potent tool in its own right, it can't do everything - there will come a time when we need to import a third-party library of some description into our project. Fortunately for us, there are several ways to achieve this, although the final answer will depend on our requirements. Throughout this chapter, we've explored those options in greater detail - let's take a moment to review what we covered in more detail.

We kicked off first with a look at the different ways we can import content into Svelte, from simply linking to files in the final build through using the likes of `svelte:head` to creating reusable actions that we can call from any location in our projects. We then used the examples to create demos to explore how they work and begin to understand some of the differences that might influence which option we would use for our requirements.

Next up, we covered off an essential point around working server side and that this will affect how we import libraries. At the same time, we explored how Svelte is different from other libraries, and for the main, we learned that working client side will suit most needs when working with Svelte.

We then moved onto adding a payment processor to our project – we used PayPal, as it was simple to set up (which suits the small size and ethos of the site). We first did a dry run-through of a demo designed for Svelte before adding the changes to our site and finally testing the result works as expected in our browser.

We then rounded out the chapter by answering a question – Rich Harris, the original creator of Svelte, claims that you can import components from other frameworks such as React into a Svelte application. We learned that it is indeed the case, and while it may not look as pretty, it can undoubtedly help migrate to using Svelte!

Okay, we've come to the end of this chapter, but don't worry, we have more to cover! It's time to get animated and see how we can add that extra special touch to our front-end design… to give it that sparkle, so to speak. Hopefully, by now, you might have an idea of where I'm heading with this: stay with me, and I will reveal it all in the next chapter.

CHAPTER 11

Animating Svelte

Until now, we've covered the core elements of Svelte as part of building our site – it's time to add a little extra sparkle! We could do this in one of several ways, but a great example is an animation. Fortunately, Svelte makes it easy to add any effect we desire; the trick is to make sure we don't overdo the effects.

In this chapter, we'll examine how Svelte supports animating, transitioning, and tweening, plus add in some custom effects to our store front-end project. We'll start first, though, with a question: what could (or should) we add to our site?

Auditing the Site

Adding any form of animation to a site – be it a transition, animation, a tween, or similar – can be a double-edged sword. Do it well, and it looks fabulous; anything else will make the site look tacky and damage the reputation of the owning company.

Take, for example, this site – `www.fournier-pere-fils.com/`. I first wrote about their site when researching for one of my other books, *Practical SVG*. The site had a fantastic picture of a vineyard with the occasional bird flying over and the sun shimmering through the trees. It might have taken a moment or two to load, but it was worth the wait!

How does that fit in here, I hear you ask? Well, in answer, on two counts: the site is advertising upmarket wine, so the animation adds a touch of class, and secondly – most importantly – it doesn't overdo the effects! Fast forward to now, and the site still runs an animation, but this time of their cellar, you can see the sun shining through the windows and slight effects of dust. It creates a really atmospheric view of something meant to be aged but, at the same time, is not overdone.

A. Libby, *Practical Svelte*, https://doi.org/10.1007/978-1-4842-7374-6_11

Okay, back to reality. Although our site is minimal, it doesn't mean we can't add anything; there are a few ideas that come to mind. Here are a few to start us off:

- Adding media such as video – granted, it's not an animation in the true sense, but providing something has become an almost de facto standard!
- How about an image carousel? I've seen dozens of different sites use a carousel of some description, particularly those selling coffee.
- We've added add-to-cart buttons in our demo, but they lack any notification when clicked – how about adding something to tell the user that the chosen product is now in the cart?
- Remember that offer modal we set up on our home page, advertising the discount? We can refine it further by animating when it appears or is closed to provide a smoother transition.
- This last idea is perfect for mobile devices – what about adding a hamburger menu? It's excellent for holding menu items in a confined location which is what we have here – we can animate the opening and closing to provide a smooth effect for our customers.

I'm sure you can think of more instances where our site could benefit from some form of animation or transition – hopefully, this handful of examples will give you an idea of what is possible!

The actual proof, though, is in the pudding (to badly quote an English saying). We can only experience it when we add it to our site and see it in the flesh. With that in mind, let's start with a demo. Don't worry too much about how it all works; it's more to show how easy it is to add animation in Svelte.

Learning a Language

Okay, I thought this was a book on using Svelte, so why are we talking about learning a language, I hear you ask? Have no fear, my dear readers – I have not lost the plot! Let me explain.

While researching this book, I was toying with ideas around how I could illustrate Svelte's animation and transition effects before adding it into our front-end project. I had a few ideas come to mind and was quite happily working through them until I came across this: `https://svelte.dev/repl/b68344fe6d0b413494905b41c25a0a3f?version=3.29.0`.

Mamma mia, I yelled – this is perfect! And why? Well, it is a port/clone of an app that I happen to have been using for some time. That app? Duolingo.

Yes, for some time now, I've been using it to learn Dutch. Okay, yes, I know – it might seem crazy since I hail from the UK, but, hey, I've always loved speaking a different language, and I thought why not: Dutch isn't the easiest, but I enjoy a challenge!

For those of you who are not familiar with it, it's an excellent app for learning a new language – it allows you to set a certain amount of time each day to learn in simple, quick exercises. The basic principle is that you drag and drop words (in this case, Dutch) from a selection at the bottom into the correct order to match a phrase in your local language. It's perfect to illustrate how Svelte uses animation, transition, and easing effects, so without further ado, let's dive in and take a look at how in more detail.

DEMO – USING ANIMATE AND TRANSITION IN SVELTE

To set up our demo, follow these steps:

1. First, go ahead and browse to `www.svelte.dev/repl` – don't forget that the URL will redirect to show the version of Svelte in use!
2. We have a fair bit of code to add, so we'll start with the script block – go ahead and add in this code to `App.svelte` on the left, which takes care of defining some initial imports and the crossfade animation:

```
<script>
 import { quintOut } from 'svelte/easing';
 import { crossfade } from 'svelte/transition';
 import { flip } from 'svelte/animate';

  const [send, receive] = crossfade({
    fallback(node, params) {
    const style = getComputedStyle(node);
    const transform = style.transform === 'none' ? '' : style.
    transform;

    return {
      duration: 600,
      easing: quintOut,
      css: t => `
        transform: ${transform} scale(${t});
```

```
            opacity: ${t}
          `
      };
    }
  });
```

3. Next comes the group of words we will use – leave a line blank, and then add this immediately below:

```
  const words = [
    { selected: false, value: "Ik" },
    { selected: false, value: "graag" },
    { selected: false, value: "Svelte" },
    { selected: false, value: "gebruik" },
    { selected: false, value: "echt" },
    { selected: false, value: "is" },
    { selected: false, value: "het" },
    { selected: false, value: "gaaf" },
  ]
  let selected = []
</script>
```

4. With the script in place, we can now focus on the markup. The first part will take care of what we drag and drop into the final answer – go ahead and add this markup, leaving a line blank first:

```
<div class="words">
  <div class="destination">
    {#each selected as word (word.value)}
      <span
        animate:flip
        in:receive={{ key: word.value }}
        out:send={{ key: word.value }}
        class="word"
        on:click={() => {
          word.selected = false;
          selected = selected.filter(w => w.value !== word.value)
        }}>
        {word.value}
      </span>
```

```
    {/each}
  </div>
```

5. We still need to add the markup for the origin, that is, where the words are dragged from. For this, skip a line after the previous block, and then add in this code:

```
  <div class="origin">
    {#each words.filter(w => !w.selected) as word (word.value)}
      <span
        animate:flip
        in:receive={{ key: word.value }}
        out:send={{ key: word.value }}
        class="word"
        on:click={() => {
          word.selected = true;
          selected = [...selected, word];
        }}>{word.value}</span>
    {/each}
  </div>
</div>
```

6. We're almost done – we need to add in the last stage, which is styling! Fortunately, it isn't too substantial – skip a line after the code for the previous step, and then add in these rules:

```
<style>
  :global(body) { display: flex; flex-direction: column; flex: 0 0
   100%; margin: 0; padding: 3rem 1rem; background: #ffffff; align-
   items: center; justify-content: flex-start; color: #000000; }

  .words { display: flex; flex-direction: column; padding: 2rem;
   border: 1px solid #596265; border-radius: 1rem; width: 350px; max-
   width: 100%; }

  .destination { display: flex; flex-flow: row wrap; align-items:
   flex-start; margin: 0 0 4rem; height: 5.5rem; background:
   repeating-linear-gradient(to bottom, transparent 0, transparent
   2.625rem, #596265 2.625rem, #596265 2.6875rem); }
```

```
    .destination .word { margin: 0 0.125rem 0.25rem; }
    .origin { display: flex; flex-flow: row wrap; justify-content:
     center; align-items: flex-start; max-width: 275px; margin: 0 auto;
     row-gap: 5px; column-gap: 5px;}
    .word { background: #c0c0c0; border: 1px solid #596265; padding:
     0.5rem; border-radius: 0.5rem;cursor: pointer; font-weight: 700; }
</style>
```

Note – for space reasons, I've compressed the styles; they are displayed properly in the code download, so feel free to copy and paste from there.

---

7. We should see something akin to Figure 11-1 appear on the right if all is well. Here, I've already moved some of the words across into the destination.

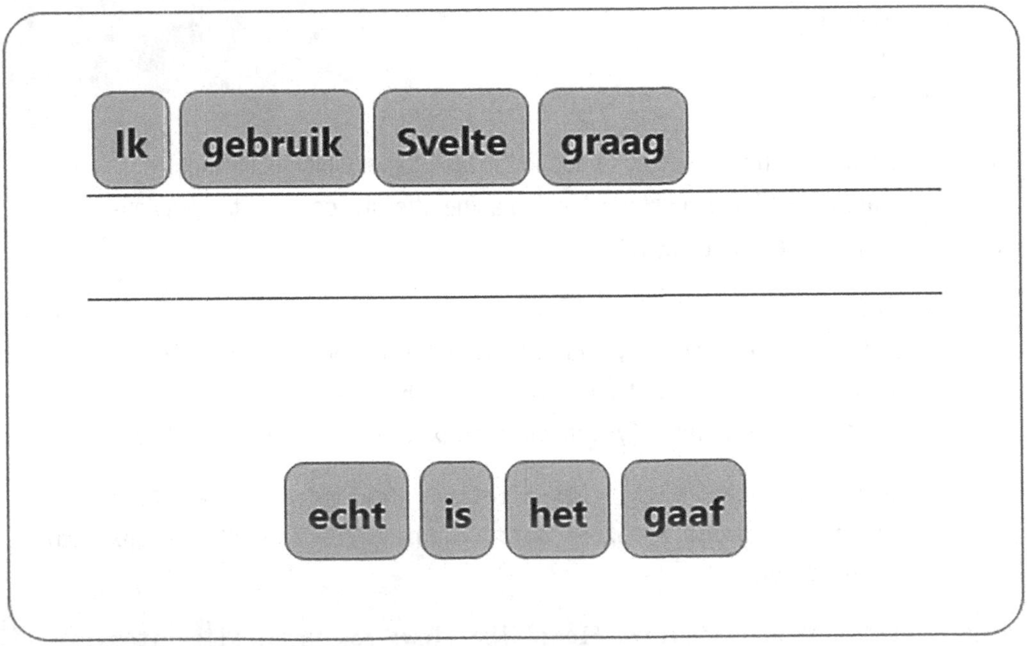

Figure 11-1. *Choosing words in the Duolingo clone*

Phew, that might seem like a lot of code, but in reality, much of it is standard markup and CSS styling! That said, it highlights a few key points we should explore in more detail ahead of updating our front-end demo. Let's dive in and review the code in more detail to see why Svelte is so powerful in animating content.

Oh, and that phrase? It's "I love Svelte, it is really cool!" in Dutch. ☺

Understanding How the Code Works

I've always loved learning a new language from an early age - over the years, I've spent time learning French, Latin, Spanish, and, more recently, Dutch. Dutch isn't the easiest to pronounce, so using the Duolingo app is a great help - when I came across an anonymous demo that replicated the effect, I just had to include it. This demo is a perfect way to show off all three critical examples of animating content in Svelte - it includes animation, transition, and easing effects at the same time.

We first import examples of each from within Svelte (so we avoid the need for third-party libraries) before creating a send/receive function. This function calculates which item is sent from the source list and where it lands in the destination list. It then works out and returns an object that contains all of the CSS style properties of each word being sent or received. We apply a `quintOut` easing effect and `transform`, `scale`, and `opacity` CSS properties as part of this function.

Next up comes the `words` object, into which we specify a mix of Dutch words that will act as the source for our demo. At the same time, we also create an empty `selected` array - this will be the target for each word we drag over when running the demo.

We then move onto the HTML markup - we start with the destination block, into which we drag words. For `#each` word we send over, we create a `span` that stores each word as it is pulled in or out (we can send back words if we get them in the wrong order). We apply a few properties such as `animate:flip`, a class of `word`, and set the `in:` and `out:` properties to determine the word order. In the next block of HTML markup, we do something similar, but this time for the origin block and for words that we select - this is our source for all of the words we can choose from in our demo.

The flip animation in Svelte is a little unique – it stands for "First, Last, Invert, Play" and is ideal for reordering animated elements, particularly if they move from one list to another.

Reviewing the Types of Animation Options

If you mentioned the word animation, you would be forgiven for thinking that it might require the services of a third-party library, right? Or oodles of CSS throughout our code... What if I said that wasn't necessary?

Not so with Svelte - the framework comes with great support for animations, transitions, and motion features, already built-in! Sure, we can use CSS animation with Svelte or just plain JavaScript, but that isn't always necessary - we can already achieve quite a bit with tools baked into the framework. To see what I mean, let's take a quick look at what Svelte has to offer when it comes to animations or transitions.

Broadly speaking, animations created using Svelte can fall into one of three categories, based on a central premise - is that element being added to or taken away from the DOM? Take animations, for example - in this instance, elements won't be static but are not transitioning out of the DOM. Here, we use the animate directive.

For elements that transition in and out of the DOM and behave differently, we use the transition directive. If we want to control the speed at which these happen or the effect of the transition, then we can use the motion directive or apply an easing effect to the animated element. We can see the differences between each in Table 11-1.

Table 11-1. *Different types of animation supported by Svelte*

Type of animation	Purpose
Animations	Add the illusion of motion to elements that are not transitioning in or out of the DOM
Transitions	Works the same as animations but used for elements that are added to or removed from the DOM
Motion	Two effects: `tween`, used to control the speed and appearance of the animation (using easing, etc.); `spring` does a similar effect but is suited more for constantly changing elements, such as playing online games or using an online drawing app

I use the term "animated element" to describe elements animated with Svelte and where we apply some form of effect to that element.

Okay, let's crack on. I want to cover one more animation effect, which is easing. Strictly speaking, it's not an animation by itself, but more of a way to control the effect of animations or transitions. We can use easings to create some funky effects with a bit of math – I will come back to that shortly, but for now, let's look at how we might apply common easing effects to a Svelte animation or transition.

Applying Easing Effects

Take a look back at the code in the *Using animate and transition in Svelte* demo near the start of this chapter – notice how in addition to using animate and transition, we also included an `easing` attribute?

As with any other library or framework that supports animation, we use easings to control the speed of animation to make it feel more natural. Real objects don't all move at a consistent rate and, likewise, won't stop or start in the same way – we can use easings to replicate the same effect in our code.

We use JavaScript or CSS to create easing effects. However, it's worth noting that if you want to create more complex effects such as Bezier curves, then you will need to use CSS for this – Svelte doesn't yet support creating them natively, and you will get better performance using CSS!

The best way to see how this all works is to dive into some code – over the following few pages, we will create two demos using Svelte. The first will cover how we can add custom easings using JavaScript, while the second will apply easings using CSS.

Creating Custom Easing Effects in JavaScript

For this demo, we will use a copy of the code from the deferred transitions demo – Svelte already has good support built-in for easings, but we will add our own using the easings provided in a Gist from Gaetan Renaudeau at `https://gist.github.com/gre/1650294`.

They have been around for some time but still work perfectly fine for our needs – creating a custom easing can be a complex matter sometimes, so anything we can do to keep things simple will be better for all!

CUSTOM EASING USING JAVASCRIPT

To add a custom easing, follow these steps:

1. From the code download that accompanies this book, extract a copy of the code for the deferred transitions demo.

Alternatively, you can copy the code from the same tab in the original demo at `https://svelte.dev/tutorial/deferred-transitions`.

---

2. Go ahead and browse to `www.svelte.dev/repl`, to create a new REPL; paste the code into the `App.svelte` tab on the left.
3. The first change to make is to remove the line starting with import { `quintOut }...` from just below the opening `<script>` tag.
4. Leave a line blank after the (now) remaining import, and then add this function:

```
function quartOut(t) {
  return Math.pow(t - 1.0, 3.0) * (1.0 - t) - 2.0;
}
```

5. Next, scroll down to the easing parameter; remove the word `quintOut`, and replace it with `quartOut`:

```
easing: quartOut,
```

6. After a few moments, we will see our demo refresh – try clicking one of the items in the to-do column on the left. If all is well, you should see a similar effect shown in Figure 11-2.

Figure 11-2. Using a custom animation

That was a simple change, but one that opens up some real opportunities for us! Leaving aside the thought of what is possible for a moment, our demo highlighted a couple of important points we should be aware of, so let's take a moment to review the code in more detail.

Exploring What Happened

At first glance, you would be forgiven for thinking that there seems to be a lot going on in this demo – our change is only a small one and barely touches the surface of what is going on!

So – to answer that question – what did we change in our demo? It all hangs around the crossfade function. We first import the `crossfade` functions from the `easing` and `transition` packages within Svelte. Next, we override the crossfade function – it is used to create a pair of transitions called send and receive. If we send one, Svelte looks for the corresponding received element and applies the transition and easing effects, using the `css:` and `easing:` parameters.

At this point, we make our change – instead of using the original `quintOut` easing, we have created one called `quartOut`, which I've taken from Gaetan's Gist. At this point, we replace the original easing name with the new `quartOut`, and the change is complete.

Okay, we've seen how to create a custom easing effect in JavaScript: what about using standard CSS? Fortunately, it's much easier to achieve – it doesn't require as much code, either! We could combine the likes of `animate:` and `transition:` CSS styles together, but I'm going to take a different approach – using Bezier curves and creating a custom keyframe animation. Intrigued? Let's dive in and explore what is involved in creating our custom easing effect using CSS.

If you would like to see the standard easings that come with Svelte, take a look at `https://svelte.dev/docs#svelte_easing`. All of the examples are available to see in action, at a REPL, at `https://svelte.dev/repl/858abbb971dc663cb9fd03f693d34e43?version=3.1.0`.

Using Styles to Create Custom Easing Effects

We explored using Svelte's in-built animation feature in the previous demo to create a custom easing effect using JavaScript. Technically, it's a great way to introduce something complex into our code while still maintaining control.

The trouble is using JavaScript can be overkill in some situations - not only is it more resource hungry, but there may be occasions where we can use a CSS-based version instead. CSS will be more performant and, at the same time, give us a cleaner solution. Fortunately, Svelte is happy to work with both - to see how I've created a simple demo that uses the Animista app (at `www.animista.net/`) to create a custom CSS easing effect. Let's take a look.

CUSTOM EASING USING CSS

To apply a CSS-based easing effect to a Svelte element, follow these steps:

1. First, go ahead and browse to `www.animista.net/` – once there, click the Scale-Up circle, and then choose scale-up-top.
2. On the right, you will see three white circles – the far right one has this symbol: {.}. Click it to get the CSS code for our demo, and take a copy for safekeeping.
3. Next, head over to `www.svelte.dev/repl` – don't forget the usual URL change to reflect the version of Svelte in use!
4. Go ahead and add an opening <script> tag at the top of the `App.svelte` tab on the left. Copy and paste in the CSS from the aminista.net website below this tag.
5. Immediately below the code from step 4, go ahead and add in two more rules:

```
.cube{ background-color: gainsboro; color: black;
font-weight: bold; width: 100px; height: 100px; display: flex;
justify-content: center; align-items:center; margin-top: 10px; }

.scale-up-top { animation: scale-up-top 2.4s cubic-bezier(0.390,
0.575, 0.565, 1.000) both; }
</style>
```

6. We can now add in our markup – for this, miss a line, and then add in this code:

```
<h2>
  Transform a box using custom CSS
</h2>
<div style="height:225px">
  <div class="scale-up-top cube">
    CSS
  </div>
</div>
```

7. After a few moments, we should see a gray box transition in on the right, as shown in Figure 11-3, although you will have to believe me when it comes to displaying the fade in effect!

Figure 11-3. *A partial image of our box fading in, using CSS*

And voilà! We have a working animation that uses CSS instead of JavaScript!

It's a perfect illustration of how we can achieve similar effects using standard CSS and that it is not always necessary to resort to using JavaScript. Sure, we won't get the same level of control over when it will fire, but we would still need to add something for that, irrespective of whether we use pure JavaScript or a mix of both. The important thing here is that Svelte can work with either, and we should consider what we use in our projects.

Although our demo doesn't use anything other than standard CSS or HTML markup, it does open up some possibilities - let's pause for a moment and explore what we can do if we are using CSS instead of JavaScript for our easings.

Taking It Further

While researching this book, I came across an intriguing website called Animista - it's available at `www.animista.net`. Why is this interesting, I hear you ask?

Well, it has something to do with the effects we can generate - I talked earlier about using cubic-bezier-based effects, which are cleaner to use than the JavaScript examples from earlier in this chapter. The trouble is they are just numbers, so it's not easy to work out what you need to use to create your desired effect. Enter Animista - it's one of several sites that takes a GUI-based approach; we can export from it both the appropriate `@keyframe` effects and the native CSS version of `cubic-bezier` code to create the overall effect.

The critical thing to note is that Svelte does not support using cubic-bezier natively (unlike the other available effects). We could use a library such as the one available at `https://github.com/gre/bezier-easing`, but this adds a lot of extra code for each easing effect! A far better option is to use the CSS equivalent as we have done, or we could have used a site such as `www.cubic-bezier.com` to achieve a similar effect.

To see the original scale-up-top effect from the Animista site that I've used here, take a look at `https://animista.net/play/basic/scale-up/scale-up-top`.

It's worth noting, though, that if for some reason we had to use CSS and JavaScript versions of the same effect, then I would recommend reconsidering the approach. Although they may have the same name, they will **not** work in the same way: this has something to do with how CSS and Svelte render easing effects. I would advise using different effects; if you use one in CSS, then don't use an equivalent in JavaScript or vice versa, as it will result in odd effects on your site.

To see what I mean, take a look at this REPL: `https://svelte.dev/repl/4b84a1a947204377b4c59e514e4e706a?version=3.24.1`.

Using Svelte Libraries

Okay, so far, we've been through some examples of how to animate content or elements in Svelte, along with applying easing effects to add that extra special touch to each effect.

I'll bet you're probably thinking, surely we could just use an animation library, right, to do most of the heavy lifting for us? Sure, we can – Svelte works fine with the likes of Anime.js, no problem.

But I'm going to shock you: there is little need for extra animation libraries when using Svelte! Svelte's animation support is excellent – so good that there is no need to add additional libraries. However, if you want to use them, then that's not a problem – there are two things to bear in mind, though:

- If we need to run scripts from a library such as GSAP (`https://greensock.com/gsap/`), then we might have to use `onMount()` – it's likely that the DOM won't have been created in time, so `onMount()` acts to defer loading until this has happened.
- When using Svelte, it's good practice not to use global CSS selectors, as Svelte will apply them to all instances of a component, not just one! It's better to reference the DOM element directly, using the `bind:this` attribute (which we will use in the Notification demo later in this chapter).

With these two points in mind, here are a few examples of libraries and animation excerpts to help get you started if you want to use a third-party animation library with Svelte:

- An example of how to create custom transitions with Anime.js: `https://dev.to/manyeya/custom-transitions-and-staggered-transitions-in-svelte-with-animejs-plm`.
- Svelte-Animation-Store – a plugin that uses Svelte's store functionality to control animation: `https://github.com/joshnuss/svelte-animation-store`.
- We can use GSAP with Svelte, but there are some catches – this StackOverflow article gives a few tips on how to use both together:

https://stackoverflow.com/questions/62780343/using-gsap-with-svelte.

- If you want to animate elements in Svelte while scrolling the page, then this plugin is for you - Svelte Animation On Scroll (SAoS), available from https://shiryel.github.io/saos/.
- When using Svelte, creating transitions will likely be done using JavaScript - this plugin allows you to build them using CSS instead: https://github.com/gawlk/svelte-class-transition.

As an aside, if you want to understand better how transitions work, then having an appreciation of the Svelte component life cycle will stand you in good stead – Christian Heine has an interesting article on this https://betterprogramming.pub/the-component-lifecycle-in-svelte-1784ecab5862, which covers lots of different aspects, including animations and transitions.

Just a few ideas - I'm sure you will find more! Okay, let's crack on. It's time we put something of what we've covered to good use and start to apply some animation effects to our front-end store demo. We can do this in a few ways, so let's dive in and look at how in more detail.

Applying Animation to Our Project

So far, we've explored examples of how we might add animation to a Svelte site: it's time to put some of this into practice and add some animation to our front-end demo.

There are various ways we can do this - there isn't necessarily a right or wrong answer as to how, but it will depend on our requirements. For example, there is no point in adding complex JavaScript transitions if we can achieve the same (or an acceptable similar) effect using CSS.

Over the following few pages, I've selected some examples of where we can benefit from adding animation; we'll start with updating the discount modal.

Adding Animation to the Banner

Remember the banner offering a 10% discount at the start? It comes in immediately at the beginning and then suddenly disappears when we click the close button. It's not very graceful - we can do better!

By itself, it's not possible within the existing component, as we can only add animations to a DOM element, not a component. Fortunately, there is a way to get around this - adding the effect is simple, but it will require some preparatory legwork beforehand. Let's take a look at what is involved in more detail.

DEMO 1: BANNER ANIMATION

To update the banner, follow these steps:

1. First, go ahead and extract a copy of `Modal.svelte` from the code download that accompanies this book – drop the file into the `\src\components` folder.

2. Next, open that file in your text editor, and then update the import at the top of `Home.svelte` with this code:

   ```
   import Modal from "../components/Modal.svelte";
   ```

3. We can now use the modal in our code – first, look for this line:

   ```
   <div class="modal-background" on:click={close}></div>
   ```

4. Add in `transition:fade`, just after the `on:click` event handler, like so:

   ```
   <div class="modal-background" on:click={close} transition:fade></div>
   ```

5. In the next line down, repeat the same step, but this time, add it just before the closing > at the end:

   ```
   ..="true" bind:this={modal} transition:fade>
   ```

6. Save the file. Next, switch to a Node.js terminal session, and then make sure your working folder is pointing to the project area.

7. At the prompt, enter `npm run dev`, and then press Enter.

8. If all is well, we should see our site appear when browsing to `https://localhost:5000`; try clicking the close button, and you should see both the modal and background fade out!

Hopefully, by now, you will have seen that the modal dialog box and background fade out with a little more grace this time – that is an improvement! It does raise an important question, though, but not around code: it's around requirements. To see why, let's take a moment to review the code changes we've made in more detail.

Breaking Apart the Code Changes

When I first started researching this book, I came across several modal components – I tried a few, as you do, and found some worked well, while others less so. Then I came across modal overlay, available from `www.npmjs.com/package/modal-overlay`. At first glance, I thought this is perfect – it's simple, doesn't require lots of configuring, and should be easy enough to add in, right?

That was the easy part. It turns out that this modal doesn't have a Git site, so there is no detail on whether it can support animations. What do I do? As it so happens, this modal is just a copy of the example from the main Svelte website but turned into an NPM package.

With the original code available from the Svelte website, we can improve on what we have – in this exercise, we dropped in a copy of the `Modal.svelte` file from the code download and then updated the import in `Home.svelte` to point to this file. All that we needed to do was add in `transition:fade` in two places – this is required to fade out both the modal background and dialog box. Otherwise, we will get some odd effects to appear!

Okay, let's move on. Next up, we're going to make a change to the cart buttons in both `Products.svelte` and `Product.svelte`. We can't have customers add products and not be told when we add them, can we? It's an excellent opportunity to add a simple notification element to tell them and a suitable animation to show and hide it on the web page.

Updating the Cart Action

When we've played with our front-end site, have you noticed anything missing, mainly when adding products to the basket?

The sharp-eyed among you should have noticed that we can add, but how do we tell the customer if the addition has been successful? Yes, we need to display some form of message. Otherwise, our customers will be none the wiser!

There are a few ways we could do this - one example is to use a callback in the button to change the state and appearance; we might choose instead to display a message on the screen for a short period. I've elected to do the latter; we could do this next to the button, but I came across an exciting package called Svelte-Notifications while researching for this book.

This plugin is available from `https://github.com/beyonk-adventures/svelte-notifications` and allows us to create a notification message on-screen, which will disappear on completion of a set timeout period. We could potentially use it for other messages, but let's begin setting it up for our add-to-cart buttons.

DEMO 2: UPDATING ADD-TO-CART ACTIONS

To rectify the omission of a notification on the add-to-cart buttons, follow these steps:

1. First, we need to install the Svelte-Notifications package – to do this, crack open a Node.js terminal, and then change the working folder to our project area.

2. At the prompt, enter `npm i -D @beyonk/svelte-notifications` and press Enter.

3. Once complete, switch to your text editor, then open `Products.svelte`, and add this import immediately below the last import statement:

```
import { NotificationDisplay, notifier } from '@beyonk/svelte-notifications';
```

4. Next, scroll down to the end of the addToCart function, and insert this line of code, as indicated:

```
    }
    $cart = [...$cart, product]
    notifier.danger('Product added!', 7000)
  }
</script>
```

5. We need to add one more change, which is to drop in this call to the `NotificationDisplay` component, immediately above the call to `CTAButton`:

```
<NotificationDisplay bind:this={n} />
<CTAButton on:click={() => addToCart(product)}>
```

6. Go ahead and save the file, and then close it. We need to make similar changes to `Product.svelte`, so go ahead and open that file in your editor.

7. As before, we need to add the import statement:

```
import { Link } from "svelte-routing";
import { NotificationDisplay, notifier } from '@beyonk/svelte-notifications';
```

8. Next, add in the call to the Notification component, as we did back in step 4:

```
  $cart = [...$cart, product]
  notifier.danger('Product added!', 7000)
}
```

9. We also need to call the component, so add in this line (highlighted):

```
<NotificationDisplay bind:this={n} />
<Button on:click={() => addToCart(product)}>
  Add to cart
</Button>
```

10. Save the changes, and then switch to a Node.js terminal session.

11. Make sure the working folder is set to our project area, and then at the prompt, enter `npm run dev` and hit Enter.

12. Try browsing to `http://localhost:5000/products` and then clicking Add to cart against a product; if all is well, we should see a notification appear top right, as indicated in Figure 11-4.

***Figure 11-4.** A notification to confirm we have added a product to the basket*

There, that's better! We can at least tell our customers that they can be assured it will be added to the basket if they add a product. It's a simple addition, but the key to maintaining a good experience for our customers. We've not added any directly in our code, but the component itself uses some great examples of animation; let's spend a moment or two to review the code in more detail to see how it uses Svelte animations.

Understanding the Changes Made

Notifying customers of an action that has taken place is essential to maintain a good customer experience. After all, customers will lose faith if they can't tell if something has happened!

In this last demo, we took the opportunity to improve the existing add-to-cart buttons by adding a notification once we add a product to the basket. To do this, we first installed the `Svelte-Notifications` plugin before adding an import for this plugin to the `Products.svelte` page. Next up, we then added a reference to trigger the notifier event, along with relevant text and a timeout period of 7000 (or 7 seconds). We then bound it to the `CTAButton` component using `NotificationDisplay`.

We then repeated the same exercise, but in the `Product.svelte` page – once added, we ran up the Svelte dev server to ensure the notification triggered as soon as we click the add-to-cart buttons on each page.

Excellent – let's crack on. We'll stay with the animation theme, but this time crank it up to something a little more obvious! How many sites have you visited where you see some form of animated banner or carousel appear?

Some developers claim it's not so good for things such as SEO, but I'm not so sure – it's perfect for adding a little visual interest and providing a link directly to a product or content. Leaving aside any thoughts on topics such as SEO for now, let's look at how we might add such a component to our site in more detail.

Iterating Through Pictures

In our next demo, we're going to step things up a little and add something I am sure you will have seen on dozens of websites: a carousel! Over the years, I've seen thousands of them in various guises, although they do get something of a mixed press. I'm not entirely sure why, as I think it's a great way to maintain a dynamic, eye-catching element to a page and provide a little visual interest.

Whatever your thoughts on them, it's a valuable tool to add - there is one question, though: which one do we use? Deciding which to use takes a little research, as many provide features that you might not need or be overkill for your site. It's worth researching to see what is available: for our next exercise, I will use one created by Jio Scon, available from `https://github.com/jioscon/svelte-image-carousel-slider`.

Okay, it may not be as feature laden as others, but that doesn't matter: it's more about how we animate that is important here! With that in mind, let's dive in and take a look at what's needed to set up our carousel in more detail.

DEMO 3: IMAGE CAROUSEL

For this exercise, you will need five images of a suitable size – I've used 640px by 427px to get a decent balance between displaying content and not taking over the whole home page.

If you don't have any images, then try a site such as Pexels.com (`www.pexels.com`) – their small image size happens to match the dimensions I've used! You need to use the horizontal ones, though, as vertical images won't work so well on our site.

Once you have these, then follow these steps:

1. First, go ahead and download a copy of `Carousel.svelte` from the code download that comes with this book – save it into the `\src\components` folder.
2. Next, we need to import this into the home page – for this, open `Home.svelte`, then scroll down to this block, and comment out all three lines:

```
<div id="banner">
  <img src="images/banner.jpg" alt="banner" />
</div>
```

3. Add in this line immediately below:

```
<Carousel />
```

4. Next, scroll to the `.welcome` class rule in the style block, and add in this extra property:

```
margin-bottom: 20px;
```

5. Save the filc and close it. Nexl, swltch to `Modal.svelte` – we need to make a change to the `.modal` class specified in the style block. Scroll down to that rule, and then add this attribute at the end:

```
  z-index: 10;
}
```

6. Go ahead and save all files, and then close them – once done, revert to a Node.js session, and then make sure the working folder is our project area.

7. At the prompt, enter npm run dev, and then switch to a browser – if we browse to `http://localhost:5000`, we should see a carousel appear once we clear the modal dialog (Figure 11-5).

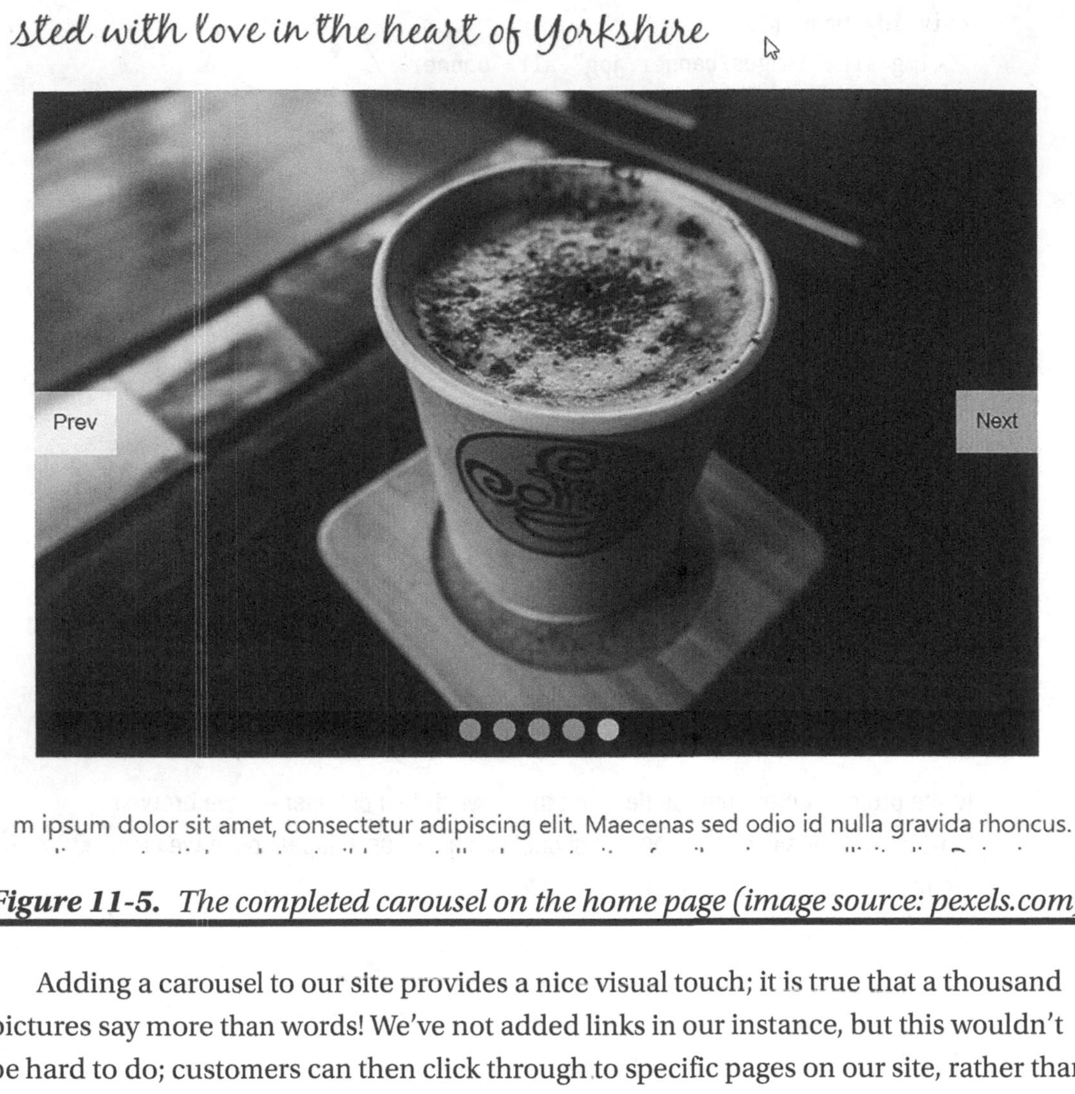

sted with love in the heart of Yorkshire
Prev
Next
m ipsum dolor sit amet, consectetur adipiscing elit. Maecenas sed odio id nulla gravida rhoncus.

***Figure 11-5.** The completed carousel on the home page (image source: pexels.com)*

Adding a carousel to our site provides a nice visual touch; it is true that a thousand pictures say more than words! We've not added links in our instance, but this wouldn't be hard to do; customers can then click through to specific pages on our site, rather than navigate manually. This particular carousel shows off some useful features, including one crucial point, so let's take a moment to review the code in more detail.

Understanding What Happened

Adding visual interest to any site is essential in today's Internet – long gone are the days of black text on gray backgrounds, reminiscent of late 1990s' web styling! (Anyone remembers that? We've come a long way since.)

One way to add in that visual content is through the use of a carousel – in the last exercise we've just completed, we used the Image Carousel Slider plugin by Jio Scon to add content on our home page. We began by installing the plugin using the typical `npm install` command before adding an import for the plugin and commenting out the original static banner image in `Home.svelte`.

We then added a call to the plugin before switching to `Modal.svelte` to tweak the `z-index` property for the modal - the latter was getting in the way of our carousel and producing some interesting effects! Once saved, we could then run up our demo and test it to ensure it animates the content as expected on our home page.

For another example of a similar component for Svelte, but with a few more features, try Svelte Carousel, available from `https://vadimkorr.github.io/svelte-carousel/`.

Summary

Phew, that has certainly been something of an animated adventure if you pardon the (terrible) pun!

Animating content in Svelte can be something of a minefield, depending on how you apply it – keep in mind that it should supplement our code and not become a dependency. That said, we've covered a lot of content over this chapter, so let's take a moment to review what we have learned.

We kicked off with a quick audit of our front-end site to see what animations we could add and maintain a refined look to the content. We then ran a demo to explore some of the types of animation we might use before going into more detail on the different types available within Svelte.

Next up, we then explored how to add in easing effects before looking at creating ones in both CSS and JavaScript. At the same time, we learned that using the same effect created in both CSS and JavaScript isn't ideal, as there are differences in how we handle them in Svelte. We then took a look at some example third-party libraries; we understood that while Svelte offers excellent support for animation and that help isn't often needed, we can still use these libraries if required.

We then rounded out the chapter by adding some effects to our front-end demo – we started by updating the discount banner before moving onto adding a notification on the add-to-basket buttons and adding in a carousel effect on the home page.

Okay, we are almost at the end of our project, but I have one more topic to cover. We've created all of our code from the ground up, albeit with some help from third-party plugins. Creating something from the ground up is perfectly acceptable, but a lot of work! What if we could have some of this already done for us? Stay with me, and I will reveal all in the final chapter.

CHAPTER 12

Adapting for Sapper

We've almost reached the end of the book, but we can't finish without touching on one essential part of using Svelte – some of the third-party libraries based on the framework. I'm thinking particularly of Sapper; it's a great framework built on Svelte and wraps many essential functions into one friendly, easy-to-install site generator tool.

Throughout this chapter, we will look at how we can use it to create a new site; we'll work through some of the differences and see how it can assist with some of the tasks we've had to complete manually. At the same time, we'll explore its upcoming replacement, SvelteKit. But first, I must start with a confession.

Introducing... Sapper?

This chapter was meant to be about Sapper, the app framework for generating Svelte sites. Sapper is a valuable tool in its own right, but as can happen, plans change: it doesn't reflect what we expect to see in today's world. There are a couple of shortcomings with the tool:

- The codebase dates from 2017 and has become a little unkempt – it was built for an age where server technology was a consideration, and things have changed dramatically since.
- The codebase differs from standard Svelte, so making it more complex and less predictable when writing code.
- There is a rising trend toward unbundling code and serving it as modules instead; it means the startup process is almost immediate, irrespective of size.

So, on that basis, sorry to disappoint if you were expecting to see Sapper; it makes much better sense to look forward to what is coming, in the form of Sapper's replacement, SvelteKit! With that in mind, the chapter will be about converting to use

A. Libby, *Practical Svelte*, https://doi.org/10.1007/978-1-4842-7374-6_12

SvelteKit; this is a more straightforward process as much of the code can be lifted and shifted as is, with only minor changes needed.

Now that we have that out of the way, let's crack on. Much of this chapter will be about converting our existing front-end site to use SvelteKit. We'll go through each part of the site to point out the changes we need to make; we'll finish with a quick look at how we can take things forward once the primary site is in place. We'll start first with a short exercise to learn how to create an initial SvelteKit site.

Migrating Our Project – Setting Expectations

Before we get started on coding, though, there is a little housekeeping admin we need to cover first - yes, I know, it's not everyone's favorite thing, but it's a necessary evil! Nevertheless, there are a few things we should be aware of for this particular chapter:

- SvelteKit is **beta** software, so do expect things won't work entirely or that we might come across bugs. That said, the framework is still pretty stable - while you may want to hold off pushing content into production for the moment (at least until it hits version 1.0), it's still worth playing with the framework, ready for when you can deploy your finished site.
- Most of the code you need for this chapter already exists in the `sveltebook` demo we created in previous chapters - I would recommend taking a copy of that site and using it as your source for this chapter.
- I will assume you are working on Windows, that the name of our project folder is `sveltekit`, and that it's located at the root of C: drive. Any time you see the words "project area," then assume it is this folder. I will refer to the original site we created using Svelte, so you may want to read through the steps first to ensure you know which folder is which!
- If you use macOS, Linux, or prefer to use a different folder or drive, please adapt accordingly.

- As far as tools are concerned, we don't need anything new - as long as you still have Internet access and your text editor, then this will be fine.
- For space reasons, we'll focus on the key changes to get the replacement SvelteKit site working; I will run through what's left to do as the next steps toward the end of the chapter.

Okay, with the housekeeping done, we can now really get started! Throughout this chapter, I will take you through a multipart demo that covers the steps required to get our SvelteKit replacement site up and running. Let's begin with creating the initial site.

Setting Up the Initial Site

The first step in our conversion project is to create an initial site - although SvelteKit was built for Svelte, there are a few changes that we need to make. It's much easier to do these from the ground up than to convert an existing site! With that in mind, let's start with our first exercise, creating a SvelteKit site.

ADAPTING OUR SITE – PART 1: CREATING THE BASE

To set up an initial SvelteKit site, follow these steps:

1. We first need to make sure we have Node 14.17.x or above – for this, fire up a Node.js terminal session, and then at the prompt, enter `node -v` and press Enter.
2. If the response back says a number **lower** than 14.17.x, you will need to update Node.js for your platform. The easiest way is to head over to `www.nodejs.org`, and then download and install the executable or package for your platform. If you have Node 14.17 or above, then please skip to step 3.
3. Assuming you have Node 14.17.x or above installed, change the working folder to be C:
4. At the prompt, enter this command and press Enter:

```
npm init svelte@next sveltekit
```

5. You will be prompted for several bits of information during the initial install – choose the highlighted options as indicated:

```
Which Svelte app template? » Skeleton project
Use TypeScript? ... No
Add ESLint for code linting? ... Yes
Add Prettier for code formatting? ... Yes
```

I've chosen not to use Typescript as a matter of preference; please feel free to select Yes for that option if you prefer, but please note that the code examples in this book are written for standard JavaScript, not Typescript.

---

6. Once completed, change the working folder to our project area, and enter this command at the prompt:

```
npm install
```

7. Node will install all of the dependencies required; when prompted, please enter `npm run dev` and press Enter at the prompt.

8. Next, go ahead and browse to `http://localhost:3000` – if all is well, we should see an initial site displayed, as shown in Figure 12-1.

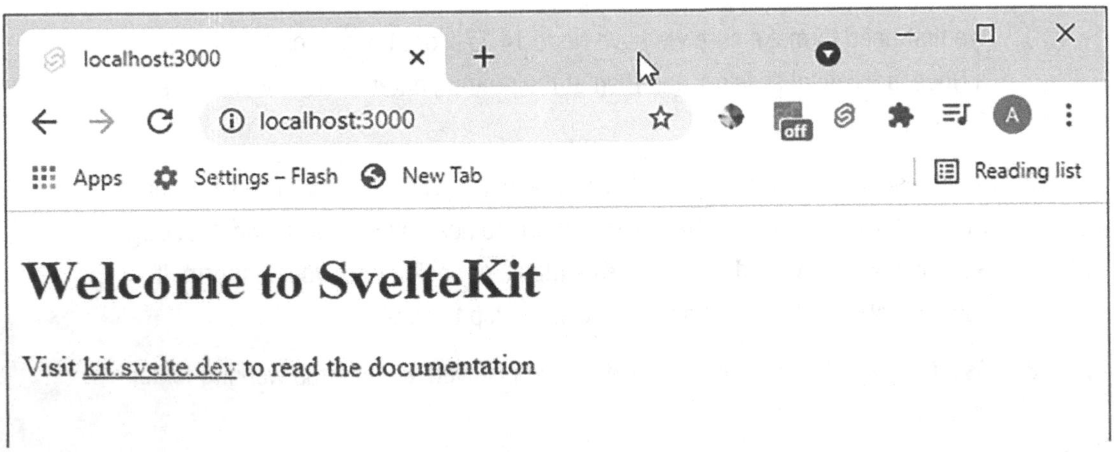

***Figure 12-1.** The initial SvelteKit site*

Excellent - we have our initial SvelteKit site in place! It might require a little more work than a standard Svelte site, but bear in mind that it includes a few more features not present in a Svelte application. Let's take a moment to review the steps in more detail before we move on to exploring our new site's file and folder structure.

Exploring the Code in Detail

Setting up a SvelteKit site is very easy - hopefully, you will have noticed that the process is similar to that we used for a standard Svelte site. Nevertheless, we need to discuss a couple of essential points - let's take a closer look at the code we used in this demo.

The first important point is the version of Node.js we used - this is where you may come unstuck if you don't have the correct version installed! The official documentation says we should use Node.js version 12 or above, but I've seen anecdotal evidence that says even this version doesn't work correctly! At the time of writing, I used version 14.17.3, which works fine; as long as you use this or newer, you should be OK.

If you try to use version 12, you will likely get this error: `SyntaxError: Cannot use import statement outside a module`. SvelteKit uses modules everywhere, which Node 12 supports, but it seems those in SvelteKit don't work unless we use Node 14 or above.

We then ran the standard command to install a new SvelteKit site - as this bundles a few packages, it prompted us for a few details. The responses we've used are a matter of preference; you may prefer to use different ones for your projects.

The final step for this demo was to run the `npm install` command - this installs all of the required dependencies for our project. We then started the SvelteKit development server and browsed to our initial site to verify all is working as expected in the browser.

Okay, let's move on. Now that we have a base site in place, it's worth taking a moment to review the file and folder structure for a typical SvelteKit site. If we were to compare it against a standard Svelte site, we would see some similarities; there are some differences though that we should be aware of, so let's dive in and take a closer look.

Understanding the Structure of a SvelteKit Site

Cast your mind back to when we created our initial Svelte site - yes, all the way back to Chapter 1, if you can remember that far back! Remember what the initial folder structure looked like once we had created the foundation site for our project?

The folder structure for SvelteKit is very similar - you will have the requisite package files, plus the `\src` folder as before. However, there are a few changes compared to a standard Svelte site, both in file names and structure - we can see them listed in Table 12-1.

***Table 12-1.** A list of critical files and folders in a SvelteKit site, with their purpose*

File or folder name	Purpose
`node_modules`	This folder is standard for any Node-based website

`src`	The main source folder – inside this, you will see (by default):
	`app.html`
	`global.d.ts`
	In this folder, we will add any content that we need to compile during the build process, such as layouts, pages, and components

`static`	Reserved for any content, media, or artifacts that we do **not** need to compile, such as style sheets, fonts, and images
`.eslintrc.cjs`	Used to configure ESLinting, which can be enabled if desired when creating a SvelteKit site
`.gitignore`	A standard file for holding exclusions that we should not merge into a Git repository

`.npmrc`
`.prettierignore`
`.prettierrc`
	Various configuration files (not specific to SvelteKit) for controlling properties

`jsconfig.json`	Configuration properties for compiling SvelteKit sites

(continued)

Table 12-1. (*continued*)

File or folder name	Purpose
package-lock.json package.json README.md	Standard files for a Node.js/Git website
svelte.config.js	A configuration file for controlling whether Google's FLoC targeted advertising technology is enabled. It is disabled by default, as it is deemed harmful by the Electronic Frontier Foundation. Most browsers (except Google) do not implement the technology

It is helpful to understand the file structure theory, but there is no substitute for getting stuck into code! The best way to get familiar with the structure is to start using the site; with that in mind, let's update the layout template that comes with each SvelteKit site.

Updating the Layout

Right, where do we start?

Well, things will be a little different for us - whereas before we were using `App.svelte` as a makeshift template, SvelteKit introduces the concept of templates proper; we can use this to build up the header, footer, and general layout of the page. We can use the `<slot />` element - this tells Svelte to add any content in pages or components into this bucket to display the compiled page on the screen.

The vital thing to note, though, is that layout filenames in SvelteKit start with a double underscore - it makes a private file, so it's not visible to end users but can still be used to create the finished pages. Let's take a look at how to set up the layout file in more detail.

ADAPTING OUR SITE – PART 2: ADDING THE LAYOUT TEMPLATE

To update the layout for our new site, follow these steps:

1. First, go ahead and extract a copy of `__layout.js` from the code download that accompanies this book – save it to `\src\routes` in our new project folder.
2. Next, copy across the `Header.svelte` and `Footer.svelte` files from the `\src\components` folder in our original project folder, and drop them into a new `\components` folder under `\src` in the new project area.
3. We also need to bring across a copy of `stores.js` and `stock.json` from the `\src` folder of our original project – save these to the `\src` folder in our new project area.
4. We need to bring two more folders – copy the `fonts` and `images` folder from within the `\public` folder in our old site to the `\static` folder in the new project area.
5. Switch to your text editor, and then crack open a copy of the `Header.svelte` file – we are going to comment out the context part for now. It's not essential to getting the site operational; we can always come back to it. Comment out lines 18–20, then 65–67, and 69 – it will show as if we are a Guest login, but that's OK for now!
6. Next, revert to a Node.js terminal session, and then make sure the working folder points to our new project area.
7. At the prompt, enter `npm install svelte-inline-svg` to install the Svelte-Inline-SVG plugin; this will reinstate support for SVGs, similar to what we did earlier in the book.
8. We also need to install `@paypal/paypal-js` for our checkout – we will use this later in this chapter. For this, enter `npm install @paypal/paypal-js` at the prompt, and then press Enter.
9. We now have the basis for our layout template – we won't be able to run it up just yet, as there will be one more component to source first! This step we will do in the next exercise when we add pages to our site.
10. At this point, save and close all open files, but you can leave the text editor open for now.

Okay, we've made a good start. We have a base layout in place, with what will be the layout for our new site. Most of what we achieved in this last exercise should be pretty self-explanatory, but let's take a moment to review the changes in more detail before moving onto the next exercise.

Understanding the Changes Made

One of the great things about SvelteKit is that building a site is similar to the original process we used earlier – there are a few things though that change, which will help make it easier for us. One of these is the introduction of a new layout template process.

We started by extracting a copy of `__layout.js`, which will act as the template for our site. Remember how we used the `App.svelte` file to build up a kind of template? The `__layout.js` is a private (denoted by the __ in the filename) file that makes this a more formal option; rather than dumping code at the very top (so to speak), we can create a layout using a file designed for this purpose. It has the added benefit of handling routing automatically – we no longer need to rely on the svelte-routing plugin we used earlier in the book!

We then copied across the original Header and Footer components from the old site; these we stored in a new components folder under `\src` in the new site. At the same time, we also brought over copies of the fonts and images library; given the existing location references for these folders were already good, we didn't have to make any changes.

Next up, we then had to edit out references to the Notification component in the layout file – this was triggering errors. The component isn't essential to getting the primary site working; as an MVP, we can focus on the core elements and come back to this later.

We then moved onto installing both Paypal and the Svelte-Inline-SVG plugins; this is something we did earlier in the book for our original site, so it's just a matter of replicating the same process for the new version.

Okay, with our new layout template in place, it's time to move on and start to add in the page content. We will do this in three parts – we'll cover adding the product gallery and product page shortly, but let's start with adding the other content pages to our new site.

Adding Pages

Any ecommerce site on the Internet will need some form of content pages - it will be for pages such as delivery questions, contact, FAQs, and more.

We've already created the base pages in the previous site, so all we need to do is move them over and adjust them, so they work within a SvelteKit environment. Let's crack on and look at what we need to do to get them working on our new site.

ADAPTING TO SAPPER – PART 3: ADDING PAGES

To set up the content pages, follow these steps:

1. First, we need to copy across the remaining content pages – for this, copy `Coffee.svelte`, `About.svelte`, and `Contact.svelte` from the `\src\pages` folder of our original site into the `\src\routes` folder in the new site.
2. Next, go ahead and rename `Home.svelte` to `Index.svelte` – this is required to ensure pages are routed correctly (more on this shortly).
3. At the same time, copy across `Modal.svelte`, `Disclaimer.svelte`, and `Carousel.svelte` from the `\src\components` folder in the old site to the `\src\components` folder in our new site.
4. Fire up a Node.js terminal session, and then change the working folder to our new project area. At the prompt, enter `npm i yup svelte-yup` and press Enter to install the form validation for the Contact page.
5. Next, we need to add a reference to the Disclaimer component into the `__layout.svelte` file – for this, go ahead and add this line of code before the closing `</script>` tag:

```
import
  Disclaimer from '../components/Disclaimer.svelte';
```

6. Go ahead and save, and then close all files – the changes are complete for this exercise.

We're starting to make more progress - if you try to run up the site now, it won't look pretty, but it should still work! We will fix the styling later in this chapter, but for now, let's review the changes we've made in more detail.

Understanding the Changes Made

So far, we've set up our base site and created a layout template - in the last demo, we started to flesh out our site with the content pages from the original demo. Unfortunately, it's not a simple case of copying files across like for like; as SvelteKit has routing built-in, we have to make a few changes!

The first change is in the copying of the files - we copied them across from `\src\components`, but put them in `\src\routes` in the new site. We could store them elsewhere, but given that we've referenced their location in `__layout.js`, it kind of makes sense to keep them with the `__layout.js` file, at least for now. SvelteKit knows where the files are stored and will automatically route to them as needed. It does raise an important point, though - the location of content-type files is something you will need to consider, particularly for larger sites.

We then renamed the `Home.svelte` file to `Index.svelte` - this fits in better with the overall structure and routing, but apart from which, the convention of calling the main index file `Home.svelte` is a little outdated! At the same time, we copied across the `Modal`, `Disclaimer`, and `Carousel` component files and stored them in the new components folder.

To round things off, we then installed the form validation components used in `Contact.svelte`; this is no different from before, but we need to do it here to retain the functionality. We also added a missing reference to the Disclaimer component in the `__layout` file - putting it here means that we maintain that banner across all pages, not just the home page.

Adding Product Gallery

We're now at the most crucial point - it's time for us to get our gallery set up, ready for use! Fortunately, we don't have too many changes to make here - let's take a look at what we need to do to get the pages working on our new site.

ADAPTING TO SAPPER – PART 4: ADDING THE PRODUCT GALLERY

To get the `Products.svelte` page operational, follow these steps:

1. First, go ahead and copy the `Products.svelte` from our old site to the `\src\routes` folder in the new project area.
2. Next, we need three additional components – copy `Cart.svelte` and `CTAButton.svelte` from the original `\src\components` folder, and drop them into the same place in the new site. Go ahead and edit the import statements at the top of `Products.svelte`, so they point to the files in the new location.
3. We can remove two imports that are now redundant – we're not using the `Link` component from `svelte-routing` nor the `Button.svelte` component so that we can remove both imports:

```
import { Link } from "svelte-routing";
import Button from "./components/Button.svelte";
```

4. Scroll down to this line of code – it contains a reference to a component we no longer need to use:

```
<h4>
  <Link to="product/{product.id}">{product.name}</Link>
</h4>
```

5. Go ahead and modify the code as highlighted:

```
<h4>
  <a href="product/{product.id}">{product.name}</a>
</h4>
```

6. We have one more step, which is to install the Svelte-notifications plugin. For this, switch to a Node.js terminal session, and then make sure to set the working folder to our new project area.
7. At the prompt, enter `npm install @beyonk/svelte-notifications` and press Enter.

8. Switch to `Products.svelte`, and comment out lines 5, 18, and 59 – this might seem a little strange given we've just installed the component, but it will throw an error. We're commenting it out until we can fix it – I will return to this step later in the code review.
9. Go ahead and save and then close all files – the changes are complete for now.

We're almost at the end of creating our replacement site - it's beginning to take shape now. We've had to make a few changes to our product gallery page to get it working, so let's pause for a moment to review the code changes in more detail.

Breaking the Code Apart

So far, we've created our initial layout and added content pages - in the last exercise, we went a step further and added one of the most important: our product gallery page.

To get this working in our new site, we first copied across the original `Products.svelte` file, along with `Cart.svelte` and `CTAButton.svelte`, before updating the import references in our code. At the same time, we then removed references to two files that were no longer needed and edited one of the links in our code to reflect that change.

There is an important point to make - notice how we dropped the page, not into the components folder (which is where it was before), but into the routes folder? It is technically a page as opposed to a component (although it contains elements of both). Given we are referencing the "page" from the navigation, it makes sense to put it with the other pages!

We then finished by installing the svelte-notifications plugin before commenting out references in our code. This last step might seem a little strange, but the plugin fell over with several errors when developing code for this book. What makes it even more bizarre is that SvelteKit was used to create the plugin! While it's a shame that the plugin doesn't appear to work, for now, we can come back to this later - it's not essential for an MVP version of our site.

Right, we're creeping ever closer to finishing our site! We have one more section to add in before we can style the site - what's left? It's the product page: let's dive in and take a look at the changes needed to get it working in our new SvelteKit site.

Adding Product Page

We need to add to our product page for this last task - we will use the one we created in the original Svelte site, but it needs a few changes to get it working on our new site.

In some cases, these changes will allow us to remove code that is no longer needed, as changes to the structure of the site make it redundant - let's take a closer look at what is involved in getting the last part of our site operational.

ADAPTING TO SAPPER – PART 5: ADDING PRODUCT PAGE

We have a few steps to work through, to get the product page operational – to do so, follow these steps:

1. First, copy across the `Product.svelte` and `Button.svelte` files from the original demo; place `Product.svelte` in the `\src\routes` folder, and put `Button.svelte` into the `\src\components` folder.
2. Crack open the copy of `Product.svelte` from our new project area – go ahead and remove this line, as it is no longer needed:

```
import { Link } from "svelte-routing";
```

3. Next, comment out lines 5, 23, and 73 – these relate to the Notifier component we set up earlier in the book, but which isn't working correctly in SvelteKit. We will come back to this later.
4. Now that we've removed the Link component reference, we need to update the link that used it to avoid throwing an error. Go ahead and find this line, and then change `Link to=` to `a href=` and `/Link` to `/a`:

```
{"<<"}<Link to="/products">{"Back to Shop"}</Link>
```

5. We used the svelte-routing component to create the dynamic link between the product gallery and the product page. We're not using this plugin here, so instead, we need to replicate the link. For this, create a new file called `[slug].svelte` in `/src/routes/product`, and then copy the contents of `Product.svelte` into this file.

You can remove the original `Product.svelte` we copied over in step 1 of this exercise if desired; it is no longer needed.

6. We need to adjust the imports in `Product.svelte` – make sure they point to the same files we've copied over into our new folder.

7. Next, go ahead and comment out or modify these lines, as indicated:

```
// let individualURL = document.location.pathname;
let individualID = (`http://${$page.path}`).split('/product/')[1];
// let individualName;
```

8. We can also remove this block too – this was a styling hack which is no longer required:

```
// hack for no product page menu item
let getShopMenuItem = document.querySelector("nav > a:nth-child(2)");

if (individualURL.indexOf("/product") != -1) {
  getShopMenuItem.style.borderBottom = "5px solid #552200";
} else {
  getShopMenuItem.style.borderBottom = "none";
}
```

9. Next, crack open `Button.svelte`, and replace the styling block at the top of the file with this – it will revert the CSS to normal CSS, as we don't have the PostCSS processor installed:

```
<style type="text/scss">
  button { background-color: #c59747; border:
none; color: white; padding: 15px 32px; text-align: center; text-
decoration: none; display:
inline-block; font-size: 18px; letter-spacing:
2.4px; width: 384px; margin-top: 10px; }

  button:hover, button:active { background-color:
#000000; color: #ffffff; box-shadow: 1px 1px
6px rgba(0, 0, 0, 0.26); }
</style>
```

10. We're done with the changes – save and close all open files.

Yes, we have finally made the transition! We now have all of our files in place, albeit the site won't look that good (but don't worry - we'll fix that shortly). We've made a few changes in this last demo to get the product page working, so let's take a moment to review those changes in more detail before moving on to styling our new site.

Understanding the Changes Made

Although we've only had to update a handful of pages, the product page is the one that needed the most changes to get it working.

In some cases, the changes were expected, such as updating import references. However, we were also able to remove a good chunk of code that was no longer required. I'm a big fan of continuous improvement, so anything that helps in this respect is a good thing!

We started by copying across the `Product.svelte` and `Button.svelte` files to the `\src\components` folder in our new site before removing a (now) redundant link to `svelte-routing`, as the functionality is covered by SvelteKit automatically. At the same time, we also updated one of the links to remove the dependency on the Link component.

Next up, we then had to comment out references to the Notification component; this isn't ideal, but as mentioned in the changes to the `Products.svelte` component, this is essential. I came across errors being generated while researching this book; in the spirit of taking an MVP approach, I decided to focus on the core elements and come back to these at a later date.

We then moved onto creating the `[slug].svelte` file - yes, it might seem an odd name, but bear in mind that this is a template file, not a regular page! Svelte will use this to create the individual product page based on the link clicked, so in reality, it would become `2.svelte` if we clicked the second product, and so on. To complete the new file, we copied the contents of `Product.svelte` into this file - we could have renamed the original file, but this would leave us without a backup if we had an issue.

We then had to make a series of changes to the code itself - first up, we updated the import references before modifying some of the code and removing that which was redundant. We then finished by updating the styling for the Button component - remember that we converted the original version to use PostCSS, which won't work until we add support for the tool.

Phew, we're done with the code changes: it's time to get artistic and style our site! This step is my favorite part - being a visual person, it's nice to see something evolve from an elementary site into something more refined. In this case, most of the styling should come across as is, although there will be some changes we need to make – let's move swiftly on and find out what we need to do to get our site looking more attractive.

Migrating Styles

When it comes to styling any site, this is where we can make a real visual impact – I know writing in the confines of a book means we can't go to town; we can only do that once we have the basic styles set!

For our last exercise, we will reuse many of the original styles from the previous version of our site; this should reduce the amount of work required to make our site presentable. Before we do so, it's worth taking a look at how the site appears now, with the code complete but not all of the styles in place (Figure 12-2).

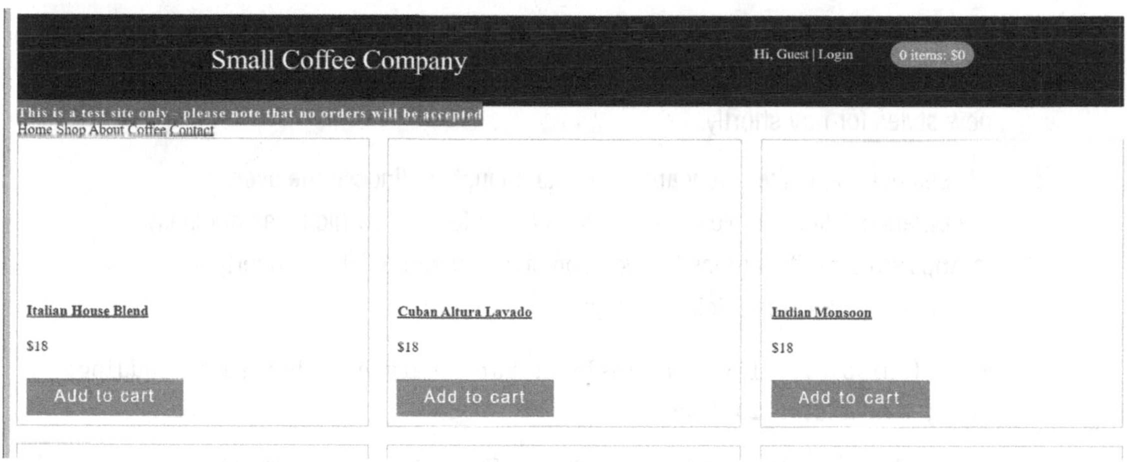

***Figure 12-2.** The site before additional styling is applied*

Okay, so it doesn't look too bad – for a straight "lift and shift," it could have been worse! Thankfully, we can improve on it, which we will do in the next exercise.

> For space reasons, I've had to compress the styles displayed in print; I would recommend viewing the versions available in the code download, as they will be in their original, uncompressed format.

ADAPTING TO SAPPER – PART 6: MIGRATING STYLES

To get the styles set up, follow these steps:

1. First, go ahead and create a new folder called `styles` in the `\static` folder. Inside of this folder, create a new style sheet called `styles.css`.
2. Next, switch to the `App.html` file, and then add in a link to the new style sheet under the link for the favicon, thus:

```
<link rel="icon" href="/favicon.png" />
<link rel="stylesheet" href="styles/styles.css">
```

3. Most of the styles we need will already exist in the original global.css file that we created – go ahead and copy the contents of `global.css` into this new `styles.css` file.
4. The exception to this is the styling for our navigation – go ahead and remove all of the entries beginning with `nav`, leaving the rest untouched. We will add in new styles for `nav` shortly.
5. We still need to make a few amendments, though, to finesse the overall appearance – first up, we need to add in a rule for main, which was originally in `App.svelte` (it includes the addition of a new `max-width` property – highlighted, not in the original design):

```
main { display: flex; margin-left: auto; margin-right: auto; padding: 20px; max-width: 1040px; }
```

6. We need to make the next change to the PayPal container referenced in `Checkout.svelte` – we need to increase the width to prevent it from jumping. Go ahead and add this rule after the code from the previous step:

```
#paypal-button-container { margin: 30px 0; width: 355px; }
```

7. We need to make two more changes – the first of which is in `Carousel.svelte`. We need to adjust the padding, so add in this extra property as indicated:

```
.papagination {
  ...
    padding: 4px;
}
```

8. The final change we need to make is to the navigation – I've not been happy with the original design, as it needed a hacky change to deal with displaying the product page. Now is a good opportunity to revamp it; go ahead and replace the <nav>...</nav> block in `__layout.js` with this:

```
<nav>
  <ul>
    <li><a href="/.">Home</a></li>
    <li><a href="/Products">Shop</a></li>
    <li><a href="/About">About</a></li>
    <li><a href="/Coffee">Coffee</a></li>
    <li><a href="/Contact">Contact</a></li>
  </ul>
</nav>
```

9. Remember how I said we would replace the styling in step 4? Well, here is the replacement – go ahead and copy the code in, block by block, at the end of the file, starting with the main <nav> element:

```
nav { background-color: #c59747; }
```

10. We need to add in a rule for the unordered list block:

```
nav ul { display: flex; align-items: start; list-style-type: none;
margin: 0; width: 420px; margin-left: auto; margin-right: auto; }
```

11. Next up comes the rule for each list item and link in that unordered list block:

```
nav ul li { padding: 6px 0; }

nav ul li a { position: relative; display:
block; text-decoration: none; transition: 0.5s;
padding: 5px 15px; font-weight: bold; color: #552200; }
```

I've set a 0.5s value for the transition, but you may find this too short; please feel free to increase the value as you see fit.

12. Finally, we have three rules in place to take care of highlighting the menu entry if we hover over it:

```
nav ul li a::after { position: absolute; content: "";
width: 100%; height: 3px; top: 100%; left: 0;
background: #552200; transition: transform 0.5s; transform: scaleX(0);
transform-origin: right; }

nav ul li a:hover { color: #000000; }

nav ul li a:hover::after { transform: scaleX(1);
transform-origin: left; }
```

13. The final step is to save and close any file we have open, ready to the results of our hard work.

14. You can leave a Node.js terminal session open, though – we will need it very shortly.

Phew, we're done with styling our site; it's time to test. Hold your horses, my dear reader! Yes, we will test very shortly, but before we do so, we should do a quick review of the code we've added and cover off a couple of essential points regarding styling code within SvelteKit.

Breaking Apart the Code

Although we've covered a lot of code in this last exercise, most of it will be self-explanatory; I've deliberately tried to reuse code from earlier to make it easier to affect the transition to using SvelteKit. This said, there are a couple of important points we should cover:

- Remember how we stored styles in various places in the original demo, such as `global.css`, or within each component? The same principle still applies, but this time as we're using static CSS, the style sheet has to go into the static folder – this is to tell SvelteKit not to compile the contents during the site's build. If we were using a tool such as PostCSS or Sass to compile our styles, the code would have to shift to a new folder that Svelte can reference during the compile and build process.

- I've taken the opportunity to refactor some of the markup during the styling process. Some of you may think this isn't a good approach; I would say that it's essential to keep a continuous improvement mindset going and that if we can improve on code, then we should. Markup will never reach the final version; if it does, then the site is no longer of any use to us - the same applies to styling!

Okay, we've now reached that point where we need to test our site! Yikes, I wonder, will it work as we expect?

Testing the Site and Next Steps

Right, we can't put it off any longer. Go ahead and switch back to that Node.js terminal session from the end of the last exercise. At the prompt, enter npm run dev (which should be very familiar by now!), and what do you get?

If all is well, we should see something akin to Figure 12-3, shown overleaf.

Figure 12-3. *Our finished SvelteKit site*

Wow, it doesn't look too bad, huh? Sure, there are a couple of changes, and we've not built in everything we had before, but it's a good start! We still have a long way to go before putting this into production use, but we have a good starting base for developing our site into something more refined and ready for customer use.

Thinking further afield, though, there are a host of features we could add or investigate for our site – here are a few ideas to get you started:

- Now that we have good routing built-in by default, what about providing something like a 404 page? I've put a brief example into the code download that accompanies this book – we would save it to the `\src\routes\` folder, and SvelteKit will take care of routing automatically.
- Accessibility is another factor – this is something we could add into the app.html file, although how we do it will depend on the size of your site.
- How about preprocessing? We built this into our original site; SvelteKit will happily work with most preprocessing tools such as Sass or PostCSS. I would recommend searching on Google for articles, which should turn up something that will help you get it set up.

Of course, we should not forget some of the areas we were not able to get in place during the migration:

- The Notifier component is one area that needs attention – it was throwing a `cannot use import statement outside a module error` when I tried to implement it while researching for this book. A check on the website didn't reveal anything at the time of writing. Could this be a candidate for replacement? Bear in mind that we are using beta software, so we should expect issues such as this in our code!
- Paypal was also complaining of an error – it flagged `Error: Document is ready and element #paypal-button-container does not exist` in `Checkout.svelte` at or around line 38. I suspect the placeholder isn't ready in time, so PayPal is unable to initialize correctly – again, it's something we should check if we develop the site into something we can put in front of customers.

- If you take a look at the console log area, you may see a few warnings regarding Svelte slots that are missing; this is one area we should revisit if only to clean up some of the alerts!

Phew, we've covered a lot! These are just a few ideas to consider; I know we've not been able to cover everything, but hopefully, what we've touched on here and earlier in the book will give you something you can use to develop your future projects.

Summary

SvelteKit may have only been around for less than a couple of years and still be beta software. Still, in that time, it has come on leaps and bounds – throughout this chapter, we've seen how easy it is to migrate the core elements from our original Svelte site to this new framework. We covered some practical steps in this chapter, so let's take a moment to review what we have learned.

We started with a quick look at why this chapter was meant to be about SvelteKit's predecessor and how it was more beneficial to look forward to SvelteKit, before working through the steps to create the initial site for our replacement front-end demo.

Next up, we then explored a high level view of a typical SvelteKit site's structure before adding a new layout template, ready for us to develop the new site. We then worked through adding pages, the product gallery, and the individual product page template before finishing with restyling the site using existing styles from the original version of our project.

We wrapped up with a look at the next steps and confirmed that our site runs; we had set expectations at the start to focus on core elements, so we worked through some ideas as to how we could develop our site into something we can put in front of customers.

Sadly, all good things must come to an end, as we've now reached the end of the book – it's been an adventure! I hope you've enjoyed reading and working on the examples as much as I have with writing them and that you'll be able to put this to good use in your future projects.

APPENDIX

Getting Help

Help, I'm stuck...!

In over 20 years of supporting family, friends, and colleagues with IT requests, this is one phrase I hear far too often – indeed, if I had had a dollar for each time, I would be on a remote island somewhere, basking in the sun, drinking whiskey...

But I digress. There may well be occasions where you do become stuck on something when working with Svelte – it might be a simpler framework to learn than the likes of Angular, but it doesn't mean that things will be plain sailing all of the time! If you do become stuck, there are a few sources you can turn to for help:

- The first port of call should be the interactive tutorial, starting from `https://svelte.dev/tutorial/basics`, or the Svelte examples page, available from `https://svelte.dev/examples#hello-world`. They may not be an exact match for your requirements, but you may find your answer with a little lateral thinking!
- If the query relates to a specific API function, then I would recommend taking a look at the extensive documentation on the Svelte site, at `https://svelte.dev/docs`.
- If things are such that you need more help (and there will be occasions when this might happen), then feel free to ask in the Svelte Discord chatroom at `https://svelte.dev/chat` or on Reddit at this URL: `https://www.reddit.com/r/sveltejs`.
- If you have a more complex query, it may be better to post a question on the Stack Overflow website, at `https://www.stackoverflow.com`. There are lots of questions tagged with the word Svelte, which may have your answer, or you can ask your own if you can't find something there that has already been asked.

A. Libby, *Practical Svelte*, https://doi.org/10.1007/978-1-4842-7374-6

I would strongly recommend reading the Code of Conduct at `https://stackoverflow.com/conduct`; this will help you get a better answer for your questions.

Hopefully, this will help you solve that burning question or conundrum - Svelte is a great framework to learn; there are thousands of people out there who already use it and who I am sure will be willing to help encourage others to come into the Svelte family.

Index

A

B

C

A. Libby, *Practical Svelte*, https://doi.org/10.1007/978-1-4842-7374-6

D

E

F, G, H, I, J, K

L, M, N, O

P, Q, R

S, T

U, V, W, X, Y, Z

Printed in the United States
by Baker & Taylor Publisher Services